Greatness *in the* Shadows

Branson, Douglas M. - Greatness in the Shadows, Larry Doby and the Integration of the American League
University of Nebraska Press, Lincoln (2016)

Douglas M. Branson

Greatness *in the* Shadows

Larry Doby and the Integration of the American League

University of Nebraska Press
LINCOLN & LONDON

Library of Congress Cataloging-in-Publication Data
Names: Branson, Douglas M.
Title: Greatness in the shadows: Larry Doby and the integration of the American League / Douglas M. Branson.
Description: Lincoln: University of Nebraska Press, [2016] | Includes bibliographical references and index.
Identifiers: LCCN 2015031802
ISBN 9780803285521 (cloth: alk. paper)
ISBN 9780803285941 (epub)
ISBN 9780803285958 (mobi)
ISBN 9780803285965 (pdf)
Subjects: LCSH: Doby, Larry. | Baseball players—United States—Biography. | African American baseball players—United States—Biography. | Discrimination in sports—United States. | American League of Professional Baseball Clubs. | Baseball—United States—History.
Classification: LCC GV865.D58 B73 2016 | DDC 796.357092—dc23
LC record available at http://lccn.loc.gov/2015031802

Set in Minion Pro by M. Scheer.

Frontispiece courtesy of the Cleveland Press Collection, Michael Schwartz Library, Cleveland State University.

*To two other professor-authors of baseball
books whose efforts inspired my own*

Robert Francis Garratt
Joseph Thomas Moore

Contents

Preface

It would really disturb me if I went into a locker room and found a black player who didn't know what players like Jackie Robinson, Larry Doby and Don Newcombe did forty or fifty years ago.

—HENRY AARON, introduction to Robinson's *I Never Had It Made*

The 2013 film *42* is the most recent Jackie Robinson movie, one of several made over the years. "It is worth the wait," said *Sports Illustrated*'s review of the film.[1] In addition to feature-length films, there have been three made-for-TV movies, one Broadway play, and fifty-plus book-length biographies of Jackie Robinson, who played second and third base for the Brooklyn Dodgers from 1947 to 1957.

Robinson's pathbreaking accomplishments are memorialized in other ways. Every April all Major League Baseball players wear number 42 in honor of his achievements, something they have done since the inaugural Jackie Robinson Day in 2004. Robinson was a six time All-Star, elected to the Baseball Hall of Fame in 1962, the first year in which he was eligible.

Robinson was the first African American to play Major League Baseball in the modern era, breaking into the big leagues on April 15, 1947. In a country where both overt and latent racism were still nearly universal, he endured taunts, epithets, vituperation, hostility, and death threats along with threatened and real acts of physical intimidation. He put up with it all, initially alone, with aplomb and dignity while achieving Hall of Fame numbers, batting .311 lifetime, with 127 home runs. He carried himself with class and dignity, but after two years of relative silence, he became an articulate, sometimes angry spokesperson for integration not only in baseball but also in the larger society.

Larry Doby, center fielder for the Cleveland Indians, was the second African American to break the color line, just eleven weeks after Robinson, on July 5, 1947. Doby too endured taunts, second-class-citizen status, hostility, avalanches of bottles and cans thrown onto the field, and other acts of physical intimidation. He was not allowed in many of the hotels in which the Indians stayed, including, until 1954, the lodgings for each year's Indians' spring training, in Tucson, Arizona. In certain southern cities, where the Indians would play a number of preseason exhibition games, cab drivers would not permit Doby to ride in their "whites only" taxis. At times Doby was forced to walk to the ballpark where the Indians were to play. Once he was there, on several occasions ushers and turnstile operators denied him admission to the park because he was black. Some ushers tried to bar him from the park even when Doby was in his Cleveland Indians uniform.

In contrast to knowing about Jackie Robinson, virtually no young—black or white—baseball players or fans know who Larry Doby was. So, too, the middle-aged are ignorant of what a great player and good man Doby was, let alone what he endured in integrating the other conference of Major League Baseball, the American League. The books on Jackie Robinson continue to come forth with one appearing even as this Doby book was being written.[2] Meanwhile, the memory of Larry Doby and what he accomplished is forgotten, or at least has faded away, much like an iceberg drifting into more temperate waters and melting to nothing.

Writing of the great Chicago Cub, Ernie Banks, Rich Cohen, a supposedly knowledgeable *Sports Illustrated* baseball writer, asserts that "along with [Hank] Aaron and Willie Mays, Banks forms a triumvirate of African-American pioneers who came up in the aftermath of Jackie Robinson, who were counseled by Jackie and rode his break through weird old racist America."[3] Not a glimmer about Larry Doby, a true pioneer, or about other African Americans like Don Newcombe, Luke Easter, and Monte Irvin who followed Doby into the big leagues, preceding Mays and Aaron.

Only a subset of a subset, a handful of the eldest baseball fans, remember who Doby was, what he accomplished, or how good a baseball player he was.[4]

Doby batted .286 in nine seasons with the Cleveland Indians (.283 overall, in a fourteen-year career), with 253 home runs. He was a seven-time All-Star (Robinson was six-timer), elected to the Hall of Fame as well—but only in 1998, and only then by the Veterans' Committee (rather than by the Baseball Writers of America), many years after Doby had become eligible. He twice led the Indians to the American League pennant (1948 and 1954).

It would be more poignant to say that no books have been written about Doby, but there has been one, by Joseph Moore of Montclair State University in New Jersey.[5] The Cleveland Indians succeeded in having a street near Jacobs Field, the Indians' home park, renamed Larry Doby Way.[6] Finally, in July 2015 the Indians dedicated a statue of Doby outside Cleveland's Progressive Field, following past dedications of similar statues of Bob Feller and Jim Thome. The U.S. Postal Service issued a series of four commemorative stamps, honoring four baseball greats: Ted Williams, Joe DiMaggio, Willie Stargell, and Larry Doby.[7]

But there have been no movies. Neither Major League Baseball nor the American League observes a "Larry Doby Day." When in 1997 Major League Baseball required all teams to retire number 42 permanently, in honor of the long-since-deceased Robinson, neither baseball nor the news media mentioned Doby's name, let alone his achievements. Nor did the baseball powers require teams to retire the number 14, which Doby had worn. At that time, in 1998, Doby was still alive, living in Montclair, New Jersey, and busy with his children and grandchildren. On a relative basis, as compared to Jackie Robinson, Larry Doby and his baseball career have slipped into obscurity.

Why? Part of the reason, of course, is that Robinson was the first. The second of anything receives but a fraction of the attention the first receives. One calloused sports writer expressed it graphically: "Second place finishers in America are suckers. . . . Those who don't come first or don't do things a certain way get lost. They disappear."[8] More eloquently, the New York Times wrote,

"In glorifying those who are first the second is often forgotten. Doby integrated all those ballparks where Jackie Robinson never appeared. And he did it with class and clout."[9]

Yet it is undeniable: the second always labors and lives in the shadow of the first. Doby himself reflected, with a trace of bitterness, "Jackie got all the publicity for putting up with [the racial taunts and slurs]. But it was the same thing I had to deal with. The crap I took was just as bad. Nobody said 'We're gonna be nice to the second Black.'"[10]

Other factors mask Larry Doby's achievements, accounting for his relatively modest historical stature. He played in the shadow of Mickey Mantle, the incomparable center fielder of the New York Yankees, who broke into the major leagues in 1951, and who was also blond haired, blue eyed, and white. In 1952 Doby hit 32 home runs, driving in 104 runs. "Looking back on Mantle's 1952 season [23 home runs and 87 RBIs], *Total Baseball* had a total player rating [for Mantle] of 4.8," second in the American League.[11] Who was first? Larry Doby of the Cleveland Indians. Even today books and retrospectives hail Mantle as one of the greatest baseball players of all time, while Larry Doby is largely is forgotten.

In 1951 another center fielder, said by many to have been the best all-around player of all time, broke into Major League Baseball. In that year Willie Mays donned a New York Giants uniform. To a degree Mays and the shadow he cast also serve to mask Larry Doby's achievement in integrating the American League and in playing thirteen years of Major League Baseball.

Doby also played the core of his career for a team perceived as a perennial also-ran. Even though the Cleveland Indians won the American League championship twice (1948 and 1954) and the World Series once (1948), the dominant theme of that era was of the Indians finishing second, sometimes third, behind the New York Yankees. The Yankees won American League pennants in seven of the nine years in which Doby played for Cleveland, winning six of the seven World Series in those years. Also in contrast with Cleveland, the Dodgers, for whom Jackie Robinson played, were perennial contenders or at least viewed that way. They won National League pennants in six of the years in which Jackie Robinson played, compared to two American League pennants for Cleveland and Larry Doby.

Cleveland, too, is not New York. Today Ohio would be classi-fied, somewhat dismissively, as one of the "flyover" states. New York, of course, is on the coast and considered by many New York-ers to be the center of not only the country but also the universe. Along with certain West Coast teams (the Los Angeles Dodgers and the San Francisco Giants), the Yankees are also known as one of the "pretty boy" teams in baseball.

One last shadow that both over time and back then obscured Larry Doby and his achievements was Satchel Paige, or perhaps, more accurately, the legend of Satchel, which is more than some-what different than Paige himself. To some Paige was a clown, a buffoon, a Stepin Fetchit character who sat in a rocking chair in the bullpen and encouraged the belief that he had been born in the nineteenth century. To many others Satchel Paige was "one of the greatest pitchers of any hue in baseball history," with a career that spanned forty years.[12]

Paige and his legend cast a particularly long shadow over Doby and his achievements because Bill Veeck, owner of the Cleveland Indians at the time, signed Satchel Paige to a Major League con-tract in July 1948. For much of 1948, 1949, and beyond, the aura—and antics—of Satchel Paige aura overshadowed Doby.

The purpose of this book is not so much to chronicle Larry Doby's life and baseball career, although certain chapters attempt a fresh look at those things. Rather, the true inspiration behind the book, and the animus that drives it, is the desire to explore just why Larry Doby remains so obscure or, if not obscure, so much in the shadows.[13]

Note on Monetary Conversions

Measuring a dollar in today's terms is trickier than it might seem because you can choose from an array of multipliers to determine how much yesterday's dollar would be worth today. Multipliers include the following:

- Consumer Price Index ($13.40 for $1.00 in 1927)
- Unskilled wage ($42.60 for a 1927 dollar)
- Production (skilled) worker compensation ($54.10)
- Nominal gross domestic product (GDP) per capita ($65.50)
- Relative share of GDP ($174)

In this book I have approximated today's equivalents of past years' baseball salaries and sums received in player trades using year-to-year increases in production (skilled) worker compensation. See generally Measuring Worth, at http://www.measuringworth .com/uscompare (last accessed May 23, 2015).

Greatness *in the* Shadows

The Coolest of Them All?

Mantle, Mays, or Doby?

That [Mays and Mantle] were the two best players of the period isn't simply a myth . . . it's a fact. . . . [It is] obvious that they are the two greatest players in the history of the game.

—ALLEN BARRA, *Mickey and Willie*

Who was the best ball player? Was it Willie Mays, center fielder of the San Francisco (then–New York) Giants, whom "a great many people consider . . . the greatest all-around player of all time?"[1] Or was it Mickey Mantle, fleet center fielder of the dominant New York Yankees, known for hitting prodigious tape-measure home runs, 535 of them over his eighteen-year Major League career? Or was it the quiet, unassuming centerfielder Larry Doby, playing in the hinterlands of Cleveland? In his book on Mantle and Mays, quoted above, author Allen Barra mentions Doby only a single time and never utters anything close to a superlative.[2]

Baseball and American Life Post–World War II

Those were the conversations and comparisons that took place in nearly every schoolyard and in many work places all across the United States. It is difficult to overemphasize the importance and the centrality of baseball in American life in the late 1940s and early 1950s. Never before, and never since, has baseball captured the attention of so many. As David Halberstam has written, "In the years immediately following World War II, professional baseball mesmerized the American people. . . . Baseball, more than anything else, seemed to symbolize normalcy and a return to life as it had been before Pearl Harbor."[3]

During the war U.S. citizens had endured over four years of privation, with scarcity and rationing of everything from eggs and butter to automobiles, tires, and gasoline. Their loved ones had been in harm's way, or at least potentially so. Nearly every American male of appropriate age served in the military; 418,500 of them died in combat. Worldwide 15 million military men and women died. No one knows for sure, but 60 million people, or more, are estimated to have died in World War II.[4]

"When Bob Feller returned from the Navy," where he had spent the four years since Pearl Harbor, "to pitch in late August, 1945, a Cleveland paper headlined the event: THIS IS WHAT WE'VE BEEN WAITING FOR . . . . The crowds were extraordinary and enthusiastic."[5] Everyone was eager to leave the war years behind. For many baseball was the vehicle to do so. "Nor was it just numbers" of fans. "There was a special intensity to it in those days."[6] When the Boston Red Sox trained down to New York for a series against the Yankees, fans crammed the station platforms in Massachusetts, Rhode Island, and Connecticut to cheer the team as its train passed thorough the station.

In 1948 the Cleveland Indians, for whom Larry Doby and Bob Feller played, and who won the AL pennant and the World Series that year, set a record, drawing 2.6 million fans in the regular season, closely followed by the New York Yankees, who drew 2.4 million. Newspapers throughout the country headlined the baseball pennant races every day. Men and women brought radios to their offices and workplaces (back then the games were played in the afternoons rather than at night).

The popularity, indeed centrality, of baseball in American life continued into the 1950s. On summer Sundays, especially in August and September, the Cleveland Indians played doubleheaders against the Yankees in Cleveland's Municipal Stadium, drawing sold-out crowds of eighty-five thousand plus. In 1951, 1952, 1953, 1955, and 1956, the Indians battled the Yankees for the American League pennant and finished second in each of those years. Only in 1954 did the Indians best the Yankees, finishing first, but in that decade at least, the Indians always contended for the pennant, and the pennant races—Cleveland versus New York, Indians versus Yankees—were filled with excitement and drama.

A Personal Take on Those "Wonder Years"

Those Indians versus Yankees doubleheaders, and the excitement swirling about them, more than anything else characterize the time in which I became a baseball fan. Those years also coincide with the years in which Larry Doby starred for the Indians: a fixture in center field, a spectacular fielder, a home run hitter, and a quiet, dignified presence on and off the playing field. Countless times I listened to longtime Cleveland announcer Jimmy Dudley after Doby had hit a towering drive: "Going, going . . . gone." But, again, only in 2013, when watching the credits for the movie 42, did I learn that Doby had also been a racial pioneer, doing in the American League what Jackie Robinson had done a few weeks earlier in the National.

In 1955 I played right field, and once in a while third base, for the South Dayton Optimist Club. (The Optimists' creed: "Talk health, happiness and prosperity to every person you meet—think only of the best, work only for the best, and expect only the best.") On practice days, like thousands of other kids, I would tie one baseball shoelace to a lace from the other shoe. Draping the shoelaces over my shoulder, one shoe in front and the other against my back, I would slide the wristband of my mitt onto my handlebars. With baseball glove hanging from the handlebars and "my spikes" swinging to and fro, I would ride off to practice at Wilmington Park, a mile away.

We—my friends, teammates, and I—all had our baseball card collections. Mine filled a cigar box and half of another. Often, even just before practice, my friends and I compared cards; traded cards; proposed, negotiated, and bought and sold cards; and filed and refiled cards, for hours. We bought packets with the Topps baseball cards inside; we kept the cards but threw the gum away (we thought it tasted like cardboard).

I saw my first Major League game in 1955, Cleveland Indians against the Baltimore Orioles, who had recently arrived in Baltimore from St. Louis, where the team had been the Browns. Mike "The Bear" Garcia pitched for the Indians; Larry Doby, my hero, played center field. My fantasy, then and for several years thereafter, was to be just like him. I was crestfallen when the Indians traded Doby to the Chicago White Sox following the 1955 season.

Doby, of course, also was African American, which I can't say made any impression on me back then. Growing up, I went to Catholic schools with students of all socioeconomic and racial backgrounds. Some of my friends were black; we played sports together. In the Catholic schools I attended, the nuns and later the brothers placed strong emphasis on racial equality and social justice.

In those moments of fantasy, unlike most other boys my age, my childhood hero was not Willie Mays and it was not Mickey Mantle, both of whom I knew about and perhaps knew, instinctively, might be better players than Doby—but not by much. My childhood hero was Larry Doby.

A Peek at Doby's Career

In 1955 Doby had hit .291 for the Indians. Mantle hit only .298 lifetime; Mays hit .302. To compare, a recent inductee (2015) into the Baseball Hall of Fame, former Houston Astro Craig Biggio, hit .283 lifetime.

The year previous, 1954, was a stellar one for Doby: 32 home runs and 126 runs batted in (RBIs), leading the American League in both categories. In 1954 he also led Cleveland to a 111-win season, then the Major League record, and to the American League pennant, which led them only to a disastrous four-game World Series sweep by the New York Giants.[7] Doby was named to the American League All-Star team in seven of the nine years he played for the Indians.

In 1948, the other year in which the Cleveland Indians won the American League pennant and the World Series as well, Doby hit .301 with fourteen home runs, in his first full year in the major leagues. Mantle hit only .267, with thirteen home runs, in his first Major League year. Doby was an athletic center fielder who made circus and highlight-reel catches.

Noteworthy, too, is that through the postwar years and the 1950s, it was only the Indians (1948 and 1954), and the White Sox (1959), the two teams for which Doby played, who offered any serious resistance to the hated New York Yankees. The Yankees won the remainder of the American League pennants and appeared in twelve World Series during that fifteen-year time span.

Latter-Day Discoveries

Only in 2013, when I went to see the movie *42*, about Branch Rickey and Jackie Robinson breaking down racial barriers for Robinson to become the first African American in Major League history, did I see Doby's name, which by then had long since passed from my consciousness. My wife and I sat in the dark theater with the ending credits rolling. Near the credits' end, fine print indicated that the American League had been integrated in the same year, 1947. Larry Doby, of the Cleveland Indians, had done it. I had never realized that my childhood hero had been a pioneer. I ordered a few books and began to read.

An Amazon search revealed that roughly fifty-five books have been written about Jackie Robinson and his and Branch Rickey's feat, beginning the integration of baseball. Hollywood has produced two, and television one, feature films about Robinson's life. Once each year players for all thirty-two Major League teams wear throwback uniforms, all with Jackie Robinson's number 42, in Robinson's memory. Robinson retired from Major League Baseball in 1958, after only a ten-year career. He was elected unanimously to the Baseball Hall of Fame five years after he retired in the first year in which he was eligible, only the sixth player in history to be so honored.

By contrast, only one book, a biography, *Larry Doby: The Struggle of the American League's First Black Player* (2011), by history professor Joseph Thomas Moore of New Jersey's Montclair State University, exists.[8] Only two memorials exist: Cleveland named a street outside Jacobs Field (now Progressive Field) after Doby, and the Indians have placed a Doby statue outside the park. Cleveland has also retired Doby's number, 14.

The Shadows

Why? As well as the fifty-five books about Jackie Robinson, thirty-five books have been written about Mickey Mantle; thirty-two books by or about Willie Mays; and thirty-one books about Satchel Paige, the lanky pitcher, humorist, and legendary character who followed Doby to the Indians. But only one book about Doby?

Arguably, in beginning the integration of the American League, Doby had a much rougher time of it than Robinson did in integrating the National League (see chapter 17). Of course, it goes without saying that neither Doby nor Robinson should have had to endure the taunts, name-calling, isolation, and other forms of discrimination they endured. To cite only a few examples, Doby could not stay with his teammates as the team traveled to many of the other American League cities. He was forced to stay in an African American hotel or in the home of a black family, even during the Indians' spring training in Tucson, Arizona. Doby lived in segregated quarters in ten of the thirteen spring-training sessions he attended, many even after he had become a star. By contrast, in spring training Robinson could enjoy the comforts of his own brick bungalow at Dodger Town, which the Dodgers built in 1949 in Vero Beach, Florida, and used for spring training each year for the remainder of Robinson's Major League career and thereafter (until 2012).

In 1947, unbeknown to Doby, Bill Veeck, owner of the Cleveland Indians, purchased Doby's contract with the Newark Eagles of the Negro Baseball League. In early July Doby received notice of the transaction and then had to parachute into Comiskey Park, Chicago, with little warning and no preparation for his Major League debut and his first Major League season.

Branch Rickey, on the other hand, brought Jackie Robinson along slowly, over an eighteen-month period. Rickey lectured Robinson and held sessions with him. He sent Robinson down to AAA baseball, with the Montreal Royals of the International League. There Robinson played a full season before largely but not completely tolerant crowds, preparing himself for what the atmosphere was likely to be once he reached "the Bigs."

Willie Mays's introduction to organized baseball and the major leagues was gradual as well, similar to Robinson's. The New York Giants sent Mays for a season to its AAA affiliate, the Minneapolis Millers. There, Mays quickly won acceptance, becoming wildly popular with tolerant, near color-blind Minnesota crowds.

Questions

This book is not a biography. Joseph Moore's book, *Larry Doby*, is a very good one, accurate, easy to read, and well documented. Even though there are some fifty-five books about Robinson, thirty-five about Mantle, and so on, one biography is enough if it's a good one.

Neither is this book an attempt to make the case that Larry Doby was better than, or even the equal of, Mickey Mantle or Willie Mays, other celebrated center fielders. Doby was not. But he was not far behind, a half notch, probably much less, below the skills and achievements of those players, and he was the equal of, if not a better baseball player than, Jackie Robinson.

Doby was a fine center fielder and also a very good hitter, who could hit for average as well as for power. He led the major leagues in slugging percentage in 1952. As noted, he also led the league in home runs (twice), in RBIs (once), and in runs scored (once). He fought in World War II. He was a through-and-through family man who, together with his wife of fifty-three years, raised five children. And he was a racial pioneer who endured as much—indeed probably much more—than his friend and fellow pioneer Jackie Robinson.

To return to my youth out in the hinterlands, both of my best friends, Jimmy Wenzke and Tom Thorton, were Yankees fans, something that seemed inexplicable to me, given their location in Dayton, Ohio. On reflection, though, it's easy enough to understand: there are fans of the "pretty boy teams" (the Yankees and the Dodgers) everywhere. But my buddies also were unabashed Mickey Mantle fans. Intermittently I made the case that Larry Doby was Mantle's equal. But they shouted me down or laughed at me. Maybe I did not even believe it myself, at least in my heart of hearts.

I would, however, make the case today that Doby was a great

player and as valuable to his team as Mays was to his and as Mantle was to the Yankees (at least for portions of his career). And during those Doby years, those Indians teams were not too shabby, winning the World Series once, the American League pennant twice, and finishing second to the Yankees in five of the seven other years in which Doby was a Cleveland Indian.

Rather, then, this book asks the question *why?* Why have Larry Doby and his career received so little attention?

2

The Branch Rickey Yardstick

"Branch, [if you integrate the National League] all hell will break loose."

"No, Lowell, all heaven will rejoice."

—Quoted in SAM ROBERTS, "Faster than Jackie Robinson"

Mr. Rickey was a Christian Man. He firmly believed that the treatment of the black man was a blot on the history of America.

—MAL GOODE, editor of the *Pittsburgh Courier*, 1955

This book backs into the treatment of beginning integration in modern-day baseball, especially the nearly forgotten Larry Doby half of it. It does so by treating first with the Wizards of Oz, the two gentlemen behind the curtain (well, not really far behind the curtain), Branch Rickey and Bill Veeck. Well-known to baseball historians, Rickey, Veeck, and their stories represent a necessary prelude to any story about the first African Americans in the major leagues.

Branch Rickey's office at 215 Montague Street in Brooklyn (today a Toronto Dominion bank), his lair when he was president and general manager of the Brooklyn Dodgers, was affectionately known as "the cave of the winds."[1] While there, as well as elsewhere, Rickey is said to have delivered every prologue or pronouncement as if he were "delivering the Gettysburg Address."[2] "He was a man of many faucets, all running at once," said a Brooklyn fan.[3] Enos "Country" Slaughter, a Hall of Fame player for Rickey, groused, "[Rickey] was always going to the vault for a nickel's change."[4]

Baseball Commissioner Kenesaw Mountain Landis called Rickey a "hypocritical Protestant bastard wrapped in minister's robes."[5] Rickey displayed "streaks of petulance, moralism and autocracy that either infuriated or endeared him to those he encountered."[6]

These quotations show but a few of the many sides of Wesley Branch Rickey, the highest, or among the very highest, paid persons in baseball, player or manager, from 1916 until his retirement in 1959. Even back in 1927, Rickey's five-year contract with the Cardinals provided him with a yearly base salary of $65,000 plus 10 percent commission on player sales, later raised to a $75,000 base, topping what already was the highest salary in all of baseball.[7] Accordingly, for instance, with commissions, Rickey made $95,000 in 1928 ($5.4 million in today's dollars), while players earned $3,500–$4,500 per year ($149,000–$243,000 today).[8] Even as late as 1951, Mickey Mantle earned just $7,000 with the New York Yankees; in 1951 the Major League rookie minimum was $6,000.[9] Rickey is, of course, best known as the man who cultivated Jackie Robinson as a baseball player, brought him into organized (white) baseball in 1946, and with Robinson integrated the Brooklyn Dodgers and the major leagues in 1947. This chapter explores but a few of those Rickey sides, perhaps the less known ones, for numerous biographies record and evaluate Rickey's career in depth.[10] This chapter's biographical section thus will be brief, a thumbnail sketch. But, first, let us delve into a less discussed aspect of Branch Rickey's long career in baseball.

Who Was Ralph Kiner?

Younger baseball fans know Kiner as the color commentator on New York Mets broadcasts and for his postgame show, *Kiner's Korner*, for decades broadcast on New York television and radio. More perceptive fans remember Kiner for his malapropisms, especially the ones mangling sponsors' names: "Manufacturers Hangover" for Manufactures Hanover, or "American Cyanide" for American Cyanamid.[11] The affection New York fans had for Kiner, however, overrode any offense he might have given sponsors, unlike one predecessor New York baseball announcer who referred to sponsor Proctor & Gamble's product (Ivory Soap) as "Ovary Soap" and was sacked forthwith.[12]

Kiner, who died in early 2014, was elected to the Hall of Fame in his fifteenth, and last, year of eligibility. The election took a number of years perhaps because although Kiner had a brilliant baseball career, it was a short one, limited to ten years as a player. In that time he won the National League home run championship seven consecutive years, a record that still stands, and was a six time All-Star. He was the player in baseball history to reach the two-hundred-home-run plateau earliest in his big league career.

Kiner was popular with teammates and fans alike. He had little or no ego. He served as advisor, mentor, and counselor to younger players. Fans delighted in the towering home runs Kiner hit to left field. He was approachable to fans, but he also had star quality. He dated movie stars, including Elizabeth Taylor (well, just one date, but there were other Hollywood stars as well).

Kiner, though, faced two drawbacks. First, he played for the hapless Pittsburgh Pirates, who in Kiner's last year with them, 1952, lost a record 112 of 154 games. Second, he played for Branch Rickey, whose Ohio Wesleyan classmate John Galbreath had been a successful real-estate developer in Columbus, Ohio; who owned the Pirates (as well as Darby Dan Farms, breeder of several Kentucky Derby winning racehorses); and who had brought Rickey in as the Pirates' chief executive after Walter O'Malley had eased Rickey out as president of the Brooklyn Dodgers after the 1950 season.

Following the 1952 season, a year in which Kiner had again captured the home run crown, Rickey traded him to the Chicago Cubs for six forgettable players (no more than "six jockstraps" according to Pirates broadcaster Bob Prince).[13] "We finished last with you and we can finish last without you," Rickey told Kiner.[14]

But Kiner was the most popular Pirate, whose presence sold tickets. According to Pirate teammates at the time, such as Vernon Law, Bob Friend, and Dick Groat, after Kiner's last at bat, the stands emptied, no matter whether the Pirates were winning or losing, no matter whether the game was close or a runaway. Kiner, though, and largely Kiner alone, had brought them in through the front door.

So why did Rickey trade Kiner away? Because in addition to six no-name players, the Pirates also received $150,000 ($2.3 million today), of which Rickey took a hefty portion. From his earliest days with the St. Louis Cardinals, to his last days with the Pirates, with the Dodgers in between, Rickey's contracts always provided that he would personally receive a portion of the profit made on any player traded. So, in addition to a $55,000 or $65,000 annual salary, which was lowered only during the war years (to $40,000), Rickey made a healthy addition to his contract salary by peddling baseball flesh.[15]

Cash for Players and Cash for Branch Rickey

Rickey always bragged of himself as a supreme judge of baseball talent. A principal plank in his platform was that it was far better to have traded a player a year early than a year too late.[16] At the latter point, the player would have lost a major portion of his market value. One of Rickey's sayings, of which he had a multitude, was "Never trust a guy with a bad ankle, knee or arm. The day you need them, something will go wrong." Rickey "could look at a player and in an instant know if he was a half-step slower . . . if he couldn't pull to his power the way he did the year before."[17]

But why cash? And why did Rickey trade away so many stars, whose presence on the field greatly bulked up the gate, like Ralph Kiner, Dizzy Dean, Rip Collins, Johnny Mize, Ducky Medwick (twice), and countless other stars, all of whom could be expected to add significantly to attendance?

A few Rickey watchers among players and at least one among sportswriters made this criticism, that Rickey churned players so that he could line his pockets with cash received, but no one particularly seems to have highlighted it. Further, no one seems to have noted the irony that the man most responsible for beginning the integration of Major League Baseball consistently made money for himself by selling baseball players.

Baseball historians write about many of Branch Rickey's attributes but two stand out. First, of course, is his role in integrating baseball and the methodical way in which he went about that. Second is his development, first in the 1920s at St. Louis, and then at Brooklyn, of the first Minor League farms systems, which had been unknown until Rickey developed the first and were sometimes referred to derisively as "Rickey's chain gang."[18] By the early 1920s, Rickey and the Cardinals had seven hundred players under contract to St. Louis.[19]

The inference that arises, though, is that Rickey developed farm clubs not only to feed talent to the Major League club. Another motivation may well have been to provide him with additional raw material for his player sales operation (except for one or two occasions, Rickey never seems to have outlaid cash for the purchase of a player, only to sell them).[20]

Rickey's trades included the following:

- Traded Jay Hanna "Dizzy" Dean in 1938, from the St. Louis Cardinals to the Chicago Cubs for three faceless players and $185,000 cash ($8.07 million today). Dean had pitched over three hundred innings per year for the Cardinals. He had won thirty, losing only seven, with a 2.66 ERA, in 1934.[21] Rickey gave as an excuse that the Deans (pitchers Dizzy and Paul) complained constantly about their salaries. Ever colorful, when holding out in 1936 Dizzy had said, "I am lopsided on one shoulder from that wheel, and the grindstone has my nose as flat as a policeman's foot."[22]

- Traded Joe "Ducky" Medwick, a star of the Gashouse Gang, from the Cardinals to the Dodgers for three players and $125,000 ($5.45 million) in 1939. In 1941, after being traded, Medwick hit .318, with 18 HR and 88 RBIs, for the Dodgers. When, in late 1942, Rickey arrived in Brooklyn, he traded Medwick again, to the New York Giants, again, for no-name players and cash.

- Sold pitcher Paul "the Dude" Derringer from the Cardinals to the Cincinnati Reds, ostensibly because Rickey did not approve of Derringer's playboy lifestyle. Rickey got the ultimate playboy of the time, shortstop Leo "The Lip" Durocher, in return. Rickey and the Cardinals received a generous cash payment as well ($75,000, or $4.75 million in today's terms).[23] Derringer went on to be a twenty-game winner for the Reds.

- In 1941 sold Hall of Fame first baseman Johnny Mize to the Giants for $50,000 ($1.89 million) and several journeymen players. Rickey opined that Mize was too slow and past his prime. The truth was that Mize had hired an agent to negotiate his salary, a rarity in those days, which Rickey attempted to stanch. In 1942 for the Giants, Mize hit twenty-six home runs, second in the National League.[24]

- While at the Dodgers, sold MVP first baseman (1941) Dolph Camilli to the New York Giants for cash, claiming that Camilli was "no longer able to pull pitches over the 32-foot screen down Ebbets Field's cozy 297-foot right-field line, and no longer demonstrate[ed] quick footwork around first base."[25] Brooklyn fans were outraged and carried "Rickey the Wrecker" and "Go Back to St. Louis, You Bum" signs outside Ebbets Field.[26]

- Traded Dodgers second baseman Billy Herman to the Boston Braves for $50,001 in 1946.

- Sold infielder Monte Basgall from the Dodgers to the Pirates for $50,001 ($901,000 today) in 1950.[27]

- At the Pirates, traded Murray Dickson to the Philadelphia Phillies for $80,000 cash in 1955.[28]

- At the Pirates, sold Daniel O'Connell to the Milwaukee Braves for six Minor League players and cash.[29]

Rickey presented a contrite facade to reporters and to the public with statements such as: "It wasn't until after I sold Dolph Camilli . . . that I realized what an idol I had peddled down the river," and "The Dizzy Dean deal broke my heart."[30] Words to the contrary, Rickey always continued his "players for cash" mode of operation alongside his receipt of one of the highest salaries in baseball. Rickey's base salary with the Pirates was $100,000 for five years ($1.62 million today), with a share of the cash received on player sales and with the contractual assurance of a five-year $50,000-per-year consultancy following retirement from active management.[31]

Contemporaneous Criticism

The list of trades Rickey engineered, which seem invariably to have included a cash element, goes on and on, with the inescapable implication that, in addition to fattening the team's treasury, Rickey was funding the add-on to his base salary. He even engineered a $100,000 finder's fee for himself if the sale of the Cardinals from Sam Breadon to Oklahoma oilman Lewis Wentz had gone through, which ultimately it did not.[32]

At the time a few critics criticized Rickey for his selfish, or at least mixed, motives in player sales. Cardinals Johnny Mize and Enos Slaughter "believed that [Rickey] didn't want to win pennants but only wanted to finish close enough to the top to draw fans and turn a profit."[33] Reporter Roy Stockton of the *St. Louis Post-Dispatch* wrote that "Rickey was 'always looking for commissions on player deals, which clouded his judgment.'"[34]

No one seems to have homed in on the duplicity of Rickey selling baseball flesh while leading the fight to integrate Major League Baseball. Rickey's biographer Lee Lowenfish calls Mize's, Slaughter's, and, by implication, Stockton's beliefs "erroneous." Yet Rickey's player deals and receipt of cash represented a conflict of interest that caused him to serve his own personal interests rather than at all times the best interests of the baseball club for which he worked. Few modern boards of director would allow such a "side job" arrangement for one of its executives.[35]

Baseball Ethics Generally

Rickey's side deal was not the first and would not be the last in the baseball world. Through some of their best years, the late 1940s and 1950s, the New York Yankees won twelve American League pennants in fifteen years. During that era the notoriously tight-fisted George Weiss was the Yankees' GM. In salary negotiations Weiss would include player's World Series checks as part of their base salaries so that Weiss could argue that players already were well compensated and thus didn't merit significant raises, or any raise at all. Then, too, after all, they were Yankees: a World Series paycheck was a routine, recurring item.

What players later discovered was that Weiss had cut a secret deal with Yankees' ownership. Dan Topping and Del Webb would give Weiss a budget, say, $1 million for salaries that year. The secret agreement then was that Weiss could pocket 10 percent of the difference (the shortfall) of actual salaries (say, $600,000) from the budgeted amount. Weiss therefore used every artifice he could think of to keep player salaries down.[36] The New York players hated George Weiss. They felt he was not only a hard bargainer but, after they learned of his side deal, that he also cheated them. Nonetheless, under Weiss and with his secret side deals, the Yankees kept winning.

Similarly, in Rickey's twenty-one years with the St. Louis team, and during the period when Rickey sold away star player after star player, the Cardinals won nine National League pennants and, in that subset of years, won six of nine world championships.[37] When Rickey assumed the reins at the Cardinals, a popular ditty about St. Louis was "first in booze, first in shoes, last in the major leagues." Budweiser was a hit, but both the St. Louis Browns (later the Baltimore Orioles of the American League) and the St. Louis Cardinals were perennial cellar dwellers. Branch Rickey changed all of that, player sales or no player sales.

Noble Motives versus Base Ones—Beginning the Integration of Baseball

The preceding discussion may have taken some of bloom off the Branch Rickey rose. Now the task becomes to add it back on— remove the tarnish, so to speak (and mix metaphors as well), for Branch Rickey was a great man.

In the 1930s and 1940s, Major League owners cited many reasons for their resistance to integration. One was that the presence of black players on the field would attract African American baseball fans. In turn, the presence of the expected substantial number of black spectators in the stands would deter white fans from attending. Gate receipts would drop significantly, and in those pretelevision contract days, gate receipts were the principal source of cash for Major League Baseball clubs.

The 1946 Wrigley Report (authored by Larry McPhail of the Yankees, Sam Breadon of the Cardinals and Phil Wrigley of the

Cubs), commissioned by the owners, also concluded that "black ball players might attract too many blacks to ballparks, threatening property values" as well as gate receipts.[38]

When Rickey brought Jackie Robinson into the big leagues, the criticism turned 180 degrees. Now the pundits, other team owners, and various other onlookers postulated that Rickey's motive was to *increase* the number of fans in the stands and thus increase the gate receipts. Brooklyn was New York City's largest borough, with a population of 2.5 million, including then as well as now, a substantial black population, which would have been lured to the ballpark by the presence of African American players.

Second-guessers also hypothesized several less noble and indeed nefarious motives behind Branch Rickey's quest to integrate the major leagues. "Jack be nimble, Jack be quick, Jack make the turnstiles click," was the popular ditty describing Rickey's motivation in integrating baseball as purely an economic, profit-seeking one.[39] "Are you stupid enough not to understand that the Brooklyn club profited hugely because of what your Mr. Rickey did?" a mythical critic asked Jackie Robinson.[40]

Critics maintained that Rickey thought of blacks in baseball only after the wartime shortage of qualified players had become acute. At one point during World War II, the Minor League Newport News (VA) Pilots had fifteen players under eighteen years of age.[41] In June 1944, desperate for players, the Major League Cincinnati Reds started pitcher Joe Nuxhall, at age fifteen the youngest big league player ever. In 1945 a one-legged player (Bert Shepard) pitched for the Washington Senators; a one-armed player (Pete Gray) patrolled the outfield for the St. Louis Browns (April 17–September 30, 1945).

In Brooklyn, when he first arrived there, Rickey faced a shortage of players not only because of the war but also because in Brooklyn he had no farm system like the one he had developed in St. Louis. Bringing black players such as Robinson on board was for Rickey a solution to the player-shortage problem, until such time as Rickey could develop a farm system. "[Rickey] maintained that the Brooklyn organization was faced with a bleak future unless radical innovations were put in place."[42]

Rickey turned to blacks as candidates because he could get them cheap. He could and did obtain them cheap, although whether that was his motivation is a different question. Rickey did not pay the Negro League's Kansas Monarchs anything when he signed Jackie Robinson to a contract with the Montreal Royals. The Monarch's longtime owners, J. L. Wilkinson and Thomas Baird, raised a stink about it, to no avail.[43] Rickey insisted, "There is no Negro league, as far as I am concerned."[44] He took advantage of the anomaly that, for the most part, Negro League teams paid players month to month. Because the players had no contracts, Rickey could scout, tamper with, and sign them, or so he felt.[45]

Soon after Rickey had signed Robinson, he raided the Baltimore Elite Giants to sign future Hall of Famer Roy Campanella and the Newark Eagles to obtain future Hall of Fame pitcher Don Newcombe. The "most singular and outspoken of the Negro League owners, Effa Manley of the Newark Eagles, a white woman who chose to pass for black," constantly expressed outrage at Rickey and what in her view were outright thefts. By contrast, when Bill Veeck acquired Larry Doby from the Newark Eagles, Veeck and the Cleveland Indians paid Manley $15,000 ($10,000 plus a $5,000 earn out; $10,000 in some accounts) if Doby stuck with the big league club for thirty days.[46] The hard-drinking, fiery Larry McPhail, general manager of the New York Yankees (and Rickey's predecessor with the Brooklyn Dodgers), contended that Rickey destroyed the Negro Leagues, in part by taking players without compensation.[47]

Social and Moral Motives

Rickey himself stated, "Putting colored players in the major leagues will accomplish something that is long overdue. It is something I have thought about and believed for a long time."[48] Based on not only his Methodist upbringing but also his lifelong religious fervor, Branch Rickey had a powerful social conscience. As early as January 1943, when addressing the membership of the New York Athletic Club, Rickey opened the door by opining that "mass scouting might possibly come up with a black player or two."[49] About the same time, Rickey consulted with George V. McLaughlin, president of the Brooklyn Trust Company and trustee for the heirs of

Charles Ebbets and Edward McKeever, who all together owned two-thirds of the Dodgers' stock. McLaughlin replied to Rickey: "Go ahead. You might turn up something."[50]

As did most other Americans, Rickey read about the 1943 race riots and smoldering racial tensions in Harlem, Detroit, Beaumont Texas, and Tulsa.[51] He sensed the irony in blacks serving and dying for their country in the war were not permitted to enter Major League baseball after they returned home.

Rickey also always recounted the story of a wrong that he had long before witnessed and always wanted to right. As a young player-coach at his alma mater, Ohio Wesleyan, in 1904 Rickey had one black player on the baseball team, Charles "Tommy" Thomas, from Zanesville, Ohio. Thomas converted from outfielder to catcher after Rickey, a catcher, had been ruled ineligible because Rickey had turned professional to play football. Fans, students, and opposing teams subjected Thomas to verbal abuse at many of the campuses the Ohio Wesleyan Battling Bishops visited. At the University of Kentucky, in Lexington, a loudmouthed fan yelled, "Get the n——r off the field." In Morgantown, at the University of West Virginia, fans hurled racial slurs at Thomas.

The apotheosis came when Rickey and his team traveled to South Bend, Indiana, to play baseball against the University of Notre Dame. The South Bend hotel clerk refused to allow Thomas to register with the rest of the owu team and obtain a room. Rickey managed to sneak Thomas into the hotel; Thomas was to sleep on a cot in Rickey's room. Once in the room, Thomas broke down sobbing, rubbing at this skin as if "to forcibly remove the stain of its color." "I never felt so helpless in my life," Rickey recalled. Though the incident occurred long before social justice had become an issue for many, "Rickey instinctively empathized with Thomas's pain of rejection."[52] Rickey and Thomas maintained a lifelong friendship even though Thomas, who had become a dentist, practiced in faraway New Mexico.[53]

Another of the many formative incidents, and a prophetic one, in Rickey's life occurred in February 1938, when Rickey attended the United Methodist Council in Chicago, Illinois.[54] There he met and discussed race and baseball with Karl Everette Downs, originally a Methodist pastor from Pasadena, California, and later the president of Sam Houston College, a small, predominantly black, Methodist school in Austin Texas. Ordinarily, the episode would be unremarkable, two scions of John Wesley's church sharing "the warming of the heart" Methodism and its practices were said to instill. But Karl Everette Downs was pastor and friend to Jackie Roosevelt Robinson, who was then and remained a lifelong Methodist. Robinson credited Downs with helping him "disassociate from the gang" and turn to the Methodist church, religion, and athletics, noting, "[Downs was a] man who influenced me powerfully."[55] Robinson would have been nineteen then, beginning to attract attention throughout Southern California because of his athletic exploits. It is the first known connection of Jackie Robinson with Branch Rickey.

Why Not Earlier?

If Branch Rickey believed so staunchly in racial equality, why did he not attempt to integrate baseball earlier? After all, the Thomas incident occurred in 1904; Rickey did not begin the process of integration until 1946–47, forty-two years later.

The answer to that question lies in St. Louis. Until Major League Baseball's westward expansion in 1958 (Dodgers to Los Angeles, Giants to San Francisco), St. Louis was the westernmost Major League team. St. Louis clubs, especially the Cardinals, drew fans from a geographical area dwarfing that of any other team, butting up against Cincinnati Reds country in western Kentucky and Tennessee, and including all of Alabama, Mississippi, Arkansas, Texas, Oklahoma, Kansas, Nebraska, Colorado, and more. Back then those areas, or certain of them, were bastions of racial prejudice and discrimination against blacks.

St. Louis was and remains a southern city, or at least it has a decidedly southern flavor to it. The *Dred Scott* case, *Scott v. Sandford* (1857), which held a slave not to be a citizen and therefore lacking standing to sue for freedom that rightfully was his, occurred in St. Louis and was in part a cause of the Civil War. Until 1944 St. Louis's Sportsman's Park, where both the Browns and the Cardinals played, segregated black and white fans, using chicken wire to relegate black baseball fans to distant and inferior seats.[56] Given the lay of the land in those years, it would have seemed to anyone who gave thought to it that beginning integration in St. Louis in the 1930s was not only a herculean but also a suicidal task.

World War II then intervened. Rickey moved on from St. Louis to Brooklyn, which he deemed more hospitable to what he intended to do. Even before the war ended, he began to lay plans for what he and Jackie Robinson would undertake.

What was Rickey's motivation? Was it to field a winning team and make money for himself and for the Dodgers? Was it to right wrongs that had smoldered in Rickey's conscience? Was it quickly to make up for the war-induced player shortage? Did the ever-frugal Rickey act because he knew that he could get talented black players on the cheap? Or did it emanate from moral and religious convictions Rickey held?

One answer, with which many but not all would agree, is that Rickey's primary motive was a deeply held sense of social justice, a firm belief that "we are all God's children." An easier answer is that it does not make any difference. According to Hall of Fame player Monte Irvin, "regardless of the motives, Mr. Rickey had the conviction to pursue it and to follow through."[57] He had the conviction, and he had the courage. "It took Branch Rickey to come up with the answers, to follow through."[58]

Wesley Branch Rickey—A Thumbnail Sketch

Rickey was born on a farm in southern Ohio on December 20, 1881. The nearest big town was Portsmouth, situated on the north bank of the Ohio River; a number of Rickeys live in Portsmouth today. The Rickeys came from an area as much southern as northern, where the local dialect consists of a nasal twang, not quite southern but not northern either. Religious belief and religious fervor were strong.

Rickey was one of four children, but two died in infancy. He and his surviving brother, Orla Edwin, played sports (Orla was a left-handed pitcher). Following high school, Rickey taught at a one-room school, Turkey Creek, several miles from his home. Southern Ohio is very hilly country, never having been flattened by Ice Age glaciers like those that scraped the northern part of the state. Rickey commuted up and down those hills, riding a bicycle to school.

At age nineteen Rickey packed up his things and traveled to Ohio Wesleyan University (owu), in Delaware, Ohio, some 105 miles away from his boyhood home and 15 miles or so northwest of Columbus, the state capital. He struggled with studies there, competing with classmates who had had the benefit of a more rounded and advanced high school education than he had. Eventually, Rickey excelled in the classroom, as he had done in sports from the beginning.

While a student at owu, Rickey played football and baseball, the latter as a catcher. By playing for the Shelby Ohio professional football team, for spending money, Rickey lost his amateur status and could no longer play for owu teams. It did not much matter. By showing leadership skills and maturity at an early age (the academics took a bit longer), Rickey became the baseball team's coach as well as a player. After he lost his playing eligibility, he continued on as the team's field manager-coach.

owu graduated Rickey in 1904. His first full-time position was as athletic director, football coach, and baseball coach at Allegheny College, in Meadville, Pennsylvania, about seventy-five miles directly north of Pittsburgh, where he spent two years and worked on a master's degree. He spent summers as a backup catcher for the St. Louis Browns.

In June 1906 he married Jane Moulton, a longtime sweetheart. The ceremony took place in Lucasville, Ohio, another southern Ohio town, fifteen miles directly north of Portsmouth. Branch and Jane were to have five daughters and a son (Branch Jr., known as "Twig") and were husband and wife for fifty-nine and a half years.

owu beckoned Rickey back from Pennsylvania, offering Rickey the position of athletic director and baseball coach if he would leave Allegheny (no more football, for which Rickey was grateful—his Allegheny teams had not done well). While at owu Rickey, ever the devout Methodist, would neither play nor coach baseball on Sundays. The teetotaling Rickey also stumped throughout Ohio, making speeches for the Anti-Saloon League, because as a good Methodist he was firmly against drink.

In 1908 Rickey's scholarly side remerged. He left Delaware, Ohio, to enter the University of Michigan School of Law in Ann Arbor, 150 miles to the north. His departure was never permanent, as Rickey remained a loyal and active OWU alumnus all his life, including many years as a trustee of the school. Burning with energy, though, Rickey also coached the University of Michigan baseball team in his years there as a law student (1909–11).

The great Hall of Famer George Sisler first played for Rickey while both were students at the University of Michigan. Sisler rejoined Rickey in St. Louis as a Brown, in 1915. After a fifteen-year All-Star career, Sisler too became a coach. He and Rickey stayed close friends all their lives.

After Rickey finished law school, Jane and Branch went west, to Boise, Idaho, where Rickey opened a law practice with two of his Michigan classmates. The strong pull of baseball, as well as the lack of gravitational pull in a faltering Idaho law practice, soon lured Rickey back to the Midwest and to professional baseball. He could not shrug off his devotion to the game.

On June 13, 1913, Rickey started work as assistant general manager and business manager of the St. Louis Browns. Rickey, though, did not get on well with the Browns owner, St. Louis ice king Phil Ball, who had recently purchased the team, so in 1916 Rickey jumped to the crosstown organization, the St. Louis Cardinals.

The Spirit of St. Louis

The Cardinals, too, had recently changed ownership. The new owner was Sam "Singing Sam" Breadon. From New York, Sam was "a boisterous, fun-loving man who loved to sing in barbershop quartets. The Bible-quoting, psalm-singing Rickey couldn't have been more different yet they functioned well together."[59] Breadon held the title of president; Rickey, who held the title of vice president, functioned as the general manager.

Breadon introduced a baseball staple, seldom seen today,

the Sunday doubleheader. Rickey managed the team, including Rogers "The Rajah" Hornsby, possibly the greatest right-handed hitter in the history of the game (.397 in 1921, .401 in 1922), and later the 1930s Gashouse Gang, the nickname for the colorful and rip-roaring Cardinal team that won the 1934 World Series.

Rickey was to manage the Cardinals and their front office for twenty-one years, interrupted only by his World War I service. In the "war to end all wars," Rickey saw extensive action in France, as a major heading up an artillery support unit that included Ty Cobb and Christy "The Christian Gentleman" Mathewson. Rickey and Mathewson, of course, go down as two prominent baseball personages who refused to play on Sundays (just as decades later, Dodgers Hall of Famer Sandy Koufax refused to pitch on the Jewish high holidays).

Rickey kept book on hundreds of baseball players, amateur and professional, carrying everywhere he went "a big, over-stuffed black loose-leaf notebook."[60] He used his book and Cardinals' money to purchase outright, or controlling interests in, twenty-eight Minor League baseball clubs: the Houston Buffaloes of the Texas League, Fort Smith of the Class C Western League, and Syracuse of the International League, all of whose players were, directly or indirectly, under contract with the Cardinals. Other Cardinals farm clubs included St. Joseph, Missouri, and Topeka, Kansas. He caused the Cardinals to conduct mass tryouts in places such as Shawnee, Oklahoma, and Danville, Illinois. Creation of the farm system is said to be "Rickey's greatest baseball innovation."[61] Incidentally, the farm system also provided Rickey with a source of ample additional income.

The 1942 Cardinals won the National League pennant. They went on to defeat the New York Yankees in the World Series. Despite the success of the team under Rickey, however, a few weeks later owner Sam Breadon and the Cardinals announced that they would not offer Branch Rickey another five-year contract. Instead, Rickey would be moving to New York to succeed Larry McPhail as president and general manager of the Brooklyn Dodgers.

From that position Rickey planned and launched the first steps at integration of Major League Baseball, overcoming numerous obstacles in his path and bringing Jackie Robinson to the Dodgers.

Rickey's Sayings

"If you worked for Branch Rickey, sooner or later you would inevitably come under a searching moral microscope."[62] Rickey often quoted favorite sayings, spouting them for his underlings, his players, and acquaintances as prescriptions for life as well as a tape measure with which to size up one's past. Rickey's aphorisms tell as much about Rickey the man as any biographical sketch can do:

Measure your conduct against "the scoreboard of life."[63]

Men who sin in haste often repent in leisure.[64]

Look for the best in everybody, but don't allow first impressions to sway you.

Men are what they make of themselves. Education never stops.

Nine times out of ten a man fashions his own destiny.

You get out of life what you put into it.

Discipline should come from within and be self-imposed.

It is not the honor you take with you but the heritage you leave behind.[65]

Coda

My father was a Wesley, Joseph Wesley, rather than Wesley Branch. He too was raised on a farm, by devout Methodist parents, George Mortimer and Ada Alice. After high school, as with Branch Rickey, Joseph Wesley taught in a one-room school up in the hills. The only difference is that Wesley Branch rode a bicycle, while Joseph Wesley rode a horse (a mean stallion named Prince) to school. My father attended a Methodist university, West Virginia Wesleyan, rather than Ohio Wesleyan in the state next door, which Wesley Branch attended. Joseph Wesley, like Wesley Branch, excelled at football and, in his youth, ran track rather than play baseball. In photos of the two men in middle age, they bear a resemblance to each other.

The similarities do not end there. I know what my father was made of. I imagine that Branch Rickey was much the same. Even given their flaws, and there do not seem to have been a few, both—Joseph Wesley and Wesley Branch—were great men who led great lives, whom I very much admire, and with whom I feel a strong and lasting bond.

3

Bill Veeck Compared

One of the most disappointing moments of his life was the moment when he learned that he was not on President Nixon's enemies list.

—MARY FRANCES VEECK, quoted in Dickson, *Bill Veeck*

[Bill Veeck] was proof positive that one man with courage constitutes a majority.

—IRV KUPCINET, *Chicago Sun-Times*, January 3, 1986

Bill Veeck was a lifelong baseball-team team owner and executive who owned one Minor League (Milwaukee Brewers) and four Major League clubs (Cleveland Indians, St. Louis Browns and Chicago White Sox, the latter twice). Baseball historians know him best as an iconoclastic, antiestablishment figure, well known for over-the-top promotions of his teams. His lesser known, more lasting achievement was as the individual responsible for beginning integration of the American League, hiring Larry Doby for the Cleveland Indians a scant several weeks after Branch Rickey, president and general manager of the Dodgers, brought Jackie Robinson aboard his Brooklyn-based National League team.

The contrasts between the two men were numerous. Branch Rickey was devout, although many said a goodly portion of Rickey's piety was hypocrisy. Bill Veeck appeared irreligious, most of his life evincing no religious fervor of any kind. Rickey dressed and acted the businessman, all pressed suits and bow ties, with an office at 215 Montague Street, in downtown Brooklyn. Veeck was an open-neck sports-shirt guy who took his shirt off when he sat in the bleachers with his team's fans. "I will not sit in a box seat in my home park," was a lodestar for Veeck.[1]

Veeck's offices were makeshift affairs, always at the ballpark. As a point of honor, the first thing Bill Veeck did at each new team (Indians, Browns, and White Sox twice) was to remove the door to his office.[2] To players, office personnel, ushers, and concession-stand workers, his introduction was the same, "Call me Bill."[3] While he owned the St. Louis Browns, Veeck, his wife, Mary Frances, and their son lived at Sportsman's Park, where they had space under the grandstands remodeled into an apartment. He had tried to do the same earlier in Cleveland, when he owned the Cleveland Indians, but zoning laws prevented him.[4]

In contrast, wherever he went, Branch Rickey had a large estate, although in New York it was the urban equivalent. Rickey sat in boxes along the third base line, hobnobbing with owners and bigwigs, while Veeck sat in the bleachers, shirt off, talking to the fans. Financially, Rickey prospered, becoming a wealthy man. Veeck, on the other hand, stumbled: he had four stints as owner of a Major League team (again, Indians, Browns, and White Sox, twice), but he never amassed the funds to hang on to any of them. He was "the last owner to purchase a Major League Baseball franchise without a personal fortune."[5]

Rickey's greatest innovations in baseball were the creation of the first farm team system, at St. Louis, and beginning the integration of the National League, by signing Jackie Robinson, at Brooklyn. History has been kind to Branch Rickey. By contrast, at most, Bill Veeck is remembered as having had a supporting role in the integration of baseball. National Public Radio Weekend host Scott Simon, who saw Bill Veeck up close in Chicago and whose memory is more vivid, disagrees with the prevailing historical review, writing: "I wanted Bill Veeck to be the Commissioner of Baseball. I wanted Bill Veeck to be the U.S. Ambassador to the United Nations. I wanted Bill Veeck to be President of the United States. He deserves to be the subject of a musical comedy . . . [or] the lead in an epic novel instead of a subordinate character in another man's memoir."[6]

Veeck the Inventive

Veeck's innovations were numerous, although at least several would not be considered of the highest order: sending a dwarf (Eddie Pagael) up to bat while at St. Louis, installing the first exploding scoreboard in Chicago's Comiskey Park (ten mortars, roman candles, flashing strobe lights, Handel's "Hallelujah Chorus," belching smoke), or promotions such as nylon stocking and orchid giveaways on Mothers' Day at Cleveland. Veeck promoted Family Night, Ladies Day, and Salute to Mexico Night. He caused giant showers to be installed in the bleachers, had games with grandstand management by fans, and preceded games with full-blown circuses or cricket games featuring his players. He staged flagpole sitting at the Cleveland ballpark. He raffled off livestock to fans attending games.

Veeck's marketing ploys ranged from the high-minded and noble ("give a pint of blood to aid the War Effort") to the riotous, nearly catastrophic (Disco Demolition Night at Chicago, with LPs flying through the air, almost decapitating players and fans, nearly as deadly as Odd Job's hat). He initiated many of the giveaways so common at ballparks today: comic books, baseball bats, decals, and batting helmets. He raffled off old cars and farm animals (a donkey once). Numbered among his door prizes were livestock, ten thousand cupcakes, and one thousand cans of beer. He promoted clear sight lines for fans in the grandstands, created by using dwarves as vendors because they would not block fans' views as taller vendors did at other ballparks.[7]

Veeck was the P. T. Barnum of baseball, a one-of-a-kind iconoclast, a gadfly, "the Baron of Ballyhoo," a fresh breeze, and a man who changed Major League Baseball for all time, despite the undying enmity and fierce opposition of owners of the other fifteen Major League teams. *Look* magazine dubbed him "baseball's number 1 screwball"; fellow owners denominated him "a shameless exhibitionist."[8] Clark Griffith, owner of the Washington Senators, openly called Veeck "a disgrace to baseball."[9]

Huey Long, the populist governor of Louisiana, promised voters "a Ford Model T in every garage and a chicken in every pot."

Bill Veeck's mantra was "Every day Mardi Gras and every fan a king."[10] At Cleveland, and before that in Milwaukee and later at St. Louis and in Chicago, Veeck followed through, implementing that mantra every step of the way. In the process he offended all the other team owners, who professed to believe that Veeck's promotions were an affront to the dignity of baseball.

In the game of baseball itself, Veeck introduced the designated hitter concept, the interleague play idea, the playoff system, free agency, and the need for league expansion.[11] His fellow owners liked Veeck's baseball innovations possibly even less than his promotional activities. Signing Larry Doby, thus beginning the integration of the American League, was an action of the highest order, a courageous and noble effort by Veeck, just as significant as Rickey's signing of Robinson to a Major League contract. In fact, the NAACP and other groups dubbed Bill Veeck "the Abe Lincoln of Baseball."[12]

Unlike Rickey, though, Veeck is best known for his unconventional and innovative marketing and management methods, not so much for baseball improvements or for what probably was his most significant achievement in baseball, scouting and signing the first African American baseball player in the American League.

Veeck and His Players

Cardinals, Dodgers, and Pirates called their team president "Mr. Rickey." Indians, Browns, and White Sox players called their president, also owner, "Bill." Veeck was a casual presence, seemingly always around the ballpark. He was taller than average, his head topped with kinky reddish blond hair (which close friends sometimes compared to a Brillo pad) that Veeck always kept short. His build was robust as well, despite his having had a leg amputated in 1946. Not only did Veeck shuffle papers in the front office, plan promotions, and trade players; he would also pick up a brush to paint a fence or help out in an overloaded concession stand.

Veeck had volunteered and served in the Marine Corps in World War II. He was never in heavy combat, though, as most Marines were; instead he injured a leg while working on Bougainville in the Pacific theater. The leg became infected, Veeck neglected it, and after two years in and out of military hospitals, Veeck consented to amputation of the leg. Loss of the leg never seemed to have made him feel sorry for himself or slowed him down in any way. On the contrary, Veeck joked about it and had an ashtray carved into his wooden prosthesis. He would amaze visitors by rolling up his pants leg and dumping ashes from his cigarette (practically everyone smoked in those days) into the carved-out ashtray.

What made Veeck approachable to players, his casual appearance and impish demeanor, contributed to the other team owners' dislike for him. He had somewhat the look of a rascal about him. A smile was always on his face and a twinkle in his eyes. He never wore a necktie. He was unconventional, one of a kind perhaps—not the typical pinstripe wearing, self-important businessman-owner with expensive tie and ostentatious pocket square.

Surprisingly, though, the men who played for Veeck, and later wrote or commented on it, have little to say about him, either praiseworthy or critical, with the exception of Larry Doby. Doby considered Veeck a second father, saying so often. In later years several times Doby and his wife, Helyn, vacationed with their family of five children at Veeck's farm, Peach Blossom Creek, on the Maryland eastern shore.[13] Veeck and Doby had a handshake trust in each other about everything, baseball included.

One player comment did concern the juxtaposition of Veeck's showmanship and circus-master image with his role as a pioneer in the integration of professional sports. In advance of the other players, Lou Boudreau, player-manager in 1946–50 and the Indians' Hall of Fame shortstop, received word that a black player would be joining the team. Boudreau recalled:

> We were in Chicago. . . . I had been unaware that Veeck had been considering a black player. My first reaction was skepticism. Knowing Bill as I did, and knowing his penchant for promotion, I immediately wondered if signing a black player was another publicity stunt, another way to sell tickets. . . .
>
> He assured me it wasn't, "Larry Doby will be a great player, you'll see," Veeck told me and anyone else who expressed doubts about his motives. Still, I had to wonder.[14]

Veeck moved quickly both to assuage doubts or fears on the Indians' part and also to head off any possible insurrection. He met with the Indians players, several of whom were southerners. "His words were forceful. 'I understand that some of you said if a "n——r" joins the club, you're leaving. Well, you can leave now because this guy is going to be a bigger star than any guy in this room.'"[15]

Doby reported to the big league club two days later, at Comiskey Park in Chicago, for a game against the Chicago White Sox. He pinch hit in his first big league game, striking out. Other Indians players of that era, or at least those who penned memoirs (Early Wynn, Al Rosen, manager Al Lopez), have little to say about Bill Veeck, other than to recount and some implicitly to praise Veeck for signing Doby.

More expansive was strikeout king Hall of Fame pitcher Bob Feller. In one of his two biographies, Feller notes that Veeck "read three and four books a week, on every subject under the sun and had a sense of history. He knew that signing Doby was significant." Veeck, though, was a businessman: "He had a sense of purpose, too. He also knew that signing Doby would put people in the ballpark and, most important, he knew that Doby had star potential, enough that he could make [the Indians] a pennant winner for the first time in 28 years."[16]

Feller gives insight into Veeck's management style. "Veeck took the doors off his office because he said that his door was always open to anyone, anyhow, so why have one?"[17] Veeck's home telephone always remained listed in the directory. After games he stood outside stadium gates, much like a pastor on the church's steps, trading notes with and thanking fans.[18] According to Feller, Veeck also "wasn't afraid to do good old-fashioned wheeling and dealing to get good players" for the team.[19]

In the other Feller biography, author John Sickels's paraphrase of Feller's comments echoes the comment that Lou Boudreau had made ten or so years earlier. "[Bill Veeck] had been interested in signing black players before" signing Doby in 1947. "[But Veeck] waited until [Jackie] Robinson was established . . . before making a move. [Veeck] was already a maverick: those who supported integration feared that if Veeck were the first owner to bring in a black ballplayer, that the whole issue would be tarred as a publicity stunt, especially if the player failed." Instead, "with Robinson successful and the bookish Branch Rickey having cleared the way, Veeck was free to move."[20]

Just how much success Robinson had had by then, late summer 1947, paving the way for Veeck's initiatives and a softer landing for Doby, might be questioned. Doby entered Major League Baseball a mere eleven weeks after Robinson and had been discovered by Veeck and his scouts a few weeks earlier than that. Veeck and Doby then integrated a different league, several of the teams in different cities, against different baseball clubs.

Undoubtedly, there were Indians, Browns, and White Sox players who would have preferred a more sedate, traditional baseball man as owner and front-office executive rather than Bill Veeck, baseball's P. T. Barnum. Those players, if there were any, seemed to have remained quiet about their preference in owners and executives, for none of their adverse commentary, if any existed, seems to have survived.

Branch Rickey and Bill Veeck

Rickey and Veeck knew and respected each other. They met at baseball meetings and conducted trade discussions and negotiations together. One anecdote is that Veeck learned never to deal face-to-face with Branch Rickey. Veeck said that he remained in his hotel room, using a bellboy to shuttle back and forth with notes, suggestions, offers, and counteroffers. To the bellhop, "Tell him [Rickey] that I'm scared of him because I know if I go up there I'll end up buying two catchers I don't need for twice as much money as I've got to spend. . . . I'm scared of him. This is one of the world's great con artists."[21]

Much like the opposing attorney who first identifies himself as "just a country lawyer" and then skins his opponent alive, in person Rickey would convey to the opposing side that he was a religious man and altogether virtuous. Beginning with a long-winded recitation of moral precepts and maxims, he would end by getting the other side to agree to what he had had no intention of doing, or finish an oration during the course of which the opponent had no idea to what he had agreed. "Rickey was the only man who could simply outtalk you, outgeneral you and out maneuver you, who could, in short, traumatize and transfix you through the sheer force of language and personality."[22]

Bill Veeck wrote three books. One is about managing the Suffolk Downs racetrack (horse racing), a task he undertook late in life.[23] Two others are autobiographies about his life in baseball, as owner-operator of four Major League and two Minor League professional baseball clubs. The better of those two, *Veeck as in Wreck*, "became an instant best seller in 1962, loved by fans but hated by owners for its belligerence toward them."[24] Sports columnist Red Smith wrote that Veeck's book "was better described as 380 pages of aggravated assault."[25]

But Red Smith must have gotten his Veeck books confused. *Veeck as in Wreck* is a compilation of good baseball and Bill Veeck stories, only a pinch acerbic here and there, a book well worth reading. By contrast, the Veeck book written three years later, *The Hustler's Handbook*, is sarcastic, irreverent, flippant, bitter at times, and difficult to read all the way through. *The Hustler's Handbook*, not *Veeck as in Wreck*, is the aggravated assault. "I have occasionally disagreed with baseball operators—publicly, privately, and semi-privately, in print and out, in summer and in winter, in sickness and in health. I have called them backward, unimaginative, and feckless. I have been known to assail a few of the more worthy as greedy and rapacious. So how come they don't like me?" Veeck asks.[26] That quotation summarizes and seemingly states the single-minded objective of *The Hustler's Handbook*.

Veeck does not spare Branch Rickey, whom he derisively refers to as "Papa Branch," from criticism.[27] Presaging his discussion of Rickey and his constant sale of players, Veeck advances the hypothesis that "baseball, like loan sharking, is a humanitarian sport."[28] Citing examples of Rickey's sales of Eddie Stanky for $100,000 and Sam Jethroe for $105,000, Veeck stands back from the individual transactions and detects a pattern: Rickey "always had that bushy-tailed crop of good young players down on the farm and he'd let them develop until, as he liked to say in his paternal humane way, they 'turned into money.' The reserve strength on the farm allowed him to sell his name players [Dizzy Dean, Paul Dean, Johnny Mize, Rip Collins, Ducky Medwick, Eddie Stanky, Ralph Kiner, Dolph Camilli, to name but a few] while their market value was still at its peak."[29] Rickey, Veeck also notes, "was always a seller."[30] He even asks, "Why?" and answers his own question, at least in part: Rickey "got a percentage on all player sales while in Brooklyn."[31] Veeck, though, never goes further to note that Rickey sold players for cash, lots of it, throughout a forty-plus-years career and that Rickey's contracts, at St. Louis, at Brooklyn, and at Pittsburgh, always gave him a generous cut of the cash proceeds received in return for players.

The last step, of course, would be to note how ironic it was that the man, Branch Rickey, given credit for integrating Major League Baseball was also far and away the greatest salesman of baseball flesh in the history of the game. Veeck did not make that leap. Maybe, though, Veeck was sniffing around it when he titled his Branch Rickey chapter "Snake Oil for Sale" and summed up Rickey as "a man who has spent his life leading sacrificial lambs to the slaughter."[32]

Veeck's other autobiography, *Veeck as in Wreck*, is unstinting in its praise for Rickey: "I think Branch Rickey is a remarkable man. He does things; he has ideas; he shakes the game up."[33]

The Bill Veeck Paradox

Bill Veeck was, as they say, "born to the purple," in Chicago in 1914. To the north of the city were (and are) some of the city's wealthiest suburbs—Kenilworth, Winnetka, and Wilmette. But there were (and still are) ritzy suburbs to the west as well—Oak Park, River Forest, Glen Ellyn, or Wheaton. Veeck and his family lived in the ritziest of the ritzy of the western suburbs, Hinsdale.

Veeck attended Phillips Exeter Academy in New Hampshire, often rated as the top prep school in the United States, uttered in the same breath with Deerfield Academy, Phillips Andover, Groton, Choate, St. Paul's, and other eastern elites. Next, Veeck attended Kenyon College in Gambier, Ohio, named after it principal sponsor, Lord Kenyon of Great Britain, who to this day still attends Kenyon

graduations. Kenyon is the college that produced President Ruth-
erford B. Hayes, poet Robert Lowell, actor Paul Newman, Swedish
prime minister Olaf Palme, and, perhaps most brilliantly, comedian Jonathan Winters, to name a few. Veeck never graduated from
Kenyon, and Exeter before that, but, then again, he did not need to.

For Veeck was born to the purple in a second sense as well,
into the world of professional baseball. Veeck's father, William
Veeck Senior, was president of the Chicago Cubs from 1917 to 1933.
Owner William Wrigley plucked Veeck Senior from the ranks
of journalists who covered the Cubs and their management or,
rather, mismanagement. So young Veeck "was raised with the
Chicago Cubs." As early as age ten, he accompanied his father to
Cubs spring training, out west and to California, at faraway Cata-
lina Island, most of which Wrigley owned. From 1933 on Veeck
became the right-hand man (lower level) of Cubs owner Phillip
K. Wrigley, who in 1933 had succeeded his father both as owner
of the Cubs and as the crown prince, nay, king, of chewing gum.
In his eight years there, Veeck did a bit of everything at the Cubs:
remodel concessions, count and sell tickets, plant ivy along the
Wrigley Field outfield wall, and paint bleacher seats.

His appetite thus whetted, in 1941 Veeck bought the Milwaukee Brewers farm team, then in last place in the American Association. In June 1946, with the help of his backers—meatpacking
heirs Lester Amour and Phil Swift, Chicago investment banker
Art Allyn, and comedian Bob Hope, originally from Cleveland,
and other investors—Bill Veeck bought the Cleveland Indians
for $1.539 million.

Lifelong Dedication to Higher Ideals

In 1947 Veeck signed Larry Doby to a Major League contract, thus
launching integration of the American League. He did so at some
personal cost: "When I signed Doby . . . we received 20,000 letters,
most of them in violent and obscene protest."[34] That rough treatment did not change Veeck's views of Doby. In the snidest book
of all snide books, *The Hustler's Handbook*, though, Veeck pens
only one positive accolade; it is about Doby, whom he describes
as "my dear friend Larry Doby."[35]

By mid-1949, under Veeck, Indians teams had fourteen African American ballplayers, including Doby, under contract.[36] Only two other of the sixteen Major League teams, the Dodgers and the Giants, had any black players at all. The best either one of those racial "pioneers" had was three.

The question that arises, or the paradox that now should be apparent, is how could one from such a privileged and elite background become the person who more than anyone else, including Branch Rickey, was the leader in bringing integration to Major League Baseball?

Reflecting back on his own animus, Veeck muses: "I have always had a strong feeling for minority groups. . . . Thinking about it, it seems to me that all my life I have been fighting the status quo, against the tyranny of the fossilized majority. I suppose that whatever impels me to battle the old fossils [other Major League team owners] also drives me to the side of the underdog."[37] Veeck's attitudes trace themselves to times long before he became a baseball team owner. As an adolescent he "used to see the Homestead Grays and Kansas City Monarchs in the old [Chicago] American Giants' park [Hollywood Park] right across the street from Comiskey Park."[38] He attended Negro League All-Star games that at that time were generally held in Chicago.[39] At that point in his life, he did those things not so much as a racial activist or pioneer but as a kid who seemed color-blind and who was intent on seeing some good baseball (for which the Negro Leagues were famous) played.

Later in life Bill Veeck joined the National Association for the Advancement of Colored People (NAACP). In Cleveland Veeck appeared in advertisements for the NAACP. He did posters with Larry Doby and with Satchel Paige: "*The NAACP gets the ball to you.*" As mentioned earlier, still later, and more seriously, the NAACP and other groups named Veeck, not Branch Rickey, "the Abe Lincoln of baseball."[40] In his autobiography Veeck waxes philosophical once again: "What offends me about prejudice . . . is that it assumes an unwarranted superiority. For as long as I can remember, I have felt vaguely uneasy when anybody tells an anti-Negro joke, an anti-Semitic or anti-Catholic joke."[41] "It only takes one leg [remember Veeck was an amputee], you know, to walk away."[42]

We either don't know or there are a myriad reasons why someone rises above and achieves far beyond where the biases and prejudices of their background might have led them. From a backward
setting in rural Texas, Lyndon Baines Johnson rose not only to be
president of the United States but also to shepherd through Congress the Civil Rights Act of 1964 and the Voting Rights Act of
1965, landmark pieces of legislation that profoundly changed the
United States for all time and righted wrongs of a past century.
So, too, from a privileged and lily-white background in Hinsdale,
Illinois, Bill Veeck emerged to lead Major League Baseball into
the twentieth century and to right wrongs that had persisted for
sixty or more years.

It is to that subject that we now turn.

Bill Veeck and Larry Doby

"Doby was as close to me as any player I have ever known. . . . I am
extremely fond of Larry and his wife, Helyn, and their children,"
Veeck wrote in his autobiography.[43] In 1947 Veeck brought Doby
aboard as the first black player in the American League. Although
it took a while, once he got his feet on the ground as an Indian,
Doby often would drop into Veeck's office to visit and chat. In
Doby's last years as a player, Veeck, then the owner of the White
Sox, traded for Doby, although in 1957 field manager and Doby
nemesis Al Lopez and assistant general manager Hank Greenberg soon conspired to do Doby in, sending him to the minor
leagues (San Diego Padres, then in the Pacific Coast League) as
a penalty for having slumped after a stellar 1956 season (from 24
home runs and 102 RBIS in 1956 to 14 home runs and 79 RBIS in
1957) (see chapter 12).

Veeck went through a divorce in 1949–50. He was forced to sell
the Indians to raise cash with which to fund the divorce settle-
ment and to establish trust funds for the three children from his
first marriage. Then, too, quick to forget Cleveland's 1948 World
Championship, in 1949 the Cleveland fans and the Cleveland press
had also turned on Veeck and the Indians, who finished third
that year despite having one of the strongest teams in baseball.

"What's Happening in Cleveland?" headlined an article written by Wendell Smith in the *Pittsburgh Courier*, a leading African American newspaper of its day. Smith, a figure greatly respected in the world of baseball, then and now, called Veeck "one of the shrewdest and most capable men in all of baseball." He did not mince his words: "The people of Cleveland should hang their heads in shame. [Cleveland] has turned out to be a city of spineless people."[44]

Veeck sold the Indians to Elis Ryan, an insurance executive. Veeck and Doby were parted. In November 1976, in Veeck's reincarnation as owner of the Chicago White Sox, Veeck hired former Cleveland pitcher Bob Lemon as manager and brought in Larry Doby, Lemon's former teammate and friend, as hitting coach.[45] Doby had been serving as hitting coach of the Montreal Expos. Thus Doby and Veeck were reunited, as they had been twice before.

In June 1978 Veeck replaced Lemon, who went on to several World Series victories as manager of the Yankees, with Larry Doby, making Doby not only the second black player but also the second black manager of a Major League team (Frank Robinson was the first). Later that year, in October, Veeck replaced Doby with former Chicago Cubs shortstop Don Kissinger, who was immensely popular in Chicago. Veeck was running out of money and in failing health. He felt he had to do something drastic to increase the gate and the cash flow, although Doby had managed the White Sox to over .500. He adopted something of a whack-a-mole approach and replaced Doby with Don Kissinger. Doby realized and accepted that Veeck had to make a change.[46]

Still later Doby and his family would spend several days each year visiting Veeck's Maryland farm. Larry Doby Jr. remembered those visits fondly as an annual family expedition.

In his autobiography Veeck provides background on the beginning of his relationship with Doby: "When I first came to Cleveland, I was almost sure I was going to sign a negro player."[47] The player's name that kept floating to the surface was Larry Doby, infielder for the Newark Eagles in the Negro League. Veeck sent out his chief scout, Bill Killifer, and then himself went to see Doby play and to investigate Doby's background. In June 1947 Veeck paid Effa Manley, who co-owned Newark with her husband, Abe,

$10,000 for Doby's contract with an additional payment of $5,000 if Doby made the Major League club.[48]

Manley was overjoyed, in part because Branch Rickey, who did not regard player contracts with Negro League teams as real contracts, just smashed and grabbed, oblivious to any piece of paper the player had signed. Rickey never paid the Kansas City Monarchs a single cent when he signed Jackie Robinson for Montreal. He never paid Manley when he signed future Hall of Fame pitcher Don Newcombe from the Newark Eagles. Manley was so impressed with Veeck's forthright dealing "that she told [him he] could have the contract of her shortstop, who she though was just as good, for $1,000." The Indians scouting reports on the shortstop were just as good as those on Doby, but the Cleveland brain trust had thought the Newark shortstop to be "too old." Veeck wryly commented, "To show how smart I am, the shortstop was Monte Irvin."[49] Irvin, of course, went on to star for the New York Giants, hitting .293 lifetime, although he did not break into the majors until age thirty, in 1948, and played only eight years—seven with the Giants and a tail year (1956) with the Cubs. Nonetheless, Irvin is today enshrined in the Hall of Fame, elected by the Negro League Committee in 1973.

Early in July 1947, Doby left his Newark Eagles teammates Monte Irvin, Don Newcombe, and others and took a train to Chicago, where the Indians were playing the White Sox. As instructed, he went straight to the Congress Hotel in downtown Chicago, where Veeck was staying. Doby met Veeck and was then was introduced to the press. Unlike the fourteen-month program through which Rickey put Jackie Robinson, Doby had a baptism by fire. The very next thing, that afternoon, Veeck and Doby took a taxicab to the ballpark for Doby's first Major League game:

> In the taxi . . . I told Larry [Veeck invariably addressed Doby as "Lawrence," which became a term of affection between the two, but he did not, apparently, at their first meeting] "If you have any troubles, come and talk them over with me. This is not the usual con, I mean this. It will take some time for the other fellows to accept you. You have to accept that. You may have to go it alone for a while. That's

why Lou Jones [an African American public relations representative Veeck had hired to help with the transition] is here.[50]

From that moment to the moment when Doby hit a "tremendous home run" to win the fourth game of the 1948 World Series, and eighty-one thousand Cleveland fans rose to their feet screaming and cheering, Doby went through a hell on earth. The ordeal was even harder to endure because of his background. Doby had been an all-sports star at Eastside High in Patterson, New Jersey: football running back, All-State in basketball, and a standout baseball player. Patterson, a blue-collar manufacturing center of one hundred thousand or so, was as integrated as any community could be back then and as thoroughly imbued with sports as most such blue-collar towns usually are. Racial prejudice was something Doby knew existed, but he had never come face-to-face with it before the big leagues. "He had not been abused as a human being. . . . He had not had his nose rubbed in it."[51] Moreover, Doby was a quiet, dignified, and sensitive person. Jackie Robinson, who endured many of the same slurs and abuse, had a fiery personality. If Robinson felt slighted, much less abused, he called it out and shouted down those who had attempted to victimize him. He had a disposition that better equipped him for what he faced than did Doby.

And Doby faced it all: hostile teammates; a segregated spring-training hotel in Tucson; segregated hotels in Baltimore, St. Louis, and Washington when on the road; whites-only taxicabs; ushers who would not admit him to ballparks (once when he was in his Cleveland Indians uniform); bottles and rocks thrown at him from the stands; racial epithets shouted by the fans; threatening letters. Through all this Veeck helped Doby as best he could. As Doby later told an interviewer on National Public Radio, "Bill Veeck was just as important to me as Branch Rickey was to Jackie Robinson. Veeck told me to curb my temper and to turn the other cheek. . . . There were places my wife, my daughter and I could not get into. Veeck would say, 'If they can't go in, I won't go in.' Veeck was quite a man, a great man. I think of Veeck as my second father."[52]

Doby also helped himself get through it. In 1948, toward the end of spring training, the Indians and the Giants were to play a series of exhibition games in the major cities of Texas: Houston, Dallas, Fort Worth, and others. The games were all sellouts. But Texas had on the books a statute making criminal any mixed racial participation on a sports field or in a sporting event. With that in mind, the Indians and the Giants had even gone to the extreme of a backup schedule in case Texas authorities tried to block the games. As Veeck later recalled,

> Doby was treated very badly in Houston. . . . He couldn't get a cab-driver to take him to the park. When he came to the plate the first time, he was roundly booed. Larry took one pitch and then he hit what very well might have been the longest ball I have ever seen hit in my life. . . . . Larry hit two home runs, two doubles and a triple that day and made a couple of sensational catches in center field. In every succeeding year, he was greeted in Houston like a favorite son.[53]

Final Evaluations

Bill Veeck helped Doby through his trials as best he could, but he could only do so much. Doby himself put too much of the weight of the world on his shoulders. "It was a very real and bitter and gnawing battle for Larry all the way," Veeck writes in one of his autobiographies. "He was possessed by the idea that he had to fight the battle for integration for his kids, Larry Jr. and Christine, so that they would never have to be bruised as badly as he had been."[54]

Theirs, Doby's and Veeck's, relationship was one of mutual admiration that lasted both men all their lives. Said Doby of Veeck, "One of the best [and most] down-to-earth human beings I've ever met. . . . I lost my father when I was eight years old. Bill Veeck was my father back then. . . . He will never get the accolades he should get." "He was quite a man, a great man."[55] Scott Simon echoes Doby: "[Veeck] was a compelling and remarkable figure in any field, who stood by his friends, lived by his principles, tried to improve himself, and didn't scrimp on fun."[56]

Writes Veeck of Doby, "It was important to Larry to make this kind of breakthrough [integration] because the problem was always in his mind. . . . With all that, his inner turmoil was such a constant drain on him that he was never able to realize his full potential. Not to my mind, at any rate. If Larry had come up just a little later, when things were just a little better, he might very well have become one of the greatest players of all time."[57]

4

Doby Breaks the Color Line in the American League

Former Negro Leagues star Larry Doby proved to be as good as everyone thought, [in 1948] batting .301 with 14 home runs in 121 games.

—ALLEN BARRA, *Yogi Berra*

[Larry] Doby became the star player that Bill Veeck had predicted he would become when he first introduced Doby to the [Indians].

—DAVID BORSVOLD, *Cleveland Indians*

Nothing could be wider of the mark than author James Hirsch's assessment in *Willie Mays* that Larry Doby was a "docile, uneducated black." Holding a bat, Larry Doby once took after a racist fan who had been baiting him all night. Lou Boudreau and other Cleveland Indian teammates restrained Doby. He was not docile. He had a temper, and once in a while, let it show.[1] Neither was Doby uneducated. He had attended college (Long Island and Virginia Union Universities) for a year. He had spent several years in the U.S. Navy during World War II, further extending his education in the school of hard knocks.

Jackie Robinson and Doby were in fact friends. They often conversed by telephone, comparing notes on the isolation they felt, the substandard food and housing they put up with, and the taunts and slurs they had to endure as the first two players of color in the major leagues:

Doby and Robinson would speak on the phone and tell one another who were the good and the bad guys and which were the good places and the bad places, and how each understood how it was to be alone. "People don't understand what that is [Doby recalled]. . . . Who do you tell about the balls you hit hard that weren't hits? Who tells you he should have had the ball you were charged with an error on? What do you do when everybody goes out of the ballpark after a game and you go out alone? . . . It's a loneliness where you are glad when the next day comes because you know you're back in the ballpark. The best time was in the field."[2]

When Jackie Robinson died a premature death in 1962, Larry Doby was a pallbearer. Based on what they went through, and the bond they formed with each other, Robinson and Doby became lifelong friends.

Doby was a dignified, articulate man who, by and large, let his on-field play set an example. When required to do so, he spoke out about the segregated state of affairs that existed both in baseball and in the wider society, but unlike Robinson, he did not do so frequently. He had a natural reserve about him.

James Hirsch demeans Larry Doby, his skills, and his achievement in integrating the American League. That Hirsch felt free to make such baseless assertions indicates how the persona of other baseball greats has come to overshadow Larry Doby, a great player and a pioneer in baseball history. Let's look at Doby's biographical facts.

Early Roots

Many of the African Americans who first broke the color line came from the American South. Henry Aaron and Satchel Paige both came from Mobile, Alabama, while Willie Mays called Westfield, Alabama (near Birmingham), his home. Ernie Banks hailed from Texas, where as a youth he actually had picked cotton. But not all came from the South. Don Newcombe was from Madison, New Jersey; Roy Campanella from Philadelphia, Pennsylvania; and Monte Irvin from Orange, New Jersey. Jackie Robinson's first years were in Florida, but his mother moved the entire family to Pasadena, California, after her husband had abandoned her, when Robinson was very young.

Larry Doby was one of the first group. He was born in Camden, South Carolina, a sleepy, segregated, but genteel southern town that lies just north of the capital, Columbia. Today a town of 6,973 souls, Camden was not appreciably smaller in August 1780, when Lord Cornwallis defeated the American Patriots in their worst single loss of the Revolutionary War (the Battle of Camden). The Patriots had their southern supply depot in Camden. Camden, then, was an old (the oldest inland town in South Carolina) and sleepy but prosperous place.

As a child Doby never knew want, although neither his surroundings nor diet were sumptuous—far from it. But he always had shoes and clean overalls to wear to school.[3] At an early age, though, both his parents left him, not for good but for long periods of time. His father, David, migrated north to Saratoga Springs, New York, where he worked with race horses, possibly as a groom, and near where he drowned while fishing on a lake at the age of thirty-seven.

According to some hearsay, David Doby was a good or even excellent sandlot baseball player in those parts (Camden), but no hard evidence exists. One of Larry Doby's earliest childhood memories was of accompanying his father to a baseball game in which the elder Doby played.

Doby's mother, Etta, went north as well, to work for better wages as a domestic in various homes in and around Paterson, New Jersey. Alexander Hamilton and the Society for the Establishment of Useful Manufactures had founded Paterson in 1790, alongside the seventy-seven-foot "Great Falls" of the Passaic River. The river and falls provided the energy source for numerous mills and plants that in those days depended on waterpower. Paterson became known as the "Cradle of the Industrial Revolution," the site at which firearms (Colt revolvers), textiles, locomotives, and other goods were manufactured. Paterson was then and is now one of the larger towns in New Jersey (currently, at a population of 149,000, the third largest in the state). Despite the ravages of the Great Depression, in the 1930s Paterson was a prosperous, mostly blue-collar, town in northern New Jersey.

Down south, Doby's maternal grandmother, "Miss Gusta" (Augusta Brooks), took over the responsibility of raising Doby when his parents moved north. When Doby's grandmother showed signs of dementia, his favorite aunt and uncle took young Doby into their home. Life had been somewhat lonely for young Larry: he was an only child and his grandmother elderly. Then he moved in with Aunt Alice, Uncle James and their five children. After he had become famous, he recollected that those years were "the happiest of his life."[4] He also reminisced about the years he lived with his grandmother: "[They] were a lot like my years in baseball: I could be me, but they were hard."[5]

Doby's mother summoned Lawrence northward when he was thirteen years old. He did not share a roof with Etta, though. From year to year, he moved among the homes of various friends of Etta. He attended Paterson's Eastside High School, an excellent secondary school of twelve hundred students, of whom twenty-five or so were black. The school and the district from which it drew were melting pots with Irish, Jews, Italians, and African Americans.

At Eastside High Doby quickly became a sports standout, winning eleven letters playing football, basketball, and baseball while also running track. He was an All-State basketball player, a sport at which he particularly excelled.[6] At the time of his high school graduation, Doby was one of only four high school players in New Jersey history who had been All-State in three sports.[7]

Doby saw few signs of racial prejudice in his high school years. Teachers, students, teammates, and fans accepted racial mixture as a matter of course. The only overt racial prejudice he experienced was when his state-champion high school football team was invited to journey south to Florida, on the condition that the team leave its single black player at home, to play in all All-Star game. Doby's teammates rallied around him and voted to reject the invitation.[8] The team did not go.

At Eastside High only one color line existed, and none spoke of it overtly: black boys were not to attempt to date white girls. To Doby it made little difference. It was at Eastside High that he met Helyn Curvy, who was a year younger and in the class behind his. In 1945 Doby and Helyn married. Their marriage lasted fifty-five years, until her death in 2000, and in the meanwhile they raised five children, four girls and one boy.

The Winds of War

From high school Doby was recruited to play college basketball. He matriculated at Long Island University, then a national basketball power under legendary coach Clair Bee. With the winds of war blowing stronger but for reasons never made clear—he had Coach Bee's blessings for the transfer—Doby transferred to Virginia Union in Richmond, Virginia, where he played for another legendary coach, Henry Hucles. Doby also played semipro baseball but under an assumed name. He did not want to lose his amateur standing, which he needed to keep his basketball scholarship. He then played, briefly, parts of two seasons (Negro League teams played short seasons anyway) with the Newark Eagles.

As the winds of war blew stronger still, Lawrence Eugene Doby enlisted in the U.S. Navy. He went through boot camp at Great Lakes Naval Training Station, north of Chicago. The navy kept Doby at the station, where he spent nearly a year as a physical-fitness instructor for "boots" coming through Great Lakes. It was there that he met future pro-football star Marion Motley. He was reunited with Motley in Cleveland, where Motley starred for the Cleveland Browns, as well as with Cleveland resident Arthur Davis, with whose family Doby lived for his first three years in Cleveland.[9]

After moving Doby around among several temporary duty stations, the navy transferred him to Ulithi Atoll in the Western Pacific. Ulithi, known as "the Barn," was where the navy's Seventh Fleet kept its floating dry docks, repair shops, and resupply facilities for the war against Japan. Doby's duty station for the duration was Mog-Mog, the largest island in the atoll.

There he met and began a lifelong friendship with Mickey Vernon, the All-Star first baseman of the Washington Senators, who was also in the navy. The two played service baseball together, prompting Vernon to write Senators owner Clark Griffith, "asking him to sign Doby."[10] After the war, Vernon sent Doby baseball bats and continued to give him batting tips. Briefly, in 1949–50, they were teammates in Cleveland, where the Indians traded Vernon back to the Senators. Vernon had played for Washington nine years previously, and after Cleveland traded him back to Washington, he played there for another six before finishing his career with stops in Boston, Cleveland, and Pittsburgh.

Back to Baseball

When the navy released Doby in the spring of 1946, he returned to the Newark Eagles, the team that he had brief stints with before he went off to war. Back then an umpire had seen Doby play a sandlot game in Paterson. He told Effa Manley, co-owner with Abe Manley of the Newark Eagles, that Doby could play. Manley asked Doby's mother if Lawrence could play for the Eagles. "Yeah," Etta replied, "if you bring him home after the game's over."[11]

After the war Doby played a year and a half for the Eagles against teams such as the Homestead Grays, the New York Cubans (waiters by day, baseball players by night), the Philadelphia Stars, the New York Black Yankees, and the Baltimore Elite Giants. He played in Yankee Stadium, the Polo Grounds, Ebbets Field, Griffith Stadium (Washington DC), and other big league ballparks. To increase their revenues, Major League owners rented out stadiums, at exploitative prices, to Negro League teams for the periods when the big league teams would be on the road.[12] Typically, black teams gave up 60 percent of their net receipts as a rental fee (gross gate receipts less expenses).[13]

Doby and others (infielder Monte Irvin, pitchers Don Newcombe, Leon Day, and Max Manning) led Newark to Negro League championships in 1946 and 1947.[14] As a rookie ballplayer in 1946, Doby made his mark. The following year was even better. By only early June 1947, Doby and his "sizzling bat" had racked up a .508 batting average, with twelve doubles, three triples, and ten home runs. He hit for the cycle (single, double, triple, and home run, all in the same game) three times.[15]

With his performance in 1947, Doby "became the consensus to become the next Negro League player to attract Rickey's attention."[16] He was a crackerjack infielder who could hit for both power and average. While Rickey had his scouts out so, too, did Bill Veeck, who had become owner and general manager of the Cleveland Indians. Veeck had long harbored a desire identical to Rickey's, that is, to begin the integration of baseball. Earlier Veeck had tried to purchase the troubled Philadelphia Phillies baseball club with the intention of stocking it with black players only to be foiled, according to Veeck, by Major League Baseball commissioner Kenesaw Mountain Landis and National League president Ford Frick (see chapter 6). According to Wendell Smith, Veeck had first heard of Doby in the 1946–47 off-season, "when Bill Nunn, managing editor of the *Pittsburgh Courier* went to Cleveland and discussed the entire idea." Nunn "urged Veeck to look the kid over real good."[17]

Then, one day in June 1947, a black public relations man named Lou Jones started showing up at Newark Eagles games. Jones was a minor celebrity in Cleveland, in part because he had been married to Lena Horne, the famous singer. Bill Veeck had hired Jones potentially to be a mentor and a handler for Doby, the putative signee. Jones identified himself to Doby as a "special assistant to Bill Veeck." He told Doby that the Indians had been scouting Doby for a couple of months, remarking, "I wouldn't be surprised if you are in Cleveland in three weeks."[18]

Clyde Sukeforth, Rickey's scout, had scouted Doby and Newcombe in Newark and Roy Campanella in Baltimore, besides having scouted Jackie Robinson. Roy Campanella, against whom Doby had played in the Negro National League (Newark Eagles versus Baltimore Elite Giants) and then with a Dodgers' farm team, "called Doby to tell him he'd soon be in Montreal where the Dodgers' farm club, the Montreal Royals, played."[19]

Looking back after Cleveland had signed Doby, African American sports writer Wendell Smith notes that "the Brooklyn Dodgers had a scout eyeing [Doby] in every [Newark Eagles] game he played in the last three weeks," that is, in the weeks before the Indians signed him. "The Dodgers planned to sign Doby and send him to Montreal."[20]

For Doby's contract Bill Veeck of the Indians offered Effa Manley $10,000 plus a potential $10,000 earn-out (or was it $5,000?—the amount is unclear) if Doby stayed with the club for thirty days, for a total of $20,000 (or $15,000). Presumably, Veeck paid the earn-out because if he had not Manley would have been heard long and loud (she was a woman who stuck up for her rights and is today the only female in the National Baseball Hall of Fame). Whatever the case, the Manleys considered the payment ($149,390.38 in 2014 dollars) paltry.[21] But compared with what Rickey paid for Negro League contracts (zero to the Kansas City Monarchs for Jackie Robinson; zero to the Newark Eagles for Don Newcombe; zero to the Baltimore Elite Giants for Roy Campanella), Veeck's proffered payment was generous. Manley also offered Veeck Monte Irvin on lesser terms, but to his later chagrin, Veeck passed on the offer, which he termed "the dumbest deal I ever did not make."[22] Horace Stoneham and the New York Giants signed Irvin shortly thereafter.

Branch Rickey said that he simply did not regard Negro League player contracts as real contracts. He termed the leagues as a whole a "racket," and he ignored the contracts.[23] Whether Rickey legitimately held that belief or was just stingy and cheap, which by all accounts he generally was, is an open question. But it was not an open question to Effa Manley. She was a persistent and vociferous critic of Branch Rickey all her life, although she softened a small bit as she lived out her days in Los Angeles.

The Cleveland Indians and the Major Leagues

When Doby joined the Indians, on July 5, 1947, he was twenty-four years old: tall rather than short for those years, but not excessively (six feet one). He was maybe two to three inches taller than the average American, but the kind of intelligence and vitality he radiated took the word *medium* completely out of the equation. He was halfway between lithe and muscular, positively thin compared to the players of today, who pump iron and some of whom ingest steroids and human growth hormones. Doby had been an All-State and college basketball player before devoting himself exclusively to baseball, a fact that helps explain his physical appearance.

Doby had a bright glow to his medium brown skin and sparkling eyes that made him look like an athlete. All the photographs of him in civilian dress show him nicely dressed, with a wool sports coat, a pocket square in the breast pocket, and pleated slacks that emphasize the trimness of his waist. He exudes confidence—but of a very modest, understated sort. He always appears reserved, in control and interested, smiling but perhaps a half step removed from the conversation.

Doby's earliest appearances as an Indian, however, were a bit shaky, incongruent with his play at Newark but perhaps not with Doby's youthful persona. Whitey Lewis, sports editor of the *Cleveland Press*, traveled to Newark. He saw Doby play in the first half of a July 4 doubleheader, a game in which Doby hit a home run. "He is fast," Lewis thought, "but so skinny. And so young. . . . He looked about sixteen years old, all arms and legs." Lewis concluded, "He's just a kid. Jackie Robinson is twenty-seven. This poor kid [Doby was 23½] has no idea what he is getting into."[24]

After Doby's July 4 Eagles game, Lewis and Doby took an all-night train from Newark to Chicago. Doby had a shaving kit and $50 from his Newark teammates. "You also have the weight of their dreams with you," Terry Pluto wrote. "For them to make it, you have to make it. Jackie Robinson isn't enough. There must be more than one, or baseball will find a reason to close the gates."[25]

In Chicago Doby went to check in at the Hotel Del Prado, where the Indians stayed. "No coloreds allowed he was told at the front desk."[26] The Indians had to scramble to find a black hotel nearby where Doby could stay. Welcome to the big leagues.

Doby met with team owner and general manager Bill Veeck at the Congress Hotel. Then Veeck and Doby rode in a taxi to Comiskey Park. At the park Doby signed his first Major League contract.[27] With Doby in tow, Veeck held a press conference where the most memorable comment was by Lou Jones, who told the assembled reporters, "I don't think we have to worry about him getting in trouble by talking too much or saying the wrong thing. He doesn't speak a half dozen words in an hour."[28] In the weeks following the press conference, and Doby's debut on the playing field, Veeck received over twenty thousand letters about Doby. For the most part the letters were "vile and racist."[29] Condescendingly, the newspapers referred to Doby as the "copper colored boy" or as "the mild mannered colored boy."[30]

After the press conference, Veeck introduced Doby to player-manager and Indian shortstop, the future Hall of Famer Lou Boudreau ("The Frenchman"). Boudreau took Doby around the Indians locker room and introduced him. Several of the Indians refused to shake Doby's hand. At least two Indians refused to turn from their lockers even to face their newest teammate. "Not a single . . . spike on the floor broke the horrible tomblike muteness. . . . Then the Indians filed out of the [locker] room. Not a single word was uttered."[31]

Doby donned his gray Cleveland Indians road uniform and then made his way onto the field. He stood there for more than a moment, looking for someone with whom he could exchange warmup tosses. Second baseman Joe Gordon, a future Cleveland manager and a future Hall of Fame player, waved his glove at Doby. "You going to stand there all day waiting for people to admire that major league uniform?" Gordon kidded. Gordon and Doby then warmed each other up, an exercise that marked the beginning of a lifelong friendship. Other Indians such as pitcher Bob Lemon and catcher Jim Hegan were also open and friendly to Doby from the beginning, as later were 1949 additions to the Indians such as Al Rosen (from Spartanburg, South Carolina, and Miami, Florida) and Early Wynn (from Hartford, Alabama), more noticeable perhaps because of their southern roots.

A Rocky Major League Start

In that half year, the second half of the 1947 season, Doby had a miserable start. In his first at bat, as a pinch hitter against the White Sox, he struck out. For the season, he appeared in only twenty-nine games, again, mostly as a pinch hitter, batting .156 with no home runs and two RBIs.

Veeck had declined to follow Branch Rickey's recipe, which called for a year in a less hostile Minor League setting (for Jackie Robinson, it had been Montreal). "I am not going to do like Branch Rickey. I'm not going to sign a Negro player and then send him to a farm club," Wendell Smith quoted Veeck as saying. "I'm going to get [a black player] I think can play for Cleveland without having to go the minors first. . . . He's going to join the club right away."[32]

Some observers, however, thought that the Indians should send their new recruit to the Minors to sand off the rough edges and to quell his nervousness. For instance, toward the end of that summer of 1947, sportswriter Wendell Smith began to doubt Veeck's strategy, as Doby continued to fail. Perhaps "the jump [from the Negro Leagues] is much too great," Smith suggested. "Doby came right up from the Negro Leagues and he had had a difficult time of it." Smith strongly hinted that the Indians should send Doby to a high-level farm team, arguing, "He hasn't . . . had a chance to adjust himself. And he won't get that chance sitting on the bench."[33] Moreover, Veeck had brought Doby up to the big club as "an infielder without any clear roster spot to fill."[34] At that point, the Indians had a set lineup. "Bill Veeck came to realize he had made a mistake. Doby was a good idea. Signing Doby in the middle of the year with no place to play was wrong."[35]

Veeck's approach righted itself in the end, however. Although manager Boudreau remained "distant," Indians coach Bill McKechnie took Doby under his wing.[36] He had Doby read Yankee great Tommy Henrich's book about play in the outfield.[37] In the 1947–48 off-season, the Indians switched Doby from the infield to center field, where he was to play for the rest of his career. They brought in all-time Cleveland great and Hall of Fame player Tris Speaker, himself once a center fielder, to school Doby on playing the outfield.[38]

Despite having to live in segregated housing for spring training, being excluded from "whites only" taxicabs and southern ballparks in which the Indians were playing exhibitions, with so-called teammates refusing to relay manager's and coaches' signals to him, having an opponent spit tobacco juice into his face while he lay on the ground after sliding into second base, and countless insults, slurs, and other hostile acts, Doby responded in the field, not with his bat (see also chapter 17). Years later Doby remembered those difficult times, saying, "You might forgive but you don't forget. . . . The things I was called did hurt me. They hurt a lot. The things people did to me, spitting tobacco juice on me, sliding into me, throwing baseballs at my head. The words they called, they did hurt." [39]

As effectively a rookie in 1948, Doby hit .301 with fourteen home runs, and sixty-six RBIs in 439 plate appearances (121 games). The Indians finished in a tie for the America League lead. To win the pennant, they then dispatched the Boston Red Sox in a one-game playoff.

The Indians faced the then-Boston Braves in the World Series. Behind the pitching of Gene Bearden, Bob Lemon, and Bob Feller, the Indians won the series four games to one. Doby hit a home run off legendary Braves pitcher Johnny Sain, to win Game Four for the Indians, 2–1. In the series Doby hit .318, with seven hits in twenty-two at-bats, including one home run, a double, and five singles. Fabled announcer Mel Allen called Doby "the leading hitter in the 1948 World Series."[40] News reports described Doby as "the outstanding star" of the Series.[41] After closing out the Braves on the road in Boston, the Indians trained home to a town gone wild, starved for a championship since the last one, in 1920. From a dismal 1947 start, Doby had climbed a steep and rocky road to become a genuine star.

Silver Linings

Doby and the Indians played in several segregated ballparks. In St. Louis and in Washington, essentially southern cities, black fans sat in separate sections, walled off by chicken-wire partitions. Doby saw through to the silver lining, however, if ever there can be a silver lining in flat-out discriminatory practices. He claimed that he had his own cheering section, a cohesive and readily identifiable one. Black fans' cheers and applause bolstered him when he took the field or came up to bat, making him feel less lonely.

Other American League city crowds were overtly hostile to the American League's first black player. The movie 42 depicts the baiting and slurs Jackie Robinson endured in Philadelphia from Phillies manager Ben Chapman, his team, and the fans, notorious throughout professional sports as judgmental, hostile, and raucous. Across town Doby experienced the same thing, for in those days Philadelphia fielded two Major League teams, the Phillies in the National League and the Athletics in the American League.

Even the Athletics organization fomented organized racism, directed toward taunting Doby. The team hired a heckler to hurl abuse and invective at him each time he came to bat against the Athletics. The episode with Doby taking a bat into the stands aside, overall Doby was unflappable, cool, and reserved in his demeanor, boiling over only in isolated instances. He ignored the Athletics' paid heckler and went about playing baseball in a "dignified and workmanlike manner."[42] The heckler followed the Indians to New York, where they were to play the Yankees; whether he was then on the As' payroll or not is unclear. After he had heckled Doby in a Yankees game, with Doby never taking the bait, the heckler approached Doby, saying, "You know, you're a good sport." The heckler subsequently disappeared; Doby never saw him again.

Philadelphia was not the only northern city where Doby encountered slurs and hostile treatment. Boston was particularly bad. The Red Sox of that era were termed the "most racist organization in baseball."[43] Owner William Yawkey proudly boasted, "There'll be no n——rs on this ball club as long as I have anything to say about it."[44]

When Cleveland first visited Boston after acquiring Doby, however, Boston stars Dom DiMaggio and Ted Williams went out of their way to welcome Doby to the big leagues. Ted Williams was a man far ahead of his generation. His friend sports announcer Curt Gowdy considered him "the least bigoted man of his time. He could not comprehend judging a player by his color. . . . Baseball [Williams thought] was a universe of its own where talent was the only thing that mattered."[45] The greeting by Ted Williams and Dom DiMaggio ("The Little Professor") was the silver lining for Doby. The remainder of the Red Sox team and the Boston fans treated him rudely, hurling catcalls and taunting him.

One of Doby's favorite people and another lifelong friend was Yogi Berra of the New York Yankees. After Doby could afford to do so, he and Helyn purchased a larger home and moved their family from Paterson to nearby Montclair, New Jersey, where they lived down the street from Yogi and Carmen Berra. When the state of New Jersey opened the Yogi Berra Museum and Interpretative Center on the campus of Montclair State University, Berra was instrumental in one area of the museum being named the "Larry Doby Wing."[46]

In their playing days Berra and Doby were rivals, albeit friendly ones. In 1954, for example, Doby led the American League in home runs (32) and RBIS (126), inching out the Yankees' Berra by two RBIS. In turn, Berra eked out a win over Doby to be voted American League MVP, at that time said to be the closest vote in MVP history. Anyway, as many baseball catchers do, Yogi Berra talked to hitters as they were at home plate. In 1948 and 1949, when Doby was still new to the league, he anticipated that Yogi's chatter would be demeaning, or abusive. Instead, it was, "How are the kids?" or "What's a good place for dinner?"[47] Yogi Berra was not only a silver lining for Doby in those early, turbulent years; he was also a friend and confidante during all their days together in baseball and afterward.

Another silver lining was Doby's relationship with Bill Veeck, who tried to take the sting out of some of the discrimination that Larry and Helyn Doby faced. Veeck took the Dobys out for dinner at nice restaurants.[48] In the off hours, Doby sat in Veeck's office, where he and Veeck carried on conversations about a wide range of topics. The story may be apocryphal, but according to David Borsvold, "When Larry Doby came to the Indians, he strongly but unsuccessfully advised the club [i.e., Veeck] to sign [Willie] Mays and two other Negro League stars, Ernie Banks and Hank Aaron."[49] What a dream team the Indians might have been had they signed other African American All-Star players.

Yankee Dynasty but Doby Comes on Strong

In 1949 the Indians were an even stronger team than they had been in 1948, when they won the World Series. They had acquired future Hall of Fame pitcher Early Wynn from the Washington Senators. With Wynn the Indians had the strongest starting rotation in baseball and one of the strongest of all time (Early Wynn, Bob Feller, Mike "The Bear" Garcia, and Bob Lemon). They had no fewer than seven future Hall of Fame players on their roster (Larry Doby, Lou Boudreau, Bob Feller, Early Wynn, Bob Lemon, Joe Gordon, and Satchel Paige).[50] To compare, the 1927 New York Yankees, called "possibly the greatest team of all-time," had only six future Hall of Famers.[51] The Indians also bought up hard-hitting third baseman Al Rosen (who was Jewish and quickly became known as the "Hebrew Hammer"), according to some, another Cleveland Indian who should be in the Hall of Fame. Yet the team finished a disappointing third behind the dreaded Yankees. For the Indians, who finished 89–65, it was a "terrible year," "a disappointing year."[52]

By contrast, the Yankees were beginning their string of American League and World Series championships. From 1947 to 1964, the Yankees won fourteen of seventeen American League pennants and ten of seventeen World Series. In 1949 the Yankees won the first of what would be five consecutive American League pennants, an integral part of the longer string. Overall, only the Indians (in 1948 and 1954) and the Chicago White Sox (in 1959) interrupted the Yankees' dominance.

To make matters worse, despite a stellar pitching staff, year after year the Indians were second to the Yankees. "The Yankees owned the fifties. The Bronx Bombers claimed every American League pennant in the decade except for 1954 and 1959 and they won the World Series six times."[53] The sting was magnified because the Indians always came so close: "The Indians were a strong team . . . but their efforts always fell a little bit short."[54]

Always the promoter, however, Bill Veeck saw some humor in all of this. In 1949, after a strong Indians team had finished third, he orchestrated a funeral ceremony in center field of Cleveland's Municipal Stadium. Wearing a stovepipe hat and a morning coat, a faux undertaker presided, and Veeck and the Indians buried the American League pennant they had won in 1948.

In 1949 Larry Doby had a good second Major League year with only a bit of a sophomore slump. He hit .280, with twenty-four home runs and eighty-five RBIs. He appeared in 147 of 154 games, with 547 at bats. The year 1950 began Cleveland's string of second-place American League finishes. By then Doby was a fixture in center field, where he exhibited a powerful throwing arm and performed highlight-reel fielding feats. He hit .326 in 1950 (25 home runs and 102 RBIs), .295 in 1951 (20 home runs and 85 RBIs), and .276 in 1952 (32 home runs, 104 runs scored, and 104 runs-batted-in). Casey Stengel listed his power hitters of that era as Mickey Mantle, Duke Snider, Ralph Kiner, and Larry Doby.[55]

After the 1951 season, baseball's bible, *Sporting News*, named its all Major League All-Star team. The outfielders were Ralph Kiner, Stan Musial, and Larry Doby.[56]

But by then, Hank Greenberg, a great player, had taken over from Veeck as Indians' general manager. Contrary to his playing career, Greenberg turned out to be a mean-spirited, miserly GM. He often used a microscope when binoculars would do, particularly in salary negotiations with Cleveland's star players. Doby was not the only victim of Greenberg's stingy and judgmental ways, but he was one of the principal ones.

5

Doby's Middle Years

World Championships, Home Run and RBI *Titles*

Doby became a force in center field, both with his glove and his powerful bat.

—TERRY PLUTO, *Our Tribe*

Larry never, ever told me who were those guys who would not shake his hand . . . He was never negative. He was always positive.

—JOE MORGAN, quoted in Moore, *Larry Doby*

Doby was "second but second to none."[1] "Larry Doby did it all—a pioneer, an All Star, a coach, a manager, an executive and Hall of Famer . . . an excellent husband and father. His story is an inspiration for all who have followed him."[2] Lou Brissie, a white pitcher from South Carolina who was a teammate of Doby's for a time, characterized Doby as the ballplayer "he admired more as an athlete and as a man" than any other.[3] Again, broadcaster Mel Allen listed the power hitters of that era as Mickey Mantle, Ralph Kiner, Duke Snider, and Larry Doby.[4]

Many a baseball player's life story turns out to be what is derisively termed a "box-score biography," a sycophantic replay, game by game and season by season. The reader may find many superlatives describing Larry Doby in this book, but in writing it I've tried to avoid the box-score, easily digested sports biography.

That said, let's pick up again with Doby's 1952 season with Indians, when he hit .276 but with 32 home runs and 104 RBIS. His average dipped to a low point in 1953, to .263, but he hit 29 home runs and batted in 102 runs. He also set an American League fielding record: 158 consecutive games and 421 chances without an error.[5]

Then came 1954, when the Indians won the American League pennant, setting a record of 111 wins in the regular 154 game season. Doby led the league in both home runs (32) and RBIs (126). He finished second to Yogi Berra in AL MVP voting.

Larry Doby had numbers and on-field achievements in the middle years of his career as well as at the beginning. Before we return to that subject, however, in the 1950s Doby encountered off-field difficulties, in particular with the Cleveland Indians front office after Bill Veeck had left and Hank Greenberg had assumed the reins. It is to that subject that we first turn.

A Downside—General Manager Hank Greenberg

Greenberg's biographers, the latest of whom has received accolades for his work, call Greenberg the "greatest Jewish baseball player of all times."[6] The biographer waxes even more superlative a few pages later, calling Greenberg simply "the greatest Jewish ballplayer—nay, athlete—of all time."[7]

Hank Greenberg was a very great baseball player, the "Jewish Babe Ruth." In the thirteen years he played, in a career interrupted by four years in military service in World War II, Greenberg batted .313 with 379 home runs, all but one year with the Detroit Tigers. He finished his career with the Pittsburgh Pirates, traded after a nitpicking dispute with despotic Detroit owner Walter Briggs Jr.

In late 1946 Greenberg's picture had appeared in *Sporting News*: the photograph was of Greenberg holding up a Yankee jersey. The caption read "Hint's He'd Like to End Career in a Yankee Uniform." After seeing the photo, Briggs traded Greenberg to Pittsburgh on the spot, despite Greenberg having hit forty-four HRs, winning the American League HR title for 1946. What made Briggs's action especially rash was that the picture dated from the war years, 1943 specifically, and was not at all of recent vintage. While home on leave from the military, Greenberg had worked out at Yankee Stadium wearing a borrowed Yankee shirt.[8]

Greenberg was tall (6 feet 3 inches), intelligent, and articulate, with bold movie-star good looks. He hit for both average and power. But the "greatest Jewish ball player—nay, athlete-of all time"?[9] Ask Sandy Koufax that. Or what about Ryan Braun or Ken Holtzman or Shawn Green? Many of my Jewish friends could name Jewish All-Star teams that have at least a few members who could give Hank Greenberg a run for his money. Be that as it may, and Greenberg was a great player, he was a mean-spirited, stingy baseball executive.

In 1947, after his playing career had ended, by chance Greenberg met up with the Indians' Bill Veeck in New York. The two closed Toots Shor's, the bar-restaurant that was the haunt of professional athletes, at four o'clock in the morning, kept up talking baseball, and, more specifically, baseball management. Having completed his one year playing for the Pirates, Greenberg ended his career with over $300,000 in savings, or $3.25 million in 2014 dollars, a rarity for Major League stars, of that or any other day.[10]

After their late-night dialogue, Greenberg and Veeck continued their conversation. Veeck, who by that time owned the Cleveland Indians, knew of a minority Indians shareholder who wished to sell. Veeck convinced Greenberg to invest $100,000 in the Cleveland ball club. The share deal fell through, but Greenberg moved to Cleveland anyway. Veeck made Greenberg an assistant to the president (Veeck himself) and later director of the Cleveland farm system.[11] When a divorce settlement forced Veeck to sell the team in 1950, new owner Ellis Ryan named Hank Greenberg general manager of the Cleveland Indians, a position Greenberg held for eight years.[12]

Greenberg, Doby, and Rosen

"Larry Doby was a special case. He was the second black player in Major League baseball, the *first* in the American League. He had nothing but talent. . . . As far as being a ballplayer, he sure could play," Greenberg wrote in his autobiography.[13]

On Doby, Greenberg continues: "Larry was obsessed with the idea that he wasn't getting the publicity that Jackie Robinson was getting. I tried to explain to him that Jackie was with Brooklyn and he was in Cleveland, and it was like night and day. Playing in Cleveland, Larry could never get the same degree of publicity

Jackie Robinson received in New York. Larry was bitter about it throughout his career."[14]

Maybe Doby had reason to be grouchy. After the 1951 season, in which Doby had hit .295 and 20 HR, Greenberg focused on Doby's 1950 production (.326, 25 HR, and 102 RBIs). He insisted on a 25 percent cut in Doby's pay (from $25,000 in 1951 to $19,000 in 1952).[15] When Doby refused to take the salary cut, Greenberg told him to take it or not play. Doby would not be welcome at the Indians spring training camp that year, Greenberg continued. Indians spring training, however, was a venue where Doby was not completely welcome anyway, forced as he was to live in seg-regated housing, even long after he had become a star.

Until the 1970s and "free agency," every Major League baseball player's contract contained a reserve clause. Because of the infa-mous reserve clause, the Cleveland Indians and general manager Hank Greenberg owned Larry Doby. Doby, as well as other Major League players, could do nothing unless the club owning their contract traded or released them. The clubs had the players not only "over a barrel" but in virtual slavery. So Doby accepted the cut in pay and reported to spring training. In 1952,he went on to hit 32 HRs, leading the American League, and 104 RBIs. But the post–1951 season salary negotiation with Greenberg was a mid-point in a deteriorating relationship.

Greenberg also ended star third baseman Al Rosen's career. In the 1950 season, "Hebrew Hammer" Rosen had hit 37 home runs and drove in 116 RBIs. In 1953 Rosen had 43 HRs, 145 RBIs, and a .326 BA. Also, in 1953 Rosen was the American League MVP. After his Hall of Fame season, Rosen went to Greenberg's office to negotiate a raise, hopefully for the 1954 season. Greenberg did not congratulate Rosen, as Rosen had expected. Instead Green-berg pulled out the little green book in which he kept the statis-tics from his own playing days. He compared his fourth Major League year to Rosen's.[16] In his fourth Major League year, Green-berg had hit three fewer home runs but had outpaced Rosen in every other category: batting average (.337 to .326); runs scored (137 to 115); total bases (397 to 367).

"He reduced me to ashes. I was absolutely devastated," Rosen recalled. Instead of a raise to $50,000, Rosen settled for $37,500. Forever thereafter Rosen nursed a grudge against Greenberg. Rosen finally quit baseball in 1956, after only a ten-year career, bound as he was to the Cleveland Indians and to Hank Greenberg by the reserve clause. He begged Greenberg to pay him or trade him. Greenberg replied that he would do neither: "If he doesn't play for me he doesn't play for anybody," Greenberg told the press.[17] In other words, Rosen could either take what Greenberg offered or quit baseball. In 1955, after Rosen had a subpar year, hitting .244 but with 21 homers and 81 RBIS, Greenberg slashed his salary 20 percent. After the 1957 season, Greenberg offered Rosen $27,500, the same as his rookie salary, when Rosen asked for $50,000.

Meanwhile, Greenberg paid aging slugger Ralph Kiner, to whom Greenberg had been a mentor the year he played for the Pirates, $40,000 when Kiner hit .243 and 18 HRS and 54 RBIS. Greenberg paid an aging Bob Feller, then entering the twilight of his career, the highest salary on the team. Perhaps smarting from the favoritism Greenberg showed certain players, Rosen said that "he would rather retire than play on [Greenberg's] terms."[18] Eventually, Rosen could take Greenberg no longer. He quit baseball prematurely and went on to a successful career heading front offices of the Yankees, the Houston Astros, and the San Francisco Giants.[19] Greenberg journeyed on, building his reputation for "contract lowballing . . . not new to baseball but Hank Greenberg [was] . . . a master at it."[20]

In his autobiography, Greenberg claims to be nonplussed by Rosen's departure from baseball: "We got into a beef and so he [Rosen] quit. He still blames me but I can't help that."[21] Years later, Greenberg told his son Stephen "that he went out of his way to make things easier for Al Rosen."[22]

Along the way, during his term as Indians' GM, which lasted until after the 1957 season, Greenberg took further potshots at Doby. In his autobiography, Greenberg states, "Doby was a grouchy person and was not popular with the team, the fans or the media. . . . Doby was as belligerent with his black teammates as he was with everyone else. In fact, I always thought Larry resented the other black players."[23] As chapter 15 chronicles, the Cleveland sportswriter fraternity seems to have ganged up on Doby late in Doby's

Cleveland career. How much of that originated in Greenberg's negative attitudes and words, which germinated much earlier, is unknown, or in the words of Donald Rumsfeld, President George W. Bush's secretary of defense, is a "known unknowable."

Greenberg as the Faux Civil Rights Advocate

Greenberg and his biographers make great claims for Greenberg as the champion of those who find themselves victims of discrimination. Biographers hail Greenberg's "determination in the front office to promote desegregation."[24] Greenberg himself describes his efforts as bordering on the heroic or even saintly.

When the Lord Biltmore Hotel in Baltimore refused registration for the five black players on the 1955 Cleveland team, GM Greenberg asserts: "I said to Spud Goldstein, our traveling secretary, 'This is not going on any longer. In 1956 we are going to write every hotel before the season opens and tell them we will not send our team there unless everyone on the team is accepted and treated as a guest with the same equal rights.'"[25] Very noble until you consider that this was in 1955. Greenberg had been general manager since 1950. In those intervening years, on road trips Larry Doby had been segregated from his teammates. He had endured discrimination since 1947 when he first broke into the major leagues. Even as late as 1955, hotels in St. Louis, Baltimore, and Washington did not allow blacks as guests.[26] Under Greenberg as well, at spring training the Indians still stayed at the Santa Rita Hotel in Tucson, Arizona. Well into the 1950s the hotel discriminated, not allowing blacks. Doby, his wife, and his children had to find a black family to house them. As reported elsewhere, the Santa Rita would not even let Helyn Doby and her baby Christina use a hotel drinking fountain when the baby was choking. Later, when it did permit "integration," the Santa Rita insisted that black players not sit in the lobby or use the main staircase.

Hank Greenberg was the Indians' general manager when all of this occurred. He did not suddenly have the responsibility bestowed on him in 1955. It is more than a bit hypocritical of Greenberg, great player that he was, and of his biographers, to present him as the champion of the oppressed, an exemplar of "broad-mindedness and compassion in race relations."[27] Greenberg could not have been much of a voice for the downtrodden, when discrimination went on right under his nose for seven or eight years and he did nothing about it.

So it is not surprising that Doby may have seemed "grouchy" or "belligerent" when he had to deal with Greenberg. Greenberg was a miser in salary and similar dealings. He was no champion, let alone martyr, for African American baseball players either. In other words, this "emperor" had no clothes. Hank Greenberg's words, and the words of his sycophantic biographer, have to be taken with not one or two but a dozen or more grains of salt. They simply do not match up with any other baseball figure's words and observations about Larry Doby.

Why Did Greenberg Have an Axe to Grind?

Well, for starters, Greenberg drove excessive, almost savagely hard, bargains with Doby as well as with others on the Indians team, such as All-Star third baseman Al Rosen. Meanwhile, he paid $40,000 per year to pitcher Bob Feller, not at the end of his career but when he was well past the peak. Greenberg had played against Feller, which may be one possible reason he was generous toward Feller while being stingy toward Doby and Rosen. Greenberg was generous toward friends such as Feller and Ralph Kiner.

Following the 1955 season, Greenberg traded Doby away "to the White Sox for two unmemorable players," outfielder Jim Busby and shortstop Chico Carrasquel.[28] Before that, in 1951, he peddled away the great Cuban player Minnie Minoso in "a questionable trade."[29] In fact, Greenberg traded Minoso whenever he was in a position to do so, that is, three times. Both Minoso and Doby were black.

Greenberg's view of Doby as jealous of Jackie Robinson also seems wide of the mark. Of course, Doby undoubtedly was jealous to a degree, but he and Robinson were friends. As Steve Jacobson observes, "[Doby] didn't get all the credit he deserved for living so gracefully in centerfield and everyplace else. Jackie Robinson was first. . . . Doby rarely let on how difficult it had been to be second. He rarely revealed his disappointment at being overlooked."[30] Then, too, "Doby survived against greater odds and obstacles than those facing Jackie Robinson. Most of us don't know that," writes Terry Pluto. "Most of us know that Larry Doby was the second African American to play major league baseball. Because he was second, it was supposed to be easier."[31] Doby himself said, "I understand what Jackie went through. Do you think it was any different 11 weeks later [against different teams, in different cities, in the more racist of the two major leagues]?"[32]

The historical depictions of Doby contradict Greenberg. "Dignity was how he conducted his life," Steve Jacobson concludes in his book *Carrying Jackie's Torch*.[33] Joe Morgan, Ken Singleton, Dusty Baker, Bill White, Yogi Berra, Bill Veeck, and scores of other baseball players, coaches, and executives who knew Doby have only praise for him as a dignified, intelligent, but reserved man who was always generous with friendship and advice. Doby was a pallbearer at Abe Manley's funeral in 1952.[34] Twenty years later he was a pallbearer at Jackie Robinson's funeral. The overwhelming weight of the evidence is against Hank Greenberg's assessments of Larry Doby.

Doby, the Indians, and the 1954 Swoon

In 1954 Bobby Avila, the Indians second baseman, won the American League batting championship, hitting .341. Third baseman Al Rosen hit .300, with 24 home runs and 102 RBIs. Larry Doby led the Indians and the American League in two important categories: he hit 32 home runs and had 126 RBIs.[35]

The Indians also had one of the best, if not the best, pitching rotations of all time.[36] The four starters (Bob Lemon, 23-7; Early Wynn, 23-11; Mike Garcia, 19-8; and Bob Feller, 13-3) won 78 games in 91 starts, losing only 29. Three of those pitchers (Lemon, Wynn, and Feller) were elected to the Hall of Fame at Cooperstown. Over the span of 1949–55, the "Big Four" won 479 games, losing only 282.[37] In naming the five toughest pitchers he ever faced, Ted Williams listed two of the three Indians Hall of Fame pitchers, Bob Feller and Bob Lemon.[38]

The Indians won 111 games in 1954, setting an American League record that stood until 1998, when the Yankees won 114 games—albeit in a 162 rather than 154 game season. In 1954 the Indians also bested the Yankees, who won 103 games but still finished second. Later that sequence of events led to the famous Casey Stengel line, "We had a splendid season, but Senor [Al Lopez] beat me *and you could look it up.*"[39] In 1949 Al Lopez, of course, had succeeded Lou Boudreau as the Indians' manager.

The Indians journeyed to the Polo Grounds to play the World Series against the New York Giants, the National League champions. "If the Indians' 1954 season looked too good to be true, that's what it turned out to be—in the World Series they were swept by the New York Giants (who had won 14 fewer games during the regular season) in four games."[40]

It was said of the Giants' Dusty Rhodes that "he was supposed to be an outfielder but he was not on speaking terms with his glove."[41] Some baseball players are like bees: one sting and then they die. Dusty Rhodes was such a player. Seemingly, Rhodes could have swept the Indians all by himself. In Game One of the 1954 World Series, Rhodes pinch hit, launching a home run in the tenth inning, with two men on, giving the Giants a 5–2 win. The game also featured "the catch" by Willie Mays of Indians first baseman Vic Wertz's four-hundred-foot line drive (see chapter 14). In Game Two Rhodes hit safely off Early Wynn and played defense. The Giants won 3–1. In Game Three Rhodes drove in two more runs. The Giants won 6–2. In Game Four Bob Lemon pitched again for the Indians, on three days' rest. He was shellacked with the Giants winning the game, 7–4, and the World Series.

Cleveland Manager Al Lopez was roundly criticized for not starting Bob Feller or otherwise using him at all in the Series. Lopez responded that Feller was "an old man," implying that he was all washed up. "He wasn't that good of a pitcher anymore."[42] But the record shows otherwise. Feller had gone 13-3 during the 1954 regular season, with a 3.09 ERA. Overall, in the 1954 World Series, Dusty Rhodes had 4 hits in 6 at bats, with 2 home runs and 7 RBIS.[43]

Many other excuses were given for the Indians spectacular no-show. Doby, the Indians' star, had an injured hamstring as well as a shoulder he had jammed sliding into a base, and he hit an anemic .154. The vaunted big three had inexplicably high ERAS: Lemon 6.75, Wynn 3.86, and Garcia 5.40.[44] Rosen had an injured hand. It was the latter, however, who gave the most cogent explanation of the Indians' flop: "It was a letdown, pure and simple. All year, people kept waiting for us to fold and the Yankees to catch us. We always [had been] the bridesmaids, and we were sick of it. The 1954 Indians drove themselves to beat the Yankees and, when we did it, it was like winning the World Series."[45] There was also Mays's spectacular catch, Lopez's failure to use his pitching staff effectively, Dusty Rhodes's improbable hitting streak, and the Indians' injuries. "You can talk about how we didn't get a break, and we didn't," Rosen concluded. "In the end, I just think the tank was empty. We had nothing left."[46]

In the Series, confirming Rosen's assessment, Doby had "nothing in the tank." He got only 2 hits in 16 ABS, for a .125 batting average. Moreover, the Indians' colossal World Series flop obscured Doby's splendid regular-season performance and more. The 1954 Cleveland Indians World Series performance stands as one of the biggest disappointments in all baseball history, unless of course you are a Giants fan.

The Other Bête Noir: Al Lopez

Lopez had always been Doby's nemesis. In 1947 Doby and Lopez played together on the Indians, Doby as a rookie and Lopez in the twilight of his career. Lopez made remarks about Doby that could be interpreted as racist (see chapter 17).

In 1950 Al Lopez succeeded Lou Boudreau as manager of the Indians. In this role Lopez alternated between hot and cold on Doby. In 1952, a year in which Doby led the league in home runs (32) and drove in 104, Lopez benched him.[47] Yet in the following year, Lopez spoke glowingly to the media, saying that Doby was his offense and that Doby "carried the team."[48]

After the debacle of the 1954 World Series, as manager of the American League's pennant winner, Lopez was entitled to be manager of the American League side in the summer classic. Doby was on the 1955 All-Star team. Yet Doby was one of the few All-

Stars whom Lopez did not play. Lopez left his own player on the bench, a seemingly intentional slap in the face.[49] Despite the slight, in 1955 Doby had another good year. He hit .295 with 26 home runs and 75 RBIS. Nonetheless, after the season concluded, Lopez and general manager Hank Greenberg traded Doby to the Chicago White Sox. Lopez's parting shot was that "he had just gotten rid of 100 strikeouts," a number typical of power hitters such as Doby (see chapter 17) and a fact of which supposed baseball expert Al Lopez seemed to be unaware.[50] Shep Jackson, a newspaper columnist, lamented the trade, calling Doby "the heart and soul of the team."[51]

Lopez then "dissed" Doby even further. To quiet Cleveland baseball fans, irate at the trade of their star player, Lopez predicted that the players received in return for Doby would outhit the former Cleveland center fielder. Together Chico Carrasquel and Jim Busby hit 19 home runs and drove in 98 runs for the Indians. Alone, in 1956 for the White Sox, Doby hit 24 HRS and batted in 102 runs.[52] He had proven Al Lopez wrong.

Doby liked being in Chicago, playing for manager Marty Marion. He recalled, "In Chicago, I was treated very, very well. I met good people in the community here, and that changed the disappointment I had felt as I left Cleveland. I had teammates that were great—Sherm Lollar, Nellie Fox, Dick Donovan, Jim Rivera, Luis Aparicio, Walt Droppo and [Minnie] Minoso."[53]

Lopez though had the last laugh. In the 1956-57, the Chicago White Sox hired Al Lopez away from Cleveland to be their field manager, replacing Marty Marion. Doby had his nemesis back as his boss once again.

In 1957, for the White Sox, Doby put up another decent year, hitting .288 with fourteen home runs, but in only 119 games. Lopez benched Doby for several skeins of games. Then after the season Lopez engineered a trade of Doby for the second time. Doby was at his home in New Jersey, in the bathroom shaving. His oldest child, Christina, was watching television. When she saw on the sports report that the Chicago White Sox had traded Larry Doby to the Baltimore Orioles, she ran in to tell her father that he had been traded.[54] Doby's manager of eight years and former teammate, Al Lopez, had not even bothered with a heads-up telephone call to Doby. Doby should have "seen the razor blade in the apple" when Lopez came over from Cleveland, but he had not.

In an article published in *Jet*, Doby told his interviewer, "I can't have any respect for a man [Lopez] who lacks respect for a man because he is a minority and acts as if we're always wrong and they're always right. I don't care to play for him." Doby told "Doc Young [of *Jet*] that Lopez's racism had affected his play [in 1958] with the White Sox."[55]

Almost like a chapter in *Alice in Wonderland*, everything was turned upside down. For Doby it could not have been worse, traded again, this time to a franchise (formerly the St. Louis Browns) only a few years removed from being relocated. Instead it got better, for a time anyway.

Travels with Larry

Doby's stop in Baltimore proved to be less than even a cup of coffee, as brief Major League player appearances are known. Doby never played a game for the Orioles. In March 1958 Baltimore general manager Paul Richards, who had insisted that Doby would be his new center fielder, traded Doby and pitcher Don Ferrarese to Cleveland for outfielder Gene Woodling, infielder Dick Williams, and pitcher Bud Daley.[56]

Larry Doby had come full circle to where his Major League career had begun. Things were looking up. Lopez and Greenberg were gone. Doby had many friends in Cleveland and knew his way around the town, but one factor, Frank Lane as the new general manager, loomed large over all the rest.

In 1958 Frank Lane had succeeded Hank Greenberg as general manager of the Indians, beginning one of the more bizarre episodes in baseball, at least insofar as general manager episodes go. Lane was known as "Trader Frank," "Frantic Frank," "The Wheeler Dealer," and by many similar names. In 1958–59 alone, as Indians GM Lane made sixty-four trades involving 140 Major League players.[57] Clevelanders know Lane as the man who traded away Roger Maris. Lane banished Maris, a promising young player, to Kansas City, where a year later the Athletics traded him to the

Yankees. With the Yankees, Maris went on, of course, to break Babe Ruth's single-season home run record.

In 1959 Lane also traded away the heartthrob movie-star-handsome slugging Rocky Colavito, a Cleveland outfielder who had hit forty-one and then forty-two home runs in the two preceding years (1957 and 1958).[58]

Lane had bought Doby back. Lane and manager Bobby Bragan planned an outfield of Minnie Minoso (also traded several times by Lopez), Larry Doby, and Rocky Colavito (soon to be gone, traded away). Plagued by injuries, Doby played only 119 games for the 1958 Indians, hitting a respectable .283, with 13 home runs. With Frantic Frank at the controls, however, Doby's numbers put him on the trading block once more.

6

It Takes a Village (and More)

Efforts at Breaking the Color Line in Baseball

By signing Jackie Robinson and other black players, [Branch Rickey] *single-handedly* thrust baseball into the forefront of the civil rights movement.

—LEE LOWENFISH, *Branch Rickey* (emphasis added)

Jackie Robinson became an internationally known figure: his name and his picture were featured in newspapers all over the world.

—HARRY FROMER, *Rickey and Robinson*

Bill Veeck and Larry Doby also broke the color line and were just as much pioneers as were Rickey and Robinson. Relatively speaking, though, Veeck, and Doby especially, remain obscure, mired in the backwash from Rickey's and Robinson's achievement. Rickey and Robinson receive the adulation, the ink, and the movie coverage.

The nature of Hollywood and the movies it makes is to simplify, simplify, and simplify more. This proclivity to simplify applies with full force to historical events and biographical details. The movie 42, as well as Robinson and Rickey biographies such as those previously quoted, represent Branch Rickey as "single handedly" accomplishing eradication of the color line. Rickey did not. Others, including most particularly Bill Veeck, played important, indeed, crucial roles. While what Rickey and Robinson accomplished truly was monumental, it is vast oversimplification to state or to intimate that they did it alone or accomplished it "single handedly."

A second myth to dispel, and one the movie 42 reinforced, again perhaps in the felt need to simplify, was that the process of integration occurred in the compressed time frame of 1946–47. It did not. Significant efforts and events aimed at spurring Major League team owners to take action occurred each and every year, as far back as 1933 and in all probability before that.

A third myth to dispel is that integration took place in 1947. What actually occurred then was the beginning of integration. The major leagues did not become truly integrated until well into the 1960s. In 1954, for example, the spring training rosters of only three of sixteen teams had more than a token black presence: the Cleveland Indians in the American League (seven black players), as well as the Brooklyn Dodgers (six) and the New York Giants (five) in the National League. Those inroads were made possible only by the forward thinking of and precedents set by three pioneers: Bill Veeck (Indians), Branch Rickey (Dodgers), and Horace Stoneham (Giants).

Yogi Berra once said, "Predicting is very difficult, especially about things in the future." But few, if any, could have predicted the long, drawn-out, and fitful process of integrating Major League Baseball. In 1950, of the eight teams in the American League, once the season began only one (Cleveland) had a black player on its roster.[1] In 1954 the majority of Major League Baseball teams still had on their inflated spring training rosters only a token black or two, out of fifty-five, sixty, or seventy players.[2] The New York Yankees had no black players on their roster until 1955. Last of the Major League teams to integrate (the Detroit Tigers were second to the last), the Boston Red Sox did not have a black player on its roster until 1959.

Accused of being a racist, Tom Yawkey, owner of the Boston Red Sox, responded to the charges of racism. With a straight face, he pointed to employment of over one hundred blacks on his South Carolina plantation: "I have no feeling against colored people. I employ a lot of them in the South. But they are clannish, and when the story got around that [the Red Sox] didn't want Negroes they all decided to sign with some other club," and not the Red Sox.[3]

African Americans in Nineteenth-Century Baseball

In the years following the Civil War, baseball was neither as prominent nor as organized as it is today. The National League existed, having been formed in 1876, but the American League did not come into existence until 1901, with the first World Series played in 1903. Back then, though, some years before the American League existed, baseball was, to a degree, integrated. One researcher found evidence of more than a sprinkling of black players, but not much more, in the 1880s: twenty-seven blacks were estimated to be playing for teams in the higher levels of organized baseball, such as they were.

Some black players achieved fame. *Sporting Life* featured John "Bud" Fowler of New Castle, Pennsylvania, as "the noted color player" and "the crack colored player."[4] The brothers Welday Wilberforce Walker and Moses Fleetwood Walker, the latter a graduate of Oberlin College, played for Toledo and other clubs. Fleetwood played games in the American South, where he endured lynching threats and constant verbal abuse, but he played. One black player from that era is now in the Hall of Fame, Cap Anson, who played for the Chicago White Stockings.[5]

All of this changed in the late 1880s, early 1890s. Formerly enlightened conferences such as the International League adopted bylaws prohibiting league teams from playing any opponent with a black on its roster.[6] An apartheid cloud descended on baseball, not to be lifted for sixty or more years. Why?

Storm Clouds Descend

In part, Major League Baseball exists in a small world of its own, but in part baseball also reflects events and attitudes in the wider world of which it is a part. Two exogenous, "wider world" events were then occurring. First were the enactments, by the southern states in particular (Texas was one of the first, in 1890), of the whites-only primary laws. Second was the accelerating adoption by states, cities, and towns of Jim Crow laws, relegating black people to inferior facilities and, by implication, inferior social status. In turn the latter was a direct outgrowth of the shameful United States Supreme Court's 1896 decision in *Plessy v. Ferguson* (discussed more extensively later). Justice Henry Billings Brown spoke for the court: "We think the enforced separation of the races, as applied to the internal commerce of the State, neither abridges the privileges and immunities of the colored man, deprives him of property without due process of law, nor denies him the equal protection of the laws, within the meaning of the Fourteenth Amendment."[7] Late in the nineteenth century a cloud of apartheid was descending elsewhere, not just in baseball, but in politics, on trains and buses, in restaurants, and at parks and drinking fountains, suddenly and quickly.

Following the War between the States, as it is called in the South, a tidal wave of northerners descended on the southern states, many in search of a fast buck. The lawyers, commercial travelers, ersatz financiers, and the like, termed carpetbaggers, changed the mix and neutralized southern whites' political power. The United States established military bases (Fort Jackson, Fort Benning, Fort Knox, Fort Polk, Fort Chafee, Fort Hood) throughout the South, so that troops might be immediately available to quell any insurrection. Those troops and those military reservations changed the landscape as well. In this changed milieu, blacks registered to and did vote. In the 1870s and 1880s, a few black politicians were even elected to office.

Then something happened. Perhaps the carpetbaggers withdrew, returning to the northern states from whence they had come, removing a leavening element from the mix. Perhaps there was a backlash to the presence of northerners in the South and to Reconstruction. Whatever caused it, one of the first steps toward de facto apartheid came in the form of enactment of whites-only primary laws. These laws stated simply that only whites could vote in political primary elections. The fiction on which such laws rested was that the only state-held elections to which the Fourteenth Amendment and the Constitution applied were the general elections. By contrast the primaries were evolutions of private political parties to which constitutional protections did not attach.

The reality was that the only elections that counted were, in fact, the primary contests. Because the entire South was dominated by one party, the Democratic Party, the primary election became, de facto, the general election. The result was that all at once apartheid characterized the political arena. Blacks could no longer vote, at least in any way that would count, let alone achieve nomination for or election to political office.[8] They were shut out of politics as completely as they were of baseball, and at nearly the same point in time too.

Beginnings of the Jim Crow Era

Homer Plessy was a young black man cited for riding in a whites-only railroad car in Louisiana. He defended his action, among other things asserting in court that he had been denied due process and equal protection of the laws. In *Plessy v. Ferguson*, the United States Supreme Court held that "separate but equal" satisfied the Constitution's demands.[9] Again, Justice Brown, speaking for the court, asserted: "Laws permitting, and even requiring, their separation into places where they are liable to be brought into contact do not necessarily imply the inferiority of one race to the other, and have generally, if not universally, been recognized as within the competency of state legislatures."[10]

The separate-but-equal lodestar spurred the adoption of "Jim Crow" laws throughout the South and in other states as well (Jim Crow was the name of a former slave, chosen at random as shorthand for these pernicious ordinances and statutes.) Blacks had to content themselves with separate (and inferior) schools, medical facilities, drinking fountains, bus and train transportation, restaurants, hotels and other lodgings, and on and on.[11] The descending cloud darkened and spread, not only in the South but through other parts of the nation as well.

Returning to its senses, in 1942 the Supreme Court struck down the whites-only primary laws.[12] Thereafter, through poll taxes, literacy tests, and residency requirements, many southern states prolonged their disenfranchisement of black citizens. Only with the enactment of the Voting Rights Act of 1964 were the storm clouds rolled back.[13] "Separate but equal" remained the law of the land until 1954. In *Brown v. Board of Education*,[14] the court held that separate but equal was never equal, reversing *Plessy v. Ferguson*.

So baseball was not completely a microcosm. It was a part of the wider world insofar as the exclusion of blacks from organized baseball may be seen as part of a wider, and unfortunate, cloud overshadowing society. The whites-only primary laws and embrace of the separate-but-equal mantra are two important facets of that dark period from roughly 1890 until after World War II, well into the 1950s.

The Counterpoint to Apartheid

Lest the reader conclude that the veil of apartheid descended completely, it is important to point out that throughout this period there also were movements against separation of the races, contrary to what the majority supported. The leading spokesperson of the day, who held much sway with wealthy northern whites (who donated millions of dollars to his college), with presidents including Theodore Roosevelt, and with educators (he received honorary degrees from Harvard, Dartmouth, and others), was Booker T. Washington.

Born into slavery in 1856, Washington clawed his way upward and graduated from Virginia's Hampton Institute.[15] At age twenty-five, he became the first president of Alabama's new Tuskegee Normal and Industrial Institute, a position he held until his death in 1915. In 1895 he made a famous speech, the "Atlanta Compromise," in which he advocated his "go slow" approach, which abjured confrontation with the white majority. Instead Washington advocated and promoted industrial education for southern blacks. One of his stated goals for Tuskegee was "not to produce farmers and tradesmen but to produce teachers of farmers and tradesmen."

The much-acclaimed George Washington Carver (1864–1943) was a nationally known Tuskegee scientist, inventor, and educator. He experimented with crops and uses for southern land long diminished by cotton growing. To promote substitutes for cotton, Carver developed over one hundred uses for the peanut, including cosmetics, dyes, plastics, and paints.

In the North, other black leaders, most notably W. E. B. Du Bois, first supported but then differed with Booker T. Washington and George Washington Carver. Du Bois believed that blacks should confront white majorities over issues of desegregation. He wanted blacks to have the same classic liberal education whites could receive instead of what he regarded as second best, an industrial arts sort of education.

On the opposition side (opposition to segregation), though, the dominant theme of the day was Washington's and Carver's because it was palatable to the well-meaning but still condescending white majority. It also held little in the way of prospects for integration of the nation's sport, Major League Baseball. Nonetheless, the existence of the Washington-Carver theses and their supporters must be noted to dispel any notion that apartheid covered the landscape completely, a heavy fog blanketing everything.

Efforts to End Baseball Apartheid

Back to baseball once more. The Great Depression saw a sudden drop in ticket sales and thus revenue for Major League teams. The drought was so severe that the pundits made guesses about the cause of as well as solutions for the revenue shortfalls. Regarding the former, one sportswriter, oblivious to the foreclosures and the unemployment around him, suggested that a cause was competition from the sport of golf, then growing in popularity.[16] Regarding the latter, famous New York sportswriter Heywood Broun proposed integrating baseball, dropping the invisible "color line" so that gate receipts might increase as a result of an additional fan base, namely, one of blacks. Broun termed the well-known but unwritten policy of segregation as "silly." "Why in the name of fair play and gate receipts should professional baseball be so exclusive?" he asked.[17]

Jimmy Powers, another New York sports columnist, was the newspaper reporter whom, paradoxically, Branch Rickey later came to loath. Powers bestowed upon Rickey the name "El Cheapo," based on the "coolie payroll" from which Rickey paid the Brooklyn Dodgers players. Powers angered Rickey over many years by using the El Cheapo label.[18] Early on, though, Jimmy Powers became "the most articulate and persistent supporter [of] the campaign to end Jim Crow baseball." Among other things, he pointed out that blacks were well integrated into college sports, including football, basketball, boxing at all levels, and track and field, noting, "There are only three popular sports today in which the dark skinned athletes are snubbed—tennis, golf and baseball."[19]

Another early advocate of integration in Major League Baseball was Frank Albert "Fay" Young, called the dean of African American sportswriters. Fay Young was sports editor of the *Chicago Defender* from 1918 to 1929 and managing editor of the *Defender* as well as other black newspapers after that. As early as 1924 Young wrote columns urging Major League Baseball to integrate.[20]

Syd Pollock owned the Cuban Stars, a semipro black baseball team playing in the Negro Leagues. Pollock proposed placing an all-black team in each of the two major leagues, "placing an entire colored club to represent a city like Cincinnati and [another to represent] Boston in the American League." He buttressed his proposal with argument: "With a colored club in either or both circuits, these feats [such as audacious base running], common among colored players, would not go unnoticed and bring greater interest in baseball, with the necessary publicity to go with it."[21]

Then there were the mixed-race barnstorming tours. Barnstorming teams, assembled on an ad hoc basis, toured after the Major League season ended. Barnstormers often drew as many or more fans than did the Major League teams' regular-season games. For example, in 1934 and later (1935, 1942), Dizzy Dean of the St. Louis Cardinals and Satchel Paige, the noted rubber-armed phenomenon, formed two teams, one white ("Dizzy Dean's All Stars") and one black ("Satchel Paige's All-Stars"), which played all over the country for two months each year after the regular season had ended.[22] They received widespread media attention. Moreover, they demonstrated to many that whites and blacks could play on the same field and probably on the same team.

In 1938 the Jake Powell affair highlighted baseball's Jim Crow stance, further infuriating the sizable contingent supporting integration in baseball. Powell, a reserve outfielder for the New York Yankees, conducted a radio interview for WGN, the powerful fifty-thousand-watt radio station in Chicago. Powell allowed that in the off-season, as a policeman or a member of the police auxiliary, his principal pursuit was "beating up n——rs and throwing them in jail." Only after outraged listeners besieged him with calls and letters did baseball commissioner Landis act, giving Powell a slap on the wrist—a ten-day suspension.

Syndicated columnist Westbrook Pegler wrote about Powell and the racist attitudes persisting in some areas of baseball, including the commissioner's office. Pegler then made a "stunning suggestion."[23] "The Yankees or one of the Chicago teams easily could try the experiment of using a star Negro player from one of the semi-pro clubs. The customers would suffer no shock, and the Southern white boys would find after a few games that it didn't hurt them much at all."[24]

Developments during World War II

Following World War II, in 1945 and 1946, Cleveland Indians pitcher Bob Feller reprised the postseason, black-white barnstorming tour, with Satchel Paige again. The two teams played all over the country, often traveling by airplane in a very sophisticated operation. In 1945 they played thirty-four games in Pennsylvania, Ohio, Illinois, Missouri, Colorado, and California, seventeen states in all, drawing 250,000 paying fans.[25] In the two barnstorming tours, 1945 and 1946, Feller's and Paige's All-Star teams played fifty-four games against each other. "Mixed race games drew audiences two to three times bigger than same-race ones. The black-versus-white encounters offered a preview of how it might work."[26]

Not all was smooth sailing, though. Either on his own motion or at the behest of the Major League owners, baseball commissioner Kenesaw Mountain Landis opposed the mixed-race, or for that matter any, barnstorming tours. In 1922, early in his career as commissioner, Landis fined Babe Ruth the equivalent of Ruth's World Series share (approximately $3,700) for barnstorming more than ten days after the season. Later he could not stop it outright, so he issued an edict prohibiting big leaguers from wearing their Major League uniforms on barnstorming tours.[27] By his restrictions on barnstorming, Landis sent a message of disapproval by the powers-that-be in Major League Baseball. The owners feared that they would lose a measure of the control they had over players and their salaries if the players could make significant amounts of money free of the Major League constraints. It was only after Landis had died, in November 1944, that Feller was able to organize his tour and the supporting organization.

Bill Veeck and the Philadelphia Gambit

Before the war, Bill Veeck had worked in the front office of the Chicago Cubs for Philip Wrigley Jr. When the young Veeck was a teenager, his father has been the Cubs general manager, in the 1920s and early 1930s. So Veeck was from a baseball family; baseball was in his blood.

Wanting to test his mettle at a level higher than an underling in the Cubs organization, the younger Veeck put together a syndicate of Chicago and Milwaukee investors to purchase control of the Milwaukee Brewers, then a struggling AAA franchise (with no connection to the current Milwaukee Brewers, who trace their lineage to the expansion Seattle Pilots, who moved to Milwaukee in 1970). Veeck turned the Brewers club around almost immediately, raising attendance with various promotions and gimmicks.

With money in his pocket, Veeck received word that the Philadelphia Phillies were in an *extremis* situation. Owned by Gerry Nugent, the team had lost 111 games in 1941, drawing only a meager 231,000 fans. Essentially the Phillies organization was bankrupt. Knowing of these matters, in 1942 Veeck telephoned Nugent, who divulged additional facts and figures about his club.

Veeck formulated a resolve to purchase the Phillies and stock the team with stars from the Negro Leagues. Earlier the *Philadelphia Record* had offered its solution to the Phillies' woes with an article headlined "Stars for A's [Philadelphia's American League team], Pep for Phils—in Negro Ranks." Phillies field manager Doc Protho had stated that all his troubles would be over if he could get permission to sign "colored stars."[28] The *Record* thought disobeying the Jim Crow prohibition and breaking through the color barrier might be the ticket: "There is even a chance—and [maybe] a whole lot more—that a few thousand fans that have been staying away from the A's and the Phils might come out to see what Paige and [Josh] Gibson and a few more like them might do in the major leagues."[29]

Thinking that it might just work, Veeck traveled to Philadelphia for face-to-face negotiations with Nugent. Having made a tentative deal, Veeck returned to Chicago to make certain his financing for the purchase, to come from several Chicago businessmen, was still in place. Having assured himself that it was, Veeck had several hours before catching the overnight train that would take him back to Philadelphia.

Then Veeck made his mistake. He allowed himself to be convinced, by John Carmichael of the *Chicago Daily News*, that he should make a courtesy call on baseball commissioner Kenesaw Mountain Landis, whose office was in the Chicago Loop. Veeck walked to the commissioner's office and informed Judge Landis (Landis was a former federal district judge) of his plan to purchase the Phillies and to add Negro League stars to the team. Commissioner Landis seemed to remain noncommittal, and early that evening Veeck caught the Broadway Limited for "The City of Brotherly Love."

When he arrived in Philadelphia early the next morning, Veeck discovered that the previous night the National League had taken over the Phillies and that a new owner was being sought. The team was eventually sold for roughly half of what Veeck had agreed to pay. Who nixed Veeck's tentative deal has never been revealed, but all fingers point to Landis and to Ford Frick, then president of the National League and later commissioner of baseball. "I had them purchased. I will always believe Landis leaked our plans to Frick. Frick [then] wouldn't talk business with us," Veeck told a leading sports columnist.[30] "His big mistake in trying to buy the Phillies was going to the Commissioner," said Hall of Famer and former New York Giant Monte Irvin. "He should have just done it."[31]

In 1942 or 1943, then, black players came very close to having an opportunity to play baseball in the big leagues. It was not only Branch Rickey who had the idea and who expended efforts to integrate the major leagues.[32]

Twists and Turns after World War II

The cataclysmic struggle of the war at an end, young men began returning home, having served in combat to defend their country. Many had been wounded; many others did not return home, having been killed in action. In that war 416,837 U.S. military men and women died, and 683,846 were wounded, many of them black.[33] When those young black men who did return home got back to their cities and towns, they found one thing still firmly in place: outside the Negro Leagues, they still could not play organized baseball. Segregation and Jim Crow were firmly in place.

At times the quest toward integration took bizarre turns. In that day and age, and given knowledge of the milieu in the years immediately following the war and of the sacrifices that had been made in that conflict, by black and white alike, it is difficult to believe, but in 1946 the owners of the sixteen Major League teams voted fifteen to one (Branch Rickey of the Brooklyn Dodgers voting "no"; Bill Veeck did not yet own a team) *against* integration.[34]

Owners of that era met periodically to engage in what Warren Buffett has referred to as "elephant bumping." They met to reconfirm that, indeed, vis-à-vis one another, they were still elephants. They did little, if anything, to refine, improve, or advance the game of baseball. Major League Baseball team owners' shortsightedness and isolation from events, or their outright bigotry in some cases, made the owners' actions in retrospect beyond comprehension.

Judge Kenesaw Mountain Landis

Perhaps the commissioner of baseball exerted an undue influence on them. Kenesaw Mountain Landis was that commissioner. His father, Abraham, had been wounded fighting for Union forces in the 1864 Civil War battle of Kennesaw Mountain, William Tecumseh Sherman's only defeat by the Confederate Army in Sherman's Atlanta campaign, which preceded Sherman's March to the Sea. At a loss to name his sixth child, and fourth son, at the suggestion of his wife, Abraham Landis named his son (with a slightly corrupted spelling) after the battle in which Abraham had fought and been wounded.[35]

Possibly because of the name, Kenesaw Mountain, many baseball writers assert that Landis was a southerner.[36] Landis was not: he was born in Ohio. His family moved to nearby Logansport, Indiana, when "Kenny" was eight, and he was reared there. He graduated from Northwestern University School of Law in Chicago in 1891. In 1905 Theodore Roosevelt appointed Landis a federal district judge, to sit in Chicago, where he had a career as a successful corporate lawyer.

The three-person National Commission (American League president Ban Johnson, National League president John Heydler, and Cincinnati owner Garry Herman) ruled Major League baseball early in the twentieth century but neither well nor effectively.

In 1919 the Cincinnati Reds played the Chicago White Sox in the World Series, then a best of nine rather than the seven-game contest it is today. The Reds won, five games to three. Later it was found that several of the White Sox players had conspired with gamblers to fix or "throw" the games. Those who fixed the games, known forever after as the "Black Sox," included pitchers Eddie Cicotte and Claude "Lefty" Williams, shortstop Swede Risberg, third baseman Buck Weaver, and outfielders Happy Felsch and Shoeless Joe Jackson, a great player who was also illiterate. The Chicago State's Attorney prosecuted the eight "Black Sox," but with their attorneys the players won acquittals.

Meanwhile, the owners of the big league teams decided that something had to be done to clean up baseball. The National Commission had proven ineffective. The Major League owners approached Judge Landis, who drove a hard bargain. He was to have near-absolute authority, including the ability to decide whether actions were detrimental to or unbecoming baseball's best interests, if he were to accept the position as the ruling authority for all baseball. The owners agreed to his demands.

In 1920 Landis resigned his judgeship, becoming the first Major League Baseball commissioner, a capacity in which he served for twenty-five years. One of his first official acts was to ban the Black Sox players from baseball for life, despite their acquittal in an Illinois criminal court. Landis is generally credited with cleaning up baseball. During his tenure he suspended fourteen players for betting on baseball.[37] His zero-tolerance rule against gambling or association with gamblers stands today, serving, for example, to bar Pete Rose from both baseball and Hall of Fame recognition.

One salient criticism of Kenesaw Mountain Landis is that he was a closet racist. Certain of his biographers recite evidence to the contrary, namely, that Judge Landis was a liberal on matters of race. But others proffer a different characterization. James Bankes concludes that Landis "made little effort to disguise his racial prejudice during 25 years in office" and that Landis "remained a steadfast foe of integration."[38] Respected baseball historian Lee Lowenfish brands Landis "the chief enforcer of the color line."[39]

A few years before World War II ended, Leo "The Lip" Durocher, then managing the Giants, told reporters that "a grapevine understanding" among Major League owners prevented teams from signing black players.[40] Reports of Durocher's comments set off a firestorm in the commissioner's office. Landis released a strong rejoinder: "Negros are not barred from organized baseball by the commissioner and never have been in the 21 years I have served. There is no rule in organized baseball prohibiting their participation and never has been. . . . If Durocher, or any other manager, or all of them, want to sign one or twenty-five Negro players, it is alright with me. That is the business of the club owners. The business of the commissioner is to interpret the rules of baseball, and to enforce them."[41]

Of course, everyone believed otherwise, holding the belief that Landis was a central cog in, if not the primary promoter of, a whites-only policy in baseball. In one black newspaper, sportswriter Butts Brown disputed Landis's assertion: "There exists . . . an implied 'Gentlemen's Agreement' which will keep everything at status quo."[42] In the leading black newspaper of the day, the *Pittsburgh Courier*, Columnist Wendell Smith described the Landis pronouncement as a cover-up for the same-old, same-old: Landis and the Major League team owners were engaging in "the perennial practice of buck-passing on the issue of color."[43]

Viewed most generously, Major League Baseball team owners had tin ears. They viewed big league owners' meetings and functions as exercises in, again, what Warren Buffett has termed "elephant bumping." Official business get-togethers presented them with opportunities to reassure themselves that, at least in the eyes of fellow owners, they were still bull elephants. Less generously, "the image of heavyweight champion Jack Johnson and his three white wives was always before them [the owners].[44] The owners thought black players would bring lasciviousness and lawlessness to the game, scaring fans (whites) away from the turnstiles. Some owners were outright bigots and racists, who made no apologies for the stances they took.

But in November 1944 Kenesaw Mountain Landis had a heart attack and died. With the new commissioner, Albert "Happy" Chandler, former governor of Kentucky, things began to change immediately, lending credence to the view that, indeed, Commissioner Landis had been behind much of the resistance to breaking the color line. Early in 1945 Commissioner Chandler made his views known: "If a black boy can make it in Okinawa and Guadalcanal, hell, he can make it in baseball. I don't believe in barring Negroes from baseball just because they are Negroes."[45]

Keeping the Pressure On

The milieu in which Branch Rickey and Bill Veeck came to operate was not a tabula rasa. Throughout the later war years and after the war, several influential forces kept up the pressure to integrate baseball. Two were committees, the LaGuardia Committee and the End Jim Crow Committee.

Paul Robeson had been an All-American football player at Rutgers. He had made the unlikely transition to opera and became a star tenor who captivated audiences with his performances in *Othello*. He was articulate and forceful, including in his advocacy for integration of baseball. On December 3, 1943, prior to Landis's death, the owners, general managers and other staff of Major League clubs held a joint meeting at the Hotel Roosevelt in New York.[46] To this meeting they invited a delegation of leading black clergy, newspaper publishers, and Urban League representatives. Landis had invited Paul Robeson as a witness, but Robeson became the principal spokesman for the delegation and what it represented.

Landis opened with a strong disclaimer that "he had not been taken in by the 'propaganda that there has been an agreement in this crowd of men [the owners] to bar negroes from baseball.'"[47] Robeson then took the floor. He warmed his audience by reminding them that he had been an All-American football player and that he had played baseball as well, noting, "I played against Frankie

Frisch when he was at Fordham and I was the catcher for Rutgers."
Turning to the subject of the day, Robeson tried hard to appeal to
the owners' enlightened self-interest:

> I never presumed there was any agreement among you gentlemen to
> bar Negro ballplayers, but merely that you hate to initiate a policy
> that has not been initiated before. We live in times when the world
> is changing very fast. . . . You might be able to make a great contri-
> bution to not only the advance of our own country but the whole
> world, because a thing like this—Negro ballplayers becoming part
> of the great national pastime of America—could make great differ-
> ence in what people all over the world would feel toward us.[48]

Others of the delegation addressed the meeting. They then presented to the assemblage a very modest four-point resolution that
clearly indicated that black players might well have to work their
way up through the minor leagues. Following their presentation,
the delegation departed.

The baseball powers then appeared about to dismiss the resolution with neither discussion nor recollection. Holding up his
hand in a hold-the-phone gesture, Branch Rickey asked, "Are we
to understand that the report from this meeting . . . is to be simply that the matter was not considered?" Wearing either his lawyer hat or his racist one, Commissioner Landis jumped in and
"retorted" to Rickey and the others. "No, no, the announcement
will have to be that the resolution was considered and you gentlemen all remember that it was considered—you each participated
in the consideration of it."[49]

Landis's forceful, suggestive comment continued the duplicity
of major league baseball's stance on integration. The episode also
indicates, however, that the pressure for integration was becoming incessant. The delegation was a forerunner of more organized
efforts to come.

In the summer of 1945, the End Jim Crow in Baseball Committee and movement took shape. The movement's mantra was
an appealing one: "Good enough to die for their country but not
good enough to play for organized baseball."[50] New York Mayor
Fiorella LaGuardia formed the Committee for Unity. Echoing and

building on the End Jim Crow Committee's work, the LaGuardia Committee's call to action was "Never a More Propitious Moment for Integration. We are just concluding a terrible war."[51] Paul Robeson and other prominent persons also continued to speak out.

Horace Stoneham of the Giants and Larry McPhail of the Yankees, among the more outspoken of the baseball potentates, assailed committee members as "professional do-gooders" and ridiculed their work.[52] McPhail went public castigating members of the LaGuardia Committee: "You do-gooders know nothing about baseball. You're just trying to stir up trouble. Negroes [aren't] interested in baseball."[53] McPhail also was one-third of a committee, along with Phillip Wrigley of the Chicago Cubs and Sam Beardon of the St. Louis Cardinals, commissioned by the Major League owners to investigate the integration question. The committee concluded that as late as 1946 the time was not ripe for integration "because a situation might be presented . . . [that] could conceivably threaten the value of Major League franchises." The meaning was that the presence of black players on the field might attract too many fans to previously all-white ballparks, thus threatening the property values of the teams' real-estate assets.[54]

The pressure for integration, though, was mounting, no longer to be ignored, or even ridiculed or belittled as McPhail or other owners attempted to do. It was against this background that Branch Rickey and Bill Veeck began plotting their respective courses of action.

In summary, then, three points can be made: First, it is inaccurate to say that Branch Rickey single-handedly broke the color line, although what he achieved was truly monumental. Second, the process leading up to what Rickey and Veeck did was a lengthy one. Integration did not come about quickly or easily or suddenly. Third, the notion that the 1947 actions of Rickey and Robinson, and by Veeck and Doby, integrated the National and American Leagues is at best misleading. More accurately, those pioneers and their courageous actions began the process of integration that ensued over the following two decades and perhaps longer.

7

The Shadow Cast by Rickey and Robinson

Blacks have excelled in all areas because Jackie Robinson
showed the way we could.

—MACK ROBINSON, quoted in Fromer, *Rickey and Robinson*

BILL VEECK: "You're part of history."
LARRY DOBY: "Part of history? I just want to play ball."

—Quoted in LEW FREEDMAN, *Early Wynn, the Go-Go White Sox,
and the 1959 World Series*

Jackie Robinson is always presented as "showing the way" and as
having done so exclusively. Almost all of today's historical accounts
do not even mention Larry Doby as a racial pioneer or otherwise.
By his outspokenness and his "in-your-face" push for racial equality (and his pugnaciousness at times), Jackie Robinson kept himself in the spotlight. Larry Doby "stood in a dimmer light," off
toward stage left, an advocate, to be sure, but a more muted and
lesser-noted one.[1] As Hall of Famer Joe Morgan said at Doby's
funeral: "There has always been the misconception that Larry was
jealous of Jackie Robinson because Jackie got most of the credit.
Nothing could be further from the truth. Larry was a big fan of
Jackie's. . . . [But] without guys like Larry Doby, the job Robinson
started would not have been finished."[2] But Doby paid a price for
his reticence in terms of how he is regarded today (or how largely
he is forgotten), and in how he was criticized and even attacked
by the media back then (see chapter 15).

Undoubtedly out of lack of knowledge, baseball author Mark Ribowsky states, correctly in part, that "spasms of excitement awaited Jackie Robinson" everywhere he went—but also very incorrectly that "players who followed him were lesser knowns . . . unimpressive on the field."[3] Hank Greenberg, Cleveland Indians' general manager through the 1950s, termed Larry Doby "grouchy" and belligerent," attributing it to Doby's jealousy of Jackie Robinson and relative lack of recognition.[4]

Certainly Doby had no reason to be envious of Robinson's on-field performance. Robinson hit .297, with twelve home runs, in his rookie season, winning Rookie of the Year honors for 1947. A year later, in his true rookie season, Doby hit .301, with fifteen home runs, leading his team to a World Series championship. Doby received no individual honors.

By the end of Robinson's career (1956), Ribowsky concludes that Robinson "had come through the ordeal with a decidedly angry streak [that] led him to see other black players as lesser men."[5] There is no evidence, however, that Robinson ever viewed Larry Doby as a lesser man. In fact the evidence is decidedly to the contrary. Doby and Robinson were friends. As the first two black big leaguers, seeking companionship, they talked often on the telephone during their first few Major League years. They commiserated with each other about the loneliness they felt being the only black players in their respective leagues; discussed their performances; told each other which cities, restaurants, and hotels were good and which were bad; and which teammates were good and which were bad. Although they played in different leagues, when the Dodgers did play the Indians in exhibitions, newspapers pictured Robinson and Doby together, laughing and talking.[6]

Postseason, Doby and Robinson were teammates, barnstorming together after the 1947, 1950, and 1951 seasons.[7] To Robinson, Larry Doby was "a good guy and a very good ballplayer."[8] When Jackie Robinson died in 1972, Larry Doby was a pallbearer at his funeral.

Nonetheless, Ribowsky's comments about the players who followed Robinson show that, merits or no, those black players, also to one degree or another racial pioneers, languish in obscurity, in the shadow of Jackie Robinson. They did so then and they do so even more so now. That is triply true of Larry Doby, who began the integration of the American League.

Two Different Persons

Like Robinson, "Doby was also college educated, rather quiet, shy and competitive, but not the sort of firebrand Jackie Robinson could be," Indians pitcher and Hall of Famer Bob Feller told his biographer.[9] In fact, "Doby went out of his way to avoid provoking incidents–if the man ahead of him [a white] hit a home run, he would wait to shake hands until both were out of sight in the dugout. He encountered so much verbal abuse on a swing through Texas that he retreated into outright aloofness."[10]

On the other hand, Doby was no wallflower or Milquetoast. He had a temper which he let show from time to time. At other times, he was taciturn: "If Doby was withdrawn, his isolation only caused his competitive fire to burn crimson hot. When racism was thrown onto the burner, or when his abilities were questioned, his bat turned molten."[11]

Robinson? Well, Robinson was near or at the opposite end of the spectrum. Jackie had a "simmering rage." "On his expense account, along with the usual items such as meals, rent and transportation, he always inserted 'humiliation.'"[12] Veteran umpire Jocko Conlan put Robinson down as "the most difficult ballplayer [he] had to deal with. . . . Almost every time he was called out on strikes, or on a close play, . . . there seemed to be words."[13]

In his autobiography, Robinson protested: "The minute I began to answer, to argue, to protest—the minute I sounded off—I became a swell head, a wise guy, an uppity nigger."[14] But his teammate, Don Newcombe, said, "[Robinson] was the type of man who had to make his presence felt. . . . Like a boiler, he could not keep it all inside him."[15]

These attributes followed Jackie Robinson even after he left baseball. In a 1968 television interview, he characterized Willie Mays as a "do-nothing Negro."[16] Earlier, in 1964, he had written, "[Mays] ignores the important issues of our time. It's a shame he's never taken part in [the civil rights movement]."[17] Mays responded diplomatically: "Great progress has been made since Jackie broke in. Jackie is a great reason behind that progress. I really admire the guy."[18]

Two points emerge. One, because he possessed a quieter, perhaps less newsworthy, persona, Larry Doby was bound to be in the shadow of Jackie Robinson. By his deferential, often understated ways, Doby put himself more in the shadow of Jackie Robinson and Jackie Robinson's achievements more than he deserved, given his on-field performance and the pioneering role he played in beginning the integration of baseball. Two, Doby is not in his rightful position today, which would still be in Jackie Robinson's shadow but with far more prominence. He is fading or has disappeared completely in many historical accounts.

Measuring Jackie Robinson's Shadow

Chapter 1 totals up the number of books, movies, and memorials to Jackie Robinson. Those totals continue to mount even today. For example, in addition to the movie 42 in 2013, noted baseball writer Roger Kahn (*The Boys of Summer*) added to the Robinson storehouse with yet another Jackie Robinson book, titled simply *Rickey and Robinson*, which appeared in 2013. Kahn's book gained currency through favorable reviews in the *Wall Street Journal* as well as elsewhere.[19]

James Earl Jones, the noted black actor with the stentorian voice, narrates *They Were All-Stars*, the introductory movie at the Negro Leagues Baseball Museum in Kansas City, Missouri. He introduces his discussion of the transition from the Negro National League to the Major Leagues with the topic sentence: "The twentieth century can be divided into halves: before Jackie, and after Jackie."[20]

That is today. But a second question must be asked and an answer attempted: what about back then? Was Larry Doby in the Robinson shadow more, less, or about the same, then as opposed to now? The answer to that question is not easy.

Today we have at least four national news publications: USA *Today*, the *New York Times*, and the *Wall Street Journal*, which appear daily, both in hard copy (print) and online, and the *Huffington Post*, which appears only via the Internet. Between 11 million and 13 million people read each on an average day. One measure of the publicity and recognition the two figures have received would involve comparing their mentions in one or more of those national publications. Who received the most attention might be a strong indication of who cast a shadow in a given field. The magnitude of the differential might also allow one to infer whether the shadow was a long one, a short one, or something in between.

But the United States had no national dailies in the late 1940s, or at least no dailies that rightfully could claim to the distinction of being national. There was, however, a national weekly, one in particular whose subject was baseball. In St. Louis, Missouri, J. G. Taylor Spink and staff each week published an approximately thirty-page news magazine that was the bible of baseball, the *Sporting News*.[21] Regarding either the Cleveland Indians or the Brooklyn Dodgers, St. Louis, Missouri, the *Sporting News*'s home, was a neutral site. Local prejudices that might result in more coverage of one player rather than another seemingly would not have been a factor in the weekly's coverage.

A computer search of the name "Jackie Robinson" in the *Sporting News* archive produced 4,490 hits on 965 different pages in the first five years of Robinson's career (1947 through 1951). A second search, this time of the name "Larry Doby," produced 1,687 hits on 425 pages, for the first five years of his career (July 1947 through July 1952). The ratio of Robinson to Doby references is 2.66. Thinking about the comparison, which is not nearly as dramatic as I expected, led to the thought that, in addition to feature stories and other blurbs, the *Sporting News* also published the box scores for every Major League game played. A portion of those hits (computer, not baseball) for Robinson and Doby, corresponding to the number of games played, did not represent articles or mentions in articles of the two men. So subtracting out the number of games played in the respective five-year periods (763 for Robinson, 653 for Doby) from the hit totals lowers the numbers: 3,737 hits for Robinson, 1,044 hits for Doby.[22] The ratio of Robinson to Doby references rises to 3.58.

But upon further examination of those old *Sporting News* editions, another thought arose. Preceding the reproduction of each box score, the *Sporting News* juxtaposed a one- or two-paragraph prose narrative about each and every game. Those narratives mentioned the names of all, or most all, players who had contributed to the result. So a second set of subtractions becomes necessary. Assuming that on most occasions, the narratives mentioned either Robinson, or Doby, as the case may be, a not unreasonable assumption given the star status of each, it behooves one to subtract the number of games in which each appeared a second time. The subtraction represents the pro forma references in the routine game-by-game narratives that preceded the box scores. For Robinson, the arithmetic is 3,737–763 = 2,974; for Doby, the arithmetic is 1,044–643 = 401. The comparison becomes more pronounced, more dramatic yet. For each mention of Doby, *Sporting News* articles of those days refer to Jackie Robinson 7.42 times.

A Second Comparison

In a very unscientific study, I went through the *Sporting News* edition by edition twice, once for the first two years of Robinson's baseball career, and a second time for the first two years of Larry Doby's career. I copied down, by hand, the headlines of all articles whose headline included either man's name. I also read all, or most all of the articles, at least until I felt I was going blind.

For those two years, "Jackie," "Jackie Robinson," or "Robinson" appears eighty-five times in headlines, more or less. In contrast, "Larry," "Larry Doby," or "Doby" appears fifteen times over reporters' bylines. Seemingly, at least one , sometimes as many as four, and on two occasions even five or seven articles about Jackie Robinson appear in every edition of the *Sporting News* in 1947–48, at least during the baseball season.

It was true at the beginning of Robinson's inaugural season:

"Just Another Game of Jackie—Negro Star Did His Thinking Night Before: 'Brooklyn Players Have Been Swell,'" April 23, 1947, p. 1 (staff)

"New York Scribe's View of Robinson's Major Bow," April 23, 1947, p. 1 (editorial)

"Let Jackie Alone, Well-Wishers Told," April 23, 1947, p. 1 (Harold Burr)

"Jackie Quick on Trigger—Stanky," April 23, 1947, p. 4 (Lester Bromberg)

"Brooklyn Dodgers–Jackie Robinson, Highlights for Major League Lidlifters," April 23, 1947, p. 13 (staff)

It was equally true toward the end of the season:

"Rookie of the Year . . . Jackie Robinson: He's 'Ebony Ty Cobb' on Base Paths," September 17, 1947, p. 1 (J. G. Taylor Spink)

"Robinson's Attitude at Position Wins Praise from N.L. Managers," September 19, 1947, p. 3 (Fred Down)

"Jackie Robinson Tabbed Best on Bases since Cobb," September 19, 1947, p. 6 (Harold Burr)

"Jackie Returns, Dodgers Sprint," September 19, p. 8 (staff)

It was true in between as well. As early as midway through the 1947 season, the *Sporting News* reported about rookie Robinson's wife and his son, Jackie Junior.[23] The paper did a second article about Robinson's spouse alone.[24] The weekly also reported about exhibition games that Robinson played.[25] *Sporting News* staff described interesting sidelights about Robinson even when there were no noteworthy baseball-centric events to report, such as his singing while playing first base, heard by opposing team's base runners.[26]

Nothing can take away from what Jackie Robinson endured or what he accomplished. There are, however, two sides to every coin, the positive and the negative. In Robinson's case, today's historical accounts of his first seasons tend to omit, overemphasize, or dwell exclusively on, the negatives. What comes through from reading the news accounts of that day is just how four-square right-thinking people, white as well as black, were behind Robinson, rooting for him and pulling for him to succeed every step of the way. The positive articles, the cheering for Jackie to have a smooth transition to the major leagues and a stellar on-field performance, outnumber the reports of mean treatment, catcalls, and discrimination ten, twelve, or more to one.

What also does not adequately come through today is the universal support of the northern news media. *Sporting News* articles appeared under the bylines of reporters from all the Major League cities of the United States as well as from the *Sporting News's* own staff. Those articles all reflect cheering for Robinson. There is not a single negative reference or a pejorative among them. Of eighty-five articles about Jackie Robinson in the period 1947–48, seventy-six of them have the Robinson name in the headline. Of those seventy-six articles, fifty-nine of them refer simply or primarily to "Jackie," all in a highly supportive and affirming way: "Jackie" this and "Jackie" that.

To be sure, newspapers reported about the negatives, the slights and taunts that Robinson had to endure. Pieces were written and published about the deplorable taunting and name-calling by Philadelphia Phillies manager Ben Chapman and his bench.[27] Reporters duly set forth both sides' version of the incident in which future Hall of Famer Enos Slaughter spiked Robinson.[28] Robinson was playing first base: his back foot was on the first base bag as Slaughter crossed the base, running out a ground ball.

In Robinson's inaugural season, opposing pitchers threw at his head or body when he batted against them. Scribes tallied the inordinate number of times this occurred, reporting it on several occasions.[29] Robinson also had to put up with segregated housing in some cities to which the Dodgers traveled when they went on the road.[30] Again, though, the positive reportage far outweighed the negative. Papers duly reported on Jackie Robinson Day at Ebbets Field, where the Dodgers awarded Robinson a new automobile, a television set, and other tokens of players' and fans' esteem at the end of his rookie season.[31] Even before the 1947 season ended, an agent was lining up off-season speaking engagements and appearances for Robinson.[32]

After the World Series, Robinson went off barnstorming (which he later did several times with Doby), as many Major League players did in those days. Unlike other players, however, Robinson was followed everywhere by the press, reporting daily on his postseason tour.[33] After his barnstorming tour, Robinson transitioned to the speaking circuit. He spoke on the West Coast.[34] He spoke on the East Coast, where he had to make apologies for being a no-show at a previously scheduled event.[35] He appeared and spoke in between the appearances on the coasts, once appearing with Branch Rickey in Chicago.[36]

The many off-season activities took a toll on Robinson. In 1948 he reported to Dodger spring training thirty pounds overweight. Back from a year's suspension from baseball, manager Leo Durocher ("Lippy" to reporters) was displeased.[37] Robinson vowed to reform, in part at least by abjuring the rubber-chicken circuit from that day forward.[38] For several years after his rookie postseason, however, Robinson did continue to be the center of attention on the barnstorming circuit. Also, by the 1948 post-season, he had been offered and had begun hosting a Manhattan-based radio talk show.[39] One of his first guests was Branch Rickey.

So Jackie Robinson had to lie, twist, and turn in a bed of thorns as the first African American to play Major League Baseball. But mixed in with those thorns, or at least on the side of them, were roses and other sweet-smelling flowers. From the very beginning of his Major League career, Jackie Robinson received extraordinary support, accolades, praise, constant press attention, and more, continuing on through his first season to the 1948–49 off-season and beyond. That, however, is all an aside. The primary purpose of the exercise is to compare Robinson's and Larry Doby's treatments in the first years of their careers. So it is to Larry Doby that we now must turn.

Doby's Media Exposure Compared

For Doby, a flurry of articles appeared when Bill Veeck signed him to be the first African American player in the American League in July 1947:

"Early Debate over Doby on Indians—Where to Play Larry in Infield," *Sporting News*, July 16, 1947, p. 3 (Ed McAuley)

"Daredevil Doby Put on Display as First Negro in American League," *Sporting News*, July 16, 1947, p. 3 (staff)

"Big Leaguer Giving Autographs" (accompanies photo of Doby), *Sporting News*, July 16, 1947, p. 4 (staff)

"Doby All-Round High School Star; Hit .358 in Puerto Rico Last Winter," *Sporting News*, July 16, 1947, p. 4 (Dan Feitlowitz)

Another flurry of articles followed fifteen months later, in October 1948, after Doby had helped lead the Cleveland Indians to victory in the World Series:

"Doby Hit 408 Foot Homer in Washington Last May," *Sporting News*, October 20, 1948, p. 2 (staff)

"Doby's Play Makes the Eagles Scream," *Sporting News*, October 20, 1948, p. 2 (J. G. Taylor Spink)

"Just Watch Larry for the Next Two Years," *Sporting News*, October 20, 1948, p. 2 (Effa Manley)

"Doby Convinces Hank [Greenberg] He Knows His Hitting," *Sporting News*, October 20, 1948 (staff)

"10,000 Turn Out for Doby's Homecoming," *Sporting News*, October 27, 1948, p. 5 (Dan Feitlowitz)

In between those milestone events, there were few articles featuring Doby, very few when compared to the near ceaseless coverage the press gave to Jackie Robinson. To be sure, there were a few articles about Doby that not only were laudatory but over the top. One veteran baseball beat writer, Lester Bromberg, termed Doby "a dream centerfielder."[40] Another writer stated, "They say Doby is the fastest mover in the American League."[41] Several pieces focused on the prodigious home runs Doby hit, musing about the source of all that power in Doby's slender body. In perhaps a bit of hyperbole, famous sports writer Shirley Povich placed Doby in a position next to Babe Ruth.[42]

Proof in the Pudding?

Perhaps Robinson's extensive exposure, much more extensive than Doby's, by a factor of 6 or 7 to 1 (see, e.g., the discussion comparison earlier in this chapter), results from superior performance? Did Jackie Robinson simply put up better numbers? Let's compare their first full seasons (1947 for Robinson, 1948 for Doby).

Doby's numbers in his first two Major League years were the following:

Year	HRS	RBI	BA	OBS
48	15	66	.301	.873
49	24	85	.280	.857

Robinson's numbers in his first two Major League years were the following:

Year	HRS	RBI	BA	OBS	
47	12	48	.297	.810	Rookie of the Year
48	12	85	.296	.820	

Surprise: Doby had better numbers almost all round, except for batting average in his sophomore season. Robinson's second-year average was superior, .296 to .280. Moreover, Doby went on a tear the following year, his third in the Majors, hitting 24 HRS, 102 RBIS, batting .326, and racking up an OBS (on-base percentage plus slugging average) at .986. But calling one man superior to the other would be quibbling. Both Robinson and Doby were very good baseball players. They accomplished much in their first years, especially given the adverse conditions and charged atmospheres in which they played.

Final Comparisons

As we've seen in this chapter, however, Larry Doby moved into the shadows early in his Major League career. And, in particular, it was in the shadow Jackie Robinson cast that Doby moved, a shadow that was undoubtedly the product of the bright glow that Jackie Robinson and his induction into the National League produced.[43] And it would be unfair to say that the overwhelming advantage in media coverage and historical treatment that Robinson and his career receive is unjustified. Jackie Robinson was a great man; what he achieved changed not only baseball but our society as a whole. What one can say is that Larry Doby's relative obscurity is not justified, not in the least. He, too, achieved much and was a fine individual and a great baseball player.

8

The Second Shadow?

A Tale of Two Cities

Between 1947 and 1957, a stretch bracketed by the arrival of Jackie Robinson and the departure of the Dodgers and Giants, New York was the nation's baseball capital.

—JAMES HIRSCH, *Willie Mays*

Nicknamed the "Mistake on the Lake," the much-maligned city [Cleveland] on the shore of Lake Erie has long had a reputation for crime, pollution and corruption.

—NANCY KEATS, "Hotter in Cleveland," *Wall Street Journal*, August 29, 2014

Cleveland or New York? Charles Dickens's recitations of the titanic events taking place in London and Paris in the late nineteenth century are the background for *A Tale of Two Cities*. In terms of either historical or literary importance, a New York–Cleveland duel in the 1950s pales by comparison. More dramatically, while New York has always been world class, the Cleveland, Ohio, of more recent times does not even make the category of "also ran."

This, however, is a book about baseball. It has been argued that Larry Doby and his achievements as a Major League center fielder have remained so long in the shadows because Doby played in Cleveland. During the same period, Mickey Mantle, Willie Mays, and Duke Snider, center fielders as well, the "kingly triumvirate," played in New York, dominating all baseball and media coverage of it.[1] "The coincidental ascendancy of Mays, Mantle and Snider announced a golden era in baseball and ratified New York's sense of itself as the center of things."[2] "[Baseball] was played more frequently, and with greater competitive fire, in New York than anywhere else. New York was the only city that claimed more than two [Major League] teams."[3] So New York versus Cleveland is a tale of two cities, simply one without capital letters.

But it is not that simple. While the Cleveland of today has engineered a makeover, including even the procurement by Cleveland of the 2016 Republican National Convention, what may be the modern reality is not the image most Americans have.[4] To them, Cleveland remains "the mistake by the lake," the city whose main waterway, the Cuyahoga River, caught fire in 1969 because the water was so polluted by chemicals and oil. It is a city losing population, a rust-belt town equidistant from Detroit and Buffalo. Back when Doby was playing, however, Cleveland was a vibrant city that through the twenties and thirties had been the fastest growing town in America. Then, in the late forties and the fifties, Cleveland was still in the hunt and the "Larry Doby not New York" story may realistically have been a tale of two cities.

The thesis, that Doby played in the shadows and that it was New York that cast some of those shadows, has to be reexamined in light of what Cleveland, Ohio, was back then, not what Cleveland may have become in its degraded state of the sixties, seventies, or eighties. That process requires that first the author and then the reader delve into not-so-ancient history.

New York at the Center of the Universe

"New York had the Broadway Theater, the Metropolitan Opera, the best museums [and] the tallest buildings."[5] And there was significantly more: the New York and the American Stock Exchanges; the Statue of Liberty; the garment district; leadership of the fashion industry; the Brooklyn Bridge; the financial center with the country's leading investment banks; Columbia, Fordham, Hunter, NYU, and many other colleges and universities; law firms and financial service firms; the best restaurants. "New York had everything any cosmopolitan would want."[6]

New York also was the center of the baseball universe, at least in the 1950s. It had, of course, Mantle, Mays, and Snider, along with the three Major League teams on which they played, the Yankees, the Giants, and the Dodgers. "New York had . . . the self-assurance of a town used to winners. It had the Yankees [which were] the perennial pennant winners. Before the Giants and the Dodgers departed [in 1958] New Yorkers had grown accustomed to an almost annual inter-borough World Series."[7] In the twelve years Casey Stengel managed the Yankees, 1949–61, the team won the American League pennant ten times, including five consecutive times (1949–53).[8]

Over in the National League, in the twelve years after World War II ended and before the moves to the West Coast, the Brooklyn Dodgers won the pennant six times (1947, 1949, 1952, 1953, 1955, 1956) and the New York Giants twice (1951and 1954).[9] The New York Major League teams were ascendant.

The Yankees also have had further winning streaks. Under Joe Torre, who took over as Yankees manager in 1996, and managed for twelve years, the Yankees won ten divisional titles, six American League pennants, and four World Series.[10] Since their move to New York from Baltimore, as the New York Highlanders (christened the Yankees in 1913) and one of the charter members of the American League, the Yankees have won forty pennants and twenty-seven World Series.[11] As of 2014 forty-four New York Yankee players and eleven managers (twelve with Joe Torre in 2014) are in the Hall of Fame.

Moses Cleaveland's Creation

North-central Ohio formed the Western Reserve for colonial Connecticut, one of the original colonies, of course. Each of the original thirteen colonies reserved tracts of land to the west. Connecticut's was in what would in 1803 become the state of Ohio.

In 1796 the Connecticut Land Company sent General Moses Cleaveland, one of its thirty-six founders, to explore and map the company's holdings, Connecticut's "Western Reserve." In his one and only foray into the Northwest Territory, as it was then known, Cleaveland did so, and he named the "capital city" after himself. The city did not drop the extra *A* and become "Cleveland" until 1831.

The area remained largely unsettled until Connecticut citizens whom the British burned out in the War of 1812 relocated there. For that reason many north-central Ohio towns have the Connecticut town names that the settlers of 1814–15 bestowed on them: Norwalk, New Haven, Greenwich, New London, Plymouth, Fairfield, and so on. The Western Reserve, after which Cleveland's principal university was named, also took on a second name: the Firelands.

During and after the Civil War, Cleveland became an industrial powerhouse. It also became a kingmaker. James A. Garfield, who was to become the twentieth president of the United States, served as pastor of the Franklin Christian Church and is buried in Cleveland's Lake View Cemetery. William McKinley, from nearby Niles, Ohio, became the second U.S. president to hail from Cleveland, his campaign the masterwork of Cleveland industrialist Mark Hanna.[12] John D. Rockefeller spent his life in Cleveland, managing his far-flung Standard Oil Trust from there. He died in 1937 and is buried in Lake View Cemetery as well.

By 1920 Cleveland had become the fifth largest city in the country, ranking behind only New York, Chicago, Philadelphia, and Boston. Led by Hall of Fame center fielder Tris Speaker, in that year the Cleveland Indians defeated the Brooklyn Robins, forerunner of the Dodgers, in the 1920 World Series. During the 1920s Cleveland was the fastest growing city in the nation, ranking fifth again in 1930. Cleveland hosted the Cleveland Air Races, in which international aviation stars Amelia Earhart and Wiley Post flew. The city was the first home of the National Space and Aeronautics Agency (NASA), than named the National Advisory Committee on Aeronautics, and home to one of the early aerospace companies, TRW.

The Vans: Oris Paxton and Mantis James Van Swerington

The most colorful narrative from those days is the history of two brothers from rural Ohio. Born in 1879 and 1881, Oris Paxton and Mantis James Van Swerington moved to Cleveland in 1890. The brothers made their first fortunes in land development and building. In 1909 they purchased a 1,399-acre tract east of the city, which they later expanded to 4,000 acres. The Society of True Believers, better known as the Shakers, had owned the property that the Van Sweringtons purchased. As early as 1822, the Shakers had bought the land for one of the nineteen communities they planned for America. They damned up Doan Brook, which ran through the Ohio property, creating millponds later know as Upper or Horseshoe, and Lower, Lakes, which still exist.[13]

Early in the twentieth century, the Vans laid out the enlarged Shaker tract as a planned upper-class community with curved streets and boulevards. A strict set of restrictive covenants and building specifications, known today as the Shaker Standards and dictating every detail of houses to be built, prevailed. The resulting community, Shaker Heights, remains today Cleveland's ritziest large suburb, the haven of the upper class.

Nothing weird so far had occurred, but it was soon to happen. The Vans decided that their suburb needed a rapid interurban railway. In turn, the "Rapid," the interurban they created, need a fitting terminus. So beginning in 1924, the Van Sweringtons caused to be constructed Cleveland's Terminal Tower (fifty-two floors, 708 feet high); when completed in 1927, it was the second tallest building in the United States and, until 1967, the tallest building outside New York.[14] Taking as their inspiration the elegant Woolworth Building in New York, the Van Sweringtons erected an elegant skyscraper that has stood the test of time, facing a large public square laid out by Moses Cleaveland in 1796.[15]

Building such a colossus for a suburban interurban evinces a touch of weirdness (megalomania?), but that touch pales by comparison with the Vans' personal lives. Neither brother ever married. The two shared a common bedroom, even though that bedchamber was in a fifty-four-room mansion, Roundwood Manor, on the grounds of Daisy Hill, their estate. They seldom gave interviews or made public appearances, but when they did, they always appeared together.

Mantis Van Swerington died in 1934. Subject to the forces of the Great Depression, their fortunes were already dwindling. The bereaved Oris was crestfallen and lost: "I don't know what to do, or how to do it, or where to go from here."[16] Two years later, he died of a coronary thrombosis.

All of that would be colorful enough, but the Van Sweringtons' railroad interests must be added to the mix. Their flagship railroad was the Nickel Plate Road, 523 miles of rail reaching New York, Chicago, and St. Louis. The brothers owned 51 percent of the Nickel Plate. At their zenith the Van Swerington brothers controlled not only the Nickel Plate and its 523 miles of track but also 30,000 miles of railroads that included the Lake Erie and Pittsburgh, the Pere Marquette, the Hocking Valley, and the Chesapeake and Ohio.[17]

The Van Sweringtons gained control of other railroad corporations by perfecting the practice of pyramiding, using only enough of their own capital to obtain control of a railroad, meaning control of the board of directors. That percentage varied from railroad to railroad but could be a low as 14–15 percent of the stock. The Van Sweringtons would then cause the directors of that railroad to expend the railroad's assets to obtain "working control," as opposed to numerical control, of a second railway. The second railway would then obtain and maintain working control of a third railway and perhaps a fourth railway as well. At the end of the day, the railroad structure resembled a pyramid, with the Van Sweringtons at the pinnacle. Three or four layers spread out below them, each layer wider than the layer above it, in a pyramidal display.

The practice became widespread in other sectors as well, for instance, in public utilities. By pyramiding, the rapacious Samuel Insull of Chicago came into control of scores of utility companies. In 1935, in fact, Congress passed the Public Utility Holding Company Act, which was recently repealed, to curb abuses associated with pyramiding.

Background for Doby's Cleveland Career

In 1950, when Doby played, Cleveland, then, was still on an ascending arc. Its population stood at 914,808. A necklace of suburbs surrounded the central city, taking the metro area population close to 2 million. The city was home to John D. Rockefeller's Standard Oil, the oil trust that monopolized the country's oil and gasoline production.

Back then Cleveland was also home to a number of the nation's railroads: the Chesapeake and Ohio and the Nickel Plate have already been mentioned. Others included the Erie Lackawanna, the Pittsburgh and Lake Erie, and the Baltimore and Ohio. Cleveland Cliffs and Pickands Mather and Company, among others, maintained large fleets of Great Lakes steam ships. Pickands Mather alone operated thirty-eight Great Lakes cargo ships, iron mines in Minnesota and Wisconsin, and several steel mills.

Those ships would load iron ore (taconite pellets) from Minnesota's Mesabi Range and then carry their cargoes across Lake Superior to the locks at Sault Ste. Marie. Down bound from there, ore ships would head through the St. Mary River to Lake Huron, then Lake St. Clair, opposite Detroit, Michigan. Turning east, the freighters would cross half of Lake Erie, stopping at Cleveland. From Cleveland the city's railroads would transship raw materials, including iron ore, to steel mills in Fort Wayne, Toledo, Middletown, Youngstown, Pittsburgh, Johnstown, and all the other points in what has now become the rust belt.

In 1947–48 Cleveland was a vibrant place. In sports it had the Cleveland Browns, who dominated the All-American Football Conference and then finished atop the National Football Conference from its formation in 1950 until 1956. In fact, Larry Doby credited Cleveland Browns players with helping ease his transition as the first African American in American League baseball. The Browns had integrated their roster after World War II, adding fullback Marion Motley and lineman Bill Willis to their 1946 squad.[18] The two black players met the Indians' train when it arrived back from the 1947 Chicago road trip in which Doby had broken into big league baseball. Doby, and the two professional football players remained friends and formed a support group for several years.[19] More importantly perhaps, Motley's 1946 debut and ensuing stardom had accustomed Cleveland sports fans to the notion of black professional athletes, assuring that fans were less harsh toward Doby, at least in Cleveland.

In fact Clevelanders had accepted black athletes as their idols earlier. Jesse Owens, who won four gold medals in Berlin's 1936 Olympics, dramatically disproving Hitler's notion of a superior race, grew up in Cleveland and graduated from Cleveland's East Technical High School.[20] Starring at Ohio State and later in the Olympics, Owens became a national hero. "One of the most significant athletes of the twentieth century," he maintained his connections with his home town.[21] He knew Larry Doby and rooted for the Indians.

We can see, then, that Cleveland still pales by comparison with New York City, in professional sports as well as everything else, but not as much as one would imagine, at least in the late 1940s and the 1950s, the decades when Larry Doby played there.

Cleveland's Misfortunes and Renaissance

Cleveland later had some rough times. In 1966, following race riots in Detroit and Los Angeles (Watts), Cleveland's eastside Hough district erupted. Cleveland's Millionaire's Row, Euclid Avenue, became a thoroughfare of weed-choked vacant lots and boarded-up buildings. With white flight to the suburbs, the central city's population dwindled to 396,000, propelling the city, which once had been the nation's fifth largest, to forty-fifth and still losing population.

Seemingly the nadir was in the 1980s. "Cleveland became the joke on Johnny Carson. A dull comic would coax a laugh from a bored audience by mentioning [Cleveland]." Things had become so bad that comedians "re-wrote the old Philadelphia jokes and made them Cleveland jokes. First prize, a week in Cleveland. Second prize, two weeks in Cleveland."[22]

Cleveland has enjoyed a comeback, as a university town (Case Western Reserve, Cleveland State, John Carroll) and as home to one of the nation's premier medical centers, the Cleveland Clinic. Two new sports stadia, the Cleveland Browns Stadium for football and Jacobs Field (now renamed Progressive Field) for baseball, have replaced the cold, wind-whipped Municipal Stadium, "the old crypt by the lakefront."[23] Today the Rock and Roll Hall of Fame dominates the lakefront. Designed by I. M. Pei, the hall opened in 1995. Because Cleveland music promoters, particularly disc jockey Alan "Moon Dog" Freed, played such a key role in the early days of rock, city powers mounted an ultimately successful campaign to bring the proposed hall of fame to Cleveland.[24]

Things seem to be on the rise again in Cleveland, reminiscent of what the city must have been like in the 1940s and 1950s, when Doby played: "Cleveland's fortunes seem to be turning around. Le Bron [James] is headed home!" to the Cleveland Cavaliers, along with all-star Kevin Love. "The 2016 Republican Convention is coming. The Browns nabbed [Heisman Trophy–winning] quarterback Johnny Manziel in the draft! There is lots of exuberance and chest thumping in Cleveland, accompanied by lofty predictions of the positive economic impacts of these events."[25]

The Indians' Ups and Downs

The Cleveland Indians' fortunes have been much the same as those of the Forest City itself, since World War II almost to a "T." The Indians trace their roots to Grand Rapids, Michigan, where in 1894 the team began its existence as the Rustlers. In 1900 the team moved east and slightly south to Cleveland, evolving through a succession of names: Cleveland Lake Shores (1900); Cleveland Bluebirds (1901), whose nickname "Blues" was preferred by fans as well as players; Cleveland Broncos (1902); Cleveland Naps (1903–4). The latter team took its moniker from its All-Star second baseman, Napoleon Lajoie (.332 BA over a twenty-one-year career), one of the greats of all time. Contrary to the Naps' namesake," the team's performance was less than stellar, prompting one wag to refer to the team as "the Napkins— because they fold so easily."[26] After Lajoie departed, the team briefly became the Cleveland Molly McGuires before settling on "Indians" in 1915.

One other significant fact from the Indians' more ancient history dates from 1915, when manager Lee Fohl traded players to the Boston Red Sox for center fielder Tris Speaker, (.345 over a twenty-two-year career), another all-time baseball great. Speaker, later Larry Doby's mentor, became Indians player-manager in 1919. Speaker led the Indians to an American League pennant and a World Series victory over the Brooklyn Robins, later Dodgers, in 1920. It was Cleveland's one and only postseason triumph until

Larry Doby came along.[27] In the interim, the Indians endured twenty-eight years of near nothingness.

The other bookend to the Doby years and Cleveland Indian history has been termed "the thirty-year slump." After Hank Greenberg and Al Lopez traded Doby to the Chicago White Sox following the 1955 season, the Indians entered another prolonged and dismal slump. The team's slump actually spanned thirty-five years, beginning in 1958 (fourth place), 1959 (second), and 1960 (fourth). From 1960 to 1993, on twenty-seven occasions the Indians finished at or near last place in the eight-team American League.

Just as Cleveland began to resurge in the early 1990s, so, too, did its baseball team. In 1994 Jacobs Field, a new, modern, and cozy ballpark, opened. Jacobs replaced the cavernous lakefront Municipal Stadium (the Crypt), in which chunks of concrete fell from pillars and walls, crowds of forty thousand felt dwarfed, and wild winds whipped off the lake.

Led by sluggers Albert Bell, Manny Ramirez, and Jim Thome, along with pitchers such as Orel Hersheiser, Jaret Wright, and Jose Mesa ("Senior Slam"), the Indians won seven divisional crowns in thirteen years. They appeared twice in the World Series (1995 and 1997), unfortunately losing on both occasions. Beginning in 1995 they reeled off five straight divisional championships. Attendance was over the moon: between June 12, 1995, and April 4, 2001, the Indians sold out 455 consecutive home games, drawing a total of 19,324,248 fans to Jacobs Field. The sellout streak was a Major League record, broken by the Boston Red Sox in 2008, for whom a sellout may be termed easier because of the much smaller capacity of Fenway Park.

The Other Era of Cleveland Dominance—The Doby Years

The 1949 Indians team numbered on its roster seven future Hall of Fame inductees (Lou Boudreau, Larry Doby, Bob Feller, Joe Gordon, Bob Lemon, Satchel Paige, and Early Wynn). Al Rosen, a power-hitting third baseman who won both American League batting and home run championships should be there as well. With Bob Feller, Bob Lemon, Early Wynn, and Mike ("The Bear") Garcia, the Indians had the best starting rotation in all baseball from 1949 until 1958, when the Indians traded Wynn to the White Sox and Feller had retired (see chapter 5). In the nine years Larry Doby played for the Indians, 1947 excluded, the Indians appeared in two World Series and finished second five times, always to the dreaded New York Yankees. They finished a disappointing third in 1949, after which Bill Veeck conducted a ceremony in which he and the team buried their 1948 pennant in centerfield.

But that era was not only an apotheosis for Cleveland, then a large and fast-paced city. It was an apotheosis for the Cleveland Indians baseball club as well. One of the undisputed leaders of those Indian teams then was Larry Doby.

The Primacy of New York: A Litmus Test

Among other things, in addition to being the baseball capital of the universe, New York was the media capital as well. Features on Jackie Robinson, Mickey Mantle, Willie Mays, Duke Snider, and other New York teams' players and managers appeared in many of the leading magazines of the day: *Look, Colliers, Saturday Evening Post, Time, Newsweek*, and others, all of which had editorial offices in Manhattan. Jackie Robinson, Mickey Mantle, and Willie Mays's visages each appeared on either the cover of *Time* or *Newsweek*.[28]

By contrast Larry Doby appeared in a national magazine once, in *Jet*, a magazine by and large marketed to and read by the African American population.[29] And that piece appeared only after most of Doby's playing days were behind him, in 1957.

New York City then also was the epicenter of the publishing and broadcasting worlds. Baseball, to be more precise New York City Major League Baseball, figured prominently in that world. A litmus test for just how marked the broadcasting presence was might be gleaned from a review of the popular television program *What's My Line?* Through the 1950 and 1960s, every Sunday night all across America families tuned in their sets to this popular show: "Each program . . . featured the appearance of at least one mystery guest, a celebrity whose face and voice were known to the masses, and who was quizzed by the blindfold-wearing panelists."[30] The panelists, who were celebrities in their own right, had to determine the identity of the mystery guest. Many of the mystery guests were baseball stars or managers. All, or almost all, of the baseball mystery guests were from the New York teams (Yankees, Dodgers, and Giants, later Mets). None was from the Cleveland Indians.

Not quite all the mystery baseball celebrities were from New York. Dizzy Dean, the star St. Louis Cardinals pitcher of the 1930s, appeared, but in 1950, long after Dean's playing days. Ten members of the Cincinnati Reds team appeared, by chance being in New York after having swept a doubleheader from the New York Giants earlier that Sunday.[31] All the other baseball mystery guests, though, appear to have been players and managers from the New York teams. A partial list would include the following:

Yankees: Joe DiMaggio, Ralph Houk, Phil Rizzuto (twice), Mickey Mantle, Roger Maris, Casey Stengel

Dodgers: Charlie Dressen, Chuck Connors, Leo Durocher, Carl Furillo, Branch Rickey, Duke Snider (twice)

Giants: Leo Durocher, Sal "The Barber" Maglie (twice), Willie Mays (twice).

Mets: Casey Stengel[32]

The litmus test may be an unscientific one, but it is another indicator that in a tale of two cities, Cleveland, even as it was in those days, finished a distant second to New York. Part of what Larry Doby accomplished in baseball and on the field has been masked from the view of subsequent generations because Doby starred in far-off Cleveland, Ohio.

9

Playing in the American League

Clark Griffith, owner of the Washington Senators [American League], called Branch Rickey a "carpetbagger," accusing Rickey of attempting to set himself up as the "czar of Negro baseball."

—MARK RIBOWSKY, *Don't Look Back*

I am not a racist. I employ dozens of blacks on my plantation in South Carolina.

—TOM YAWKEY, owner of the Boston Red Sox, quoted in Fromer, *Rickey and Robinson*

The Boston Red Sox and the Detroit Tigers, both American League teams, were the last Major League Baseball teams to integrate, with Boston being the very last, in 1959.[1] In that year the Bosox added Elijah Pumpsie Green to their roster.[2]

In less guarded moments Boston owner Tom Yawkey had said, "There will be no niggers on this ball club as long as I have anything to say about it."[3] Boston was termed "the most racist organization in baseball."[4] The entire Boston management as well as many of the players and fans were imbued with an unrefined, rough-cut brand of racism. "The top management of the Red Sox was Irish, the most powerful group in Boston": Their "established pecking order . . . in essence regarded WASPs with respect and admiration." They regarded "Jews with admiration" but with "suspicion for being smart." They treated "Italians with disdain for being immigrants and Catholic" yet not Irish. Last of all, at the bottom of the pecking order, or even below it were blacks, "well below the Italians."[5]

A short way south, in New York, Yankees general Manager George Weiss and field manager Casey Stengel were racists.[6] Stengel used racist language openly (see, e.g., chapter 17). The Yankees elevated a black player, Elston Howard, to their team only in 1955. According to some they did so only after determining that Howard fit the same mold that the Yankees applied to their white recruits: "He was the perfect Yankee, soft-spoken, well-mannered, well-educated, dedicated to excellence, a proven team player [and] also black."[7]

The Yankees' attitude was not only the product of latent racism but racism mixed with arrogance or hubris. The hubris part: "The Yankees thought of themselves as the elite team of baseball. They did not need black players (as their poor cousins in Brooklyn, the Dodgers, did) because their teams were already so good."[8] The racist part: "The [Yankees] whites-only policy reflected the attitudes of men who felt that the use of black players [would taint] their operation."[9] Black players, Yankees management felt, would draw black fans, which, in turn, would scare away good middle-class white fans. In Brooklyn Jackie Robinson told the press, "I feel the New York Yankees' management is prejudiced against black ballplayers."[10] Even in the late 1950s, Casey Stengel openly continued to call Elston Howard "my n——r."

In Contrast: The National League

Meanwhile, over in the senior circuit (National League), black players garnered Rookie of the Year honors in six of the seven years since Jackie Robinson broke in: Robinson (1947), Sam Jethroe (1949), Don Newcombe (1950), Willie Mays (1951), Joe Black (1952), and Junior Gilliam (1953).[11]

The American League did not have an African American as Rookie of the Year until nineteen years after Robinson broke in with the Dodgers (Tommy Agee, 1966).[12] In fact, from 1947, the year in which Robinson and Doby broke in, until 1960, the National League had eight black Rookies of the Year and nine African American MVPs. In the same period the American League had none, zip, in either category, and only one black player of note, Larry Doby.[13]

In all respects regarding integration, the National League was far ahead of the American League:

In 1949 five blacks played Major League Baseball.[14] Doby was the sole American League player.

By 1950 eleven blacks played Major League Baseball.[15] Larry Doby and Luke Easter, both Cleveland Indians, were the sole American League players.

In 1953 twenty-three black players populated Major League rosters, six of eight rosters in the National League and only one of eight in the American League (only the Cleveland Indians again).[16]

In 1955 half of the Major League teams still had completely white rosters. Seven of the eight lily-white teams were in the American League, only one (the Phillies) in the National.[17]

"In 1964 the National League had fifteen .300 hitters. Twelve of them were [black]. The year before, the National League had eleven .300 hitters. Ten of them were [black]."[18]

By 1960 fifty-seven African Americans held Major League roster spots, of four hundred then available (14 percent), which included several in the American League.[19] Only then, in 1960 or so, many years after the Dodgers had signed Jackie Robinson and the Indians had signed Larry Doby, could it be argued that integration of the major leagues had begun in earnest.

But the latter point is somewhat beside the focus of this chapter. Rather, here we have two hypotheses to be tested. The first hypothesis is that, over the intermediate or longer term, being the first black in the American League (Doby) was more difficult than being the first black in the National (Robinson). The alleged differential in difficulty would be because the National League, and by implication National League fan bases and National League ball clubs, were more accustomed and therefore receptive to black players.

The second hypothesis to be tested is that Doby played in the shadows because he played in the American rather than National League. The counterhypothesis is that, to the contrary, Doby stood out because he was at times the only black player, and at other times one of only a few black players, in the American League. A footnote to the counterhypothesis is that, for most of his career, Doby worked at not standing out. By nature a somewhat reserved and retiring player (some said "aloof"; see chapter 15), Doby would not have attracted the attention bestowed on National League players such as Jackie Robinson, Willie Mays, or Roy Campanella.

The First Hypothesis: Breaking into the American versus the National League

The eight teams in the National League were the Boston (later Milwaukee, still later Atlanta) Braves; the New York Giants; the Brooklyn Dodgers; the Philadelphia Phillies; the Pittsburgh Pirates; the Cincinnati Reds; the Chicago Cubs; and the St. Louis Cardinals. The American League teams were the Boston Red Sox; the New York Yankees; the Philadelphia (later Kansas City, still later Oakland) Athletics; the Washington Senators (now Minnesota Twins); the Cleveland Indians; the Detroit Tigers; the Chicago White Sox; and the St. Louis Browns (now Baltimore Orioles).

Although a northern city and home to Harvard, MIT, Tufts, Wellesley, Brandeis, Simmons, Babson, and many other colleges and universities, Boston had a reputation of being very racist. Whether that is true or not, in their beginning years both Doby and Robinson played there, against the Red Sox and the Braves, respectively. They faced similar opponent attitudes and fan bases.

Similarly, St. Louis, although located in a border state, is considered a southern city in which racial bias may have been frequently encountered. But, again, this represented an advantage to no one because both Doby and Robinson had to play there, against the Browns and the Cardinals, respectively.

We can suppose New York and Chicago to have enlightened and relatively cosmopolitan populations. In their early years and for the rest of their careers, both Doby and Robinson made an equal number of yearly appearances playing baseball there.

Philadelphia has a reputation of having the meanest crowds in sports. The Ben Chapman (Phillies' manager in 1947) incident in which Chapman and his team baited and hurled racist comments at Jackie Robinson was graphically depicted in the movie *42*.[20] But in Philadelphia Doby experienced something of the same thing. The Philadelphia Athletics hired a full-time heckler not only to distract and possibly disarm Doby when he came to bat but also to follow him to at least one other city (see chapter 4). But both Doby and Robinson had to play ballgames in Philadelphia. Advantage to neither.

So that leaves Detroit and Washington for Doby, Pittsburgh and Cincinnati for Robinson. The latter noted that he always had particularly good-sized supporting black crowds in Cincinnati, St. Louis, and Pittsburgh.[21] For two or three decades before Robinson played there, Pittsburgh had been home to the Pittsburgh Crawfords and the Homestead Grays, two of the more powerful teams in the Negro Leagues. In particular, then, Pittsburgh was an epicenter of Negro League baseball, used to seeing African Americans take to the playing field.

Doby said similar things about Washington DC as Robinson said of Cincinnati, St. Louis, and Pittsburgh. Although Washington was a city southern in character, and black fans were relegated to a certain area of the stands, fenced off with chicken wire, the black fan base was large and supportive. Larry Doby always stated that he enjoyed playing before the Washington black fans.

So who, Doby or Robinson, had it tougher? Based on the lineup of cities in which they had to play, and an amateurish review of those cities, the results are inconclusive. Jackie Robinson did say that "in a number of cities, we [black baseball players on the Dodgers team] had very little pressure."[22]

But in most cities in which they played, both Larry Doby and Jackie Robinson had to endure insults and discrimination the likes of which no one ever should have to tolerate. But again and on balance, both Doby and Robinson probably had to put up with roughly equal amounts of it, at least on the playing fields and in Major League stadiums. We can't with any certainty say that breaking in as the first black was tougher or more arduous in the American as opposed to the National League, or vice versa.

Was Doby Lost in the Shadow the National League Cast over the American League?

Yes, he was, but it is difficult to unpack that fact and its ramifications from other confounding events that surround the issue, such as the semi-obscurity resulting from playing in Cleveland, Ohio, as opposed to playing in New York City, seen in the preceding chapter.

Willie Mays, a great ballplayer who played in New York, received national publicity while Doby, who played in Cleveland, received none. Author Allen Barra calls Mays "the greatest centerfielder in baseball history."[23] Hall of Fame pitcher Bob Feller, undoubtedly biased, thought the contrary, thinking Doby the best center fielder in baseball, qua fielder.[24]

In early August 1955, in a game against the Yankees, Doby set the record for consecutive games by an outfielder without an error, 421 chances in center field without a miscue.[25] The record held for seventeen years, finally broken by Al Kaline of the Detroit Tigers.[26] Nonetheless, Doby's record is routinely ignored.

Authors also term Mays, who broke in in 1951, the first black "five tool player," and no one questions that assertion.[27] But Larry Doby, who broke in four years earlier, was in reality the first five-tool black player in the major leagues, another fact seemingly ignored or sloughed over by knowledgeable baseball historians and authors alike.

Mays appeared on the cover of *Time*, under the caption "A Boy in a Hurry": "He plays baseball with a boy's glee, a pro's sureness, and a champion's flair."[28] He appeared repeatedly on national television: *Ed Sullivan*, *The Today Show*, and *What's My Line?* A network featured an hour of programing following Mays's day as he went about Harlem.[29] *Collier's* and *Look*, highly polished magazines that in those days reached scores of American households, ran features on Willie Mays. In its feature on Mays, *Newsweek* headlined the article "The Hottest Thing since Babe Ruth."[30]

Larry Doby received very little, almost none, of that media attention.

Other confounding events were, for instance, that Mays was

a great player but only a notch or two above Doby. A second, or third, confounding condition was that Doby was reserved and quiet, while Mays played the game and seemed to approach life with abandon and glee.

The contention, not provable, is that part of Doby's obscurity resulted from his being the only black star playing in the American League, and an understated person and player at that. Meanwhile, the buzz surrounded and the attention went to the flamboyant Willie Mays; the outspoken Jackie Robinson (magical on the base paths); the large, lanky Don Newcombe; the smooth, intelligent, and well-spoken Monte Irvin; the sparky Roy Campanella; and the other talented black players, soon to number a dozen, and then a score, and then still more, all in the National League. The effect of that would be felt for years to come, as the National League came to dominate the All-Star Game year after year.[31] One reason certainly was the National League's much earlier and more pervasive efforts at integrating Major League Baseball.[32]

Playing his entire career in the laggard American League cast another shadow over the accomplishments and achievements of Larry Doby. Another factor must also be added to those discussed here: the marginal relevance of being the only noteworthy black player in the American League. It is undoubtedly a reason, unquantified though it may be, why baseball history retains so little memory of Cleveland All-Star center fielder Larry Doby.

10

The Long Shadow of Satchel Paige

The stories about Satchel are legendary and some of them are even true.

—Hall of Fame Cleveland Indians pitcher BOB BELLER

His unerring control and his ability to change speeds made him, according to some experts, the greatest pitcher of all time—any color, any league.

—JAMES HIRSCH, *Willie Mays*

According to some baseball historians, Satchel Paige was "the most celebrated moundsman in the history of our national pastime"; "the greatest pitcher who ever caressed the seams of a baseball."[1] Buck O'Neil, the Negro League star, said not all hyperbolically that "Satchel Paige wasn't just one franchise. He was a whole lot of franchises."[2] *Chicago Defender* sportswriter Eddie Murphy called Satchel "the greatest baseball pitching attraction in the entire world."[3] Noted sports author Allen Barra calls Paige "the man who might be the greatest pitcher in baseball history."[4]

Larry Doby's achievements have been masked by the legend of Satchel Paige not only in recent times. Doby also played on the Cleveland Indians with Paige, when briefly, for the second half of the 1948 and all of the 1949 seasons, Paige pitched for the Tribe. Although Paige's first Major League career was short, he became the darling of the media and crowded out much else, not only in his single good year (6-1 in 1948) but in his less-than-mediocre year (4-7 in 1949) and beyond.[5]

He could fire a baseball "as fast as a shooting star."[6] His fastball could "beat a bullet to the plate."[7] To a batter, the heater simply disappeared as it came toward him, reappearing with a "pop" in the catcher's glove. "Like Babe Ruth in the Major Leagues, Satchel single-handedly moved team ledgers from red to black."[8] A black sportswriter credited Satchel Paige with "turning out more Negroes than Lincoln freed."[9] Paige "cobbled together . . . part Cy Young, part B. T. Barnum, Stepin Fetchit, Will Rogers and Frank Merriwell."[10] Six feet four, 140 pounds, with arms and hands that hung below his knees and great oversized hands, Satchel seemed an exclamation point that had jumped off a printed page.[11] His face had sagging, almost basset hound features. But, oh, could he throw a baseball.

To other historians, however, Satchel Paige was a liar, a philanderer extraordinaire, a showoff, a clown, and a buffoon. He showed little or no loyalty to teammates, owners, and fans. Ignoring any contractual ties that should have bound him, he would jump to any baseball club that offered him a few dollars more. He pitched for 250 teams (his estimate) in his career. He would miss complete games or arrive late to them. He would rent himself out for single games to semipro and other professional teams for $250, $500, or $1,000 in extra compensation, many times for pitching only three innings, his regular team and its players be damned.

Once he could afford it, Paige purchased big, showy cars, Packard convertibles or Cadillac's in garish colors, red or gold. Not only would he never ride the bus with his team; he would wait until most of the team had boarded the lumbering behemoth, in those days never air-conditioned (christened the "Iron Lung" by members of the Birmingham Barons) and spewing exhaust and fumes.[12] Pulling abreast of the parked bus, Paige would toot his flashy convertible's horn. After arousing the jealousy of his teammates, he would squeal off to the city where his team would play its next baseball game.[13]

On outside assignments, and sometimes with his regular team, after tossing his allotted three innings, Paige would not return to the dugout. Instead, he would wade into the stands to enjoy his celebrity and receive onlookers' adulation. He would spend his time signing autographs and visiting with his fans, "preferably ones with shapely legs."[14]

The long shadow Satchel Paige cast results from no fewer than three factors: his amazing longevity, his nearly unrivaled skill set as a baseball pitcher, and the colorful image he projected, and still projects today, as one of the baseball's greatest and quirkiest players of all time. Most particularly, the shadow he casts obscures the accomplishments of Larry Doby, for Cleveland team owner Bill Veeck added Satchel Paige to the Indians pitching staff for the latter half of the celebrated 1948 Indians season. In that year, Doby's sophomore season, Larry Doby hit .301 (.396 down the stretch) and fifteen home runs, leading Cleveland to the American League pennant and then the world championship. Most baseball historians, at least the amateur ones, however, remember only Satchel Paige and recall Larry Doby only dimly, if at all. One leading Paige biographer refers to Doby as "obscure."[15]

An Extraordinarily Long Career

Paige also pitched three seasons, 1951, 1952, and 1953, for the St. Louis Browns, forerunner of today's Baltimore Orioles. He made a last Major League appearance, a token one, for Charley Finley's Kansas City Athletics, in 1965. His last game of organized profession baseball came with the Minor League Peninsula Pilots in Hampton, Virginia, on June 21, 1966, when he was fifty-nine years old. He had pitched his first with the Chattanooga, Tennessee, White Sox in 1926.

Over a forty-year career, Paige, who claimed to have kept accurate records, pitched in 2,500 games, winning 2,000 of them. He threw 250 shutouts and 50 no hitters.[16] He claimed to have struck out twenty-two of twenty-seven hitters several times. He once recorded twenty-nine starts in a month, including pitching three full games in a single day. The modern record (post 1920) for longevity belongs to the knuckleball pitcher Phil Niekro, of the Atlanta Braves, who threw 5,404 innings. Even conceding that many of Paige's "guest appearances" involved only three innings of pitching, and late in his career only a single inning, over his career Paige must have pitched as many as 20,000 or more innings of baseball. No one knows even the approximate number.

But, of course, Paige accomplished these feats and compiled awesome statistics pitching for the likes of Bismarck, North Dakota; Ciudad Trujillo, Dominican Republic; Guayama, Puerto Rico; and various teams over nine seasons with the California Winter League. He did pitch all or part of seventeen seasons in the fabled Negro Leagues, 1927–47, compiling a 103-61 record, pitching mostly for the Pittsburgh Crawfords and the Kansas City Monarchs. Of course, in all those years, Leroy Robert Paige could not rise to the highest level, the major leagues, because until 1947 the color barrier remained firmly in place, barring black players from the big leagues.

Baseball statisticians cannot resist attempts at modeling what Satchel Paige's record might have been had the major leagues granted entrance to African American athletes and had Paige pitched there from a relatively young age. One statistician's model projected a 391-246 lifetime Major League record for Paige, ranking him number three all time in wins, after Cy Young (511-316) and Walter "Big Train" Johnson (417-279) but ahead of Christy "The Christian Gentleman" Mathewson (373-188). Another historian rates Satchel the seventeenth best Major Leaguer of all time, several spots higher than Cy Young. Henry "Hammerin' Hank" Aaron, all-time home run leader and, like Satchel, a native of Mobile, Alabama, goes the statisticians one better, saying that Satchel might have won three hundred Major League games lifetime "with his outfielders sitting down."[17]

Legends and Legerdemain

His "outfielders sitting down" evokes a Paige legend. On numerous occasions Paige is rumored to have begun an inning by waving his outfielders in to the edge of the infield, motioning for them to sit on the grass. He would then proceed to strike out the opposing side. Of course, in doing so he had no need of outfielders.

Paige would intentionally walk the first three batters he faced. He would then strike out the next three, often on nine or ten pitches. In a demonstration of pitching prowess before a game, Paige would have an assistant place a board with five or six nails, hammered part but not all the way into the wood an inch or two apart, sixty feet, six inches away from the mound. Then, with five or six fastballs, Paige would drive all those nails completely into the wood. There were no speed guns in those days, but experts rate his fastball at over one hundred miles per hour, in the same category as Nolan Ryan, Justin Verlanger, Steven Strasberg, and very few other flamethrowers of the modern era.

Paige would fold over a handkerchief, place it on home plate, and throwing nine out of ten or ten out of ten fastballs over the cloth.[18] Satch threw a fastball, a curve, a sinker, a "slow sinker," a knuckleball, a "blooper," a zigzag pitch, and a "whipsy-dipsy-do."[19] Two favorites were his "nothing ball," a fastball but with no rotation, like a knuckleball with speed, and the hesitation pitch.[20] The latter would leave Satchel's right hand after a tantalizing hesitation midway through his windup, traveling toward the batter and home plate and then seem to accelerate and dive downward as it covered the last twenty feet.

Satch's windup had a very high leg kick, with his left foot coming almost to shoulder level. One story is that Paige would have "FASTBALL" lettered on the sole of his left shoe, where the batter could catch a glimpse of it, but later in life he denied ever having done that. He threw overhand, side arm, and submarine style (almost underhand). Like the black pitcher Joe Black, who became famous for it, Satchel Paige also threw a "crossover pitch." Stepping off with his left foot not toward home plate but on a diagonal pointed midway between home and third base, Satch would further extend his long arm toward the third-to-home baseline, throwing sidearm. He thus would slingshot the baseball toward the hitter's body. Very much thinking that the ball might hit him, many a hitter would bail out, stepping back from the batter's box. The pitch would sail toward home on a diagonal, inside to a right-handed batter but crossing the plate, or the rear part of the plate, on an angle, for a strike.

Sometimes Paige would pitch with no windup. But on the very next pitch, or in the following inning, he might go through his windup motion three times before throwing the ball toward the plate. In between he might wind up once or twice. There are no records of his winding up four times, but he may have done that as well.

He described his repertoire as follows: "I got bloopers, loopers and droopers. I got a jump ball, a be ball, a screw ball, a wobbly ball, a whipsy-dipsy-do, a hurry-up ball, a nothin' ball, and a bat dodger. My be ball is a be ball cause it be right where I want it, high and inside. It wiggles like a worm. . . . My whipsy-dipsy-do is a special forkball I throw underhanded and sidearm that slithers and sinks."[21]

Paige was colorful in describing his pitches. As he got older, his pitches slowed. He admitted that his fastball had gone from "blinding speed" to "just blazing speed."[22] The "barber pitch" grazed the chin of batters who leaned in too close to home plate. The "bow tie pitch" was similar but lower, glazing the batter's Adam's apple. Fastballs were "long Toms" (all out) and "short Toms" (a bit slower). The "trouble ball" was so slow that the hitter grew impatient, swinging long before the ball reached the plate. Paige's names for his pitches included "the four day rider," "slow gin fizz," "butterfly," "step-n-pitch-it," "the two hump blooper," "midnight creeper," "alley oops," drop ball," "single curve," "double curve," and "triple curve." His catcher for eight seasons, Joe Green, said, "I don't know what they mean." Perhaps Satchel did not either, at least completely.

Paige kept a constant chatter of trash talk to batters and base runners alike while also pantomiming for the benefit of the fans in the stands. Bill Veeck, who face-to-face always called Paige "Leroy," never "Satchel," recalls: "Satchel had all kinds of different deliveries. He'd hesitate before he'd throw. He'd wiggle the fingers of his glove. He'd wind up three times. Satchel was always a practicing psychologist. He'd get the batter overanxious, then he'd get them mad, and by the time the ball was there at the plate, he'd have them way off balance."[23]

The Age Myth

Central to the Satchel Paige legend is that he pitched well into old age or, indeed, that he was ageless. He had teams' game programs list his birth year as "1900? 1902? 1904? 1906?" He never allowed himself to be pinned down about his birth date. He encouraged sports reporters' comparisons of him to Rip van Winkle, Grandma

Moses, and Moses. "Methuselah was my first bat boy," he was fond of saying. He cooperated with teams in putting rocking chairs in the bullpen or outside his team's dugout. He would sit in those chairs, rocking way until the manager called upon him to enter the game. He would then shuffle toward the pitcher's mound, evincing no hurry at all to get there. "Satchel stoked that hoopla [about his age] by dishing out estimates of his age that were even more baffling than his pitches."[24] He pushed "his own PR designs of Paige as a literally ageless legend."[25]

In Mobile, Alabama, where Satch was raised, it was hit or miss (mostly miss) whether a black child's birth would be entered into the official records. Also, his mother, Lula, had twelve children, eleven of whom lived into adulthood (Satchel's brother Eugene died as an infant). But Lula insisted that each of her children's births be noted in the official records. After the Cleveland Indians brought Paige aboard in mid-1948, team owner Bill Veeck had the Mobile birth records searched. There Veeck found that Leroy Robert Paige's birth certificate listed July 7, 1906, as the date of birth. *Sports Illustrated* later confirmed that date. Even after those belt-and-suspenders confirmations, Satchel would prevaricate about this birth date.

Thus the legend continued to trump reality: the ageless pitcher myth not only survived but flourished. The legend gave Satch more of an edge, allowing him to romance sportswriters and sports fans. "They want me to be old," he said. "Seems like they get a big kick out of an old man throwing strikeouts."[26]

Debunking the Satchel Paige Legend (a Little Bit)

Satchel Paige's legend is so strong, so colorful, so vibrant that his biographers tend to be apologists for his wrongdoing and bad behavior. For instance Paige married Janet Howard, a minister's daughter whom he met while pitching for the Pittsburgh Crawfords in the mid-1930s. His marriage, however, never much deterred him from continuing womanizing, much of it emanating from the many late nights he spent at the Crawford Grill in Pittsburgh's Hill District. Gus Greenlee, known as "Gasoline Gus" from when he sold bootleg whiskey out of his car's trunk, was a leading Pittsburgh gangster; he owned not only the Pitts-

1. Larry Doby.

2. Branch Rickey with Brooklyn manager Leo Durocher.

3. Branch Rickey in his Brooklyn lair.

4. Jackie Robinson.

5. Ralph Kiner.

6. Cleveland owner
Bill Veeck.

7. A young Larry Doby. The Cleveland Press Collection, Michael Schwartz Library, Cleveland State University.

8. Loss of a limb never stopped Veeck.

9. Lou Boudreau,
Cleveland player-manager.

10. Larry Doby in action.

11. Larry Doby as a pied piper. The Cleveland Press Collection, Michael Schwartz Library, Cleveland State University.

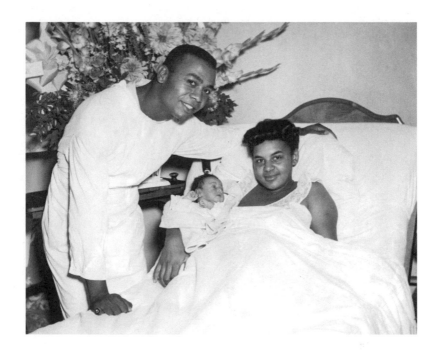

12. (*Opposite top*) Larry Doby with
Cleveland pitcher Early Wynn.

13. (*Opposite bottom*) Cleveland third
baseman Al Rosen with Larry Doby.

14. (*Above*) Larry Doby, his first daughter,
Christina, and his wife, Helyn. The Cleveland
Press Collection, Michael Schwartz Library,
Cleveland State University.

15. Mickey Mantle.

16. Former Newark
Eagles teammate
Monte Irvin.

17. Edwin "Duke" Snider.

18. The Cleveland Indians, 1954
American League Champions.

19. Manager Al Lopez
with Cleveland ace
Bob Lemon.

20. The great
Willie Mays.

21. The Three M's: Maris, Mays, and Mantle.

22. Bill Veeck and a mature Larry Doby. The Cleveland Press Collection, Michael Schwartz Library, Cleveland State University.

burgh Crawfords Baseball Club but the Crawford Grill as well, after which he named the team. Paige spent many hours at the grill, dancing, drinking, and flirting. "It was hard to number the women Satchel got to know at the Crawford Grill. He was a honeypot, luring the queen bees."[27]

In the winter of 1939–40 and again in 1940–41, Satchel pitched for the Guayama Witches in the Puerto Rico League. He had a gold Cadillac shipped there for his use in Puerto Rico. He also married again, to Luz Maria Figueroa. The only difficulty was that Satchel was still married to Janet Howard Paige, who was up north, living in Pittsburgh. Paige's biographers note the bigamy but excuse it or make light of it. "Well, that's Ole Satch," they say. The leading and most compendious biography, *Satchel* by Larry Tye, explains it all away: "In his mind his marriage to Janet Howard had been over for years, no matter that there was no divorce or formal separation. Formalities like that were as malleable as the baseball contracts [he signed and then] ignored. . . . He also relished the idea of being an outlaw."[28]

So, too, do they explain away Satchel Paige's disrespect for fellow players and team owners. "That he was an introvert" supposedly explains away his aloofness, his arrogance, and his missing games or not showing up at all. His travel by luxury automobile rather than in the team's bus must have galled the other players, but according to the biographers Satch, like Greta Garbo, needed "to be alone." "He was a hypnotic storyteller who drew a dugout full of listeners. . . . Performing in the middle of a mob masked the fact that intimate relationships were difficult for him."[29]

The search for a psychoanalytic explanation for Paige's avarice, greed, womanizing, and disrespect for fans, teammates, and owners goes on and on, seemingly without end. "He was a needy man, far more than he would ever let on." One girl friend, Bertha Wilson, could "see Satchel's vulnerable side, see and feel his pain."[30] Satchel Paige "was a man with a hurt inside that he could not address."[31]

Going AWOL

In August 1933, without explanation, Paige left his hometown team, the Pittsburgh Crawfords of the Negro League, for Bismarck,

North Dakota, where he pitched against the likes of Jamestown and Fargo, North Dakota.[32] He then returned to Pittsburgh. Without apology he resumed pitching for the Crawfords, then locked in the second half of the league pennant race.

In 1933 fans elected Paige to the Negro League All-Star team. He neither played nor even showed up for the game. One biographer states that Paige did not receive sufficient votes, which directly contradicts statements that Paige "was the most indelible black player in the land" and that "at age 26 Satchel Paige was the single biggest name in Negro entertainment, on a par with Joe Lewis and Satchmo Armstrong."[33] More probably than not, based on his track record, Paige simply did not bother to appear.

In 1935, in a dispute with Crawford's owner Gus Greenlee, Paige again absconded to North Dakota. In between he had run off to play several games in Wichita, Kansas. Biographers ballyhoo his record in Bismarck (35-2). In fact, an entire book, *Color Blind*, has been written about the Bismarck episodes, but scant attention is given to his lack of loyalty and disrespect of his Pittsburgh teammates that the episodes represent.[34]

Ultimately, Satchel signed a two-year contract to pitch for the Pittsburgh Crawfords. Then he simply walked away again, among other things, traveling to the Dominican Republic to pitch for the Dragones de Ciudad Trujillo. Pittsburgh owner Greenlee had Paige banned from the Negro League for the 1935 season. He called Paige "AWOL," an "ingrate," and worse.

A few years later when Greenlee tried to reconcile with Paige, Satchel instead signed with Abe and Effa Manley's Newark Stars (Larry Doby's Minor League team in 1946–47) for $5,000 more than Greenlee offered, but the Manleys could not reel him in either. Paige simply walked away from that contract as well. The Manleys tried but failed to persuade the Negro League to ban Paige for life. Paige's life as a "jumper" ended when Kansas City Monarchs owner J. L. Wilkinson told him, "If you even think about jumping, I'll put you out of baseball. You won't play again in the United States."[35]

With not an iota of justification, Paige's biographers nonetheless excuse his behavior. For example, Larry Tye concludes that "his teammates saw the [antics and] special treatment, but they were used to it and to him."[36] But Paige's antics must have been difficult for his teammates to tolerate, at least at times. To Negro League shortstop Jake Stephens "Paige was the most overrated player God ever put breath into" and a "pariah" among other black players.[37] "Paige thought he was the greatest, that there was nobody like Satchel. But [his egoism] made him somewhat unapproachable. He was not easy to get used to."[38]

Somewhat unapproachable? Hilton Smith was the Kansas City Monarchs' pitching star. Over twelve years he had been 161-22. When Paige arrived in Kansas City, Monarchs' management ousted Smith from his starting role and replaced him with the crowd-pleaser Paige. They relegated Smith to pitching the remainder of games after Paige had gone his usual three opening frames. Fans began to call Smith "Satchel's Caddy." It is difficult to believe that Smith and at least some of his teammates did not resent the special treatment given Satchel Paige. "It really hurt me . . . but there was not much I could do about it," Hilton Smith recalled.[39]

More accurate depictions by the biographer peek through here and there: "[His] Pittsburgh teammates resented his absences and antics [and his 'shameless behavior']. His shuffle to the mound was a slow-motion spectacle. His windmill windup made him look like a tin lizzie. He talked trash to batters and pantomimed with fans. He bragged . . . not just about his pitching but about prized possessions like his green Packard convertible."[40] If you have ever been on a team, you can easily identify and sympathize with Paige's teammates and the revulsion they must have felt at his greed, his sense of superiority and entitlement, and his antics.

Over-the-Top Historical Assessments

Apologists for Satchel Paige cannot resist returning to over-the-top statements about the legendary baseball pitcher. By going 14-2, with a 2.16 ERA in 1934, Paige had, according to the leading biographer, "the best season of his life and perhaps anyone else's."[41] True, his nonleague games, pitching for the House of David in a Denver tournament, and in the California Winter League, elevated his record to 35-2. But ask Bob Gibson (22-9 and 23-7 in 1968 and

1970, ERA 1.12) or Sandy Koufax (25-5, ERA 1.88 in 1963) or any number of other Major League pitchers whether Satchel Paige's 1934 was the best season of anybody's life.

Another wildly over-the-top assessment is that Paige's "down home demeanor belied the sagacity of a Rhodes Scholar and the cunning of a corporate titan."[42] But such is the strength and persuasiveness of the Satchel Paige legend that the legend, even though based not completely on historical facts, leads writers to make such statements. It was in intimate contact with the Paige legend, and under the shadow it cast, that in only his second Major League season Larry Doby led the Cleveland Indians to the World Championship.

Paige and Doby as Teammates

Not only were Paige and Doby teammates after team owner Veeck signed Satchel to a contract on July 7, 1948; they were roommates as well. "Veeck had hoped that Satchel would make things easier for Doby, who felt enormous pressure as the first black in the American League."[43] Seemingly, having another black on the roster and sharing a room with him would ameliorate one of the less noted features of being the first to break the color barrier, that is, not racial taunts and epithets but isolation and loneliness accompanying being the only black player on the team. Doby missed "not having another player to communicate with, talk the game over with after it's over, and start [him] thinking about the next game."[44] Doby could not socialize with teammates earlier in the evenings either. He recalled, "I wasn't invited out by the other players. They might go to a place where I wouldn't be served, so they didn't do it."[45]

In spring training Jackie Robinson could retreat to his bungalow in Dodgertown, the state-of-the-art baseball facility in Florida, which the team owned and operated from 1949 onward. By contrast the Cleveland Indians trained in leased facilities in Tucson, Arizona. The team stayed in the Santa Rita Hotel, which, while in the seemingly more enlightened Southwest, would not admit blacks.[46] So Chester Willis, a black who supplied laundry services to the Santa Rita, and his family took Doby into their home. Until

1954 each year during spring training, Doby was segregated from teammates. He had to make it to the training facility on his own each morning. The same was true for obtaining transportation to ballparks in the southern cites in which the Indians played exhibitions. Hotels and many taxicabs in southern cities would not admit blacks. Doby was on his own.

So the addition of another black player, in this case, Satchel Paige, and the assignment of him as roommate to Doby, would seem to eliminate some of the sense of isolation, giving Doby a companion. And "what a roomie! Satch arrived with twenty suits of clothes, a big smile and no advice."[47] Paige did everything large: he owned fifteen shotguns, twenty-two hunting dogs, several luxury cars, and more. He brought not only a luxury car to Cleveland but a chauffeur as well.

One of the Paige characteristics that particularly alarmed Doby was that Satchel carried a loaded handgun in his luggage. Satch's handgun habit carried over from his barnstorming days. Then he often carried thousands of dollars in his suitcase.[48] But that would have made no difference to Doby, raised in integrated urban settings in New Jersey rather than in the rough-and-tumble world of barnstorming.[49]

Another unappealing habit from his barnstorming days was that Paige cooked catfish in the hotel room. "He would set up his small electric stove in their hotel room, buy catfish from the nearest fish store, and fry it up in their room. As soon as Doby got his first whiff of Paige's dinner, he would look for company elsewhere."[50]

Usually, however, it was Paige staying out late, leaving Doby alone in the room, not vice versa. Contrary to Doby's and the Indians' expectations for the rooming arrangement, in Doby's words, "Supposedly I roomed with Satch while he was in Cleveland, but in reality I roomed with his luggage."[51] And what luggage it was. Paige traveled with a "huge steamer trunk," in which he carried his suits, twenty-four ties, "an abundance of toiletries, silk underwear and sports shirts." He fitted into the trunk a collapsible heat lamp, an electric massage machine, and a portable cooking grill, among other things.[52]

As it turned out, Doby and Paige had little influence on each other.[53] There was little chance that the forty-two-year-old Paige would change his style and persona to act as a big brother or confidante to his more serious twenty-five-year-old roommate. On Doby's part, he stated, "I never paid that much attention to [Satch]. In the clubhouse, Satch would start telling stories and the guys would start laughing. I would ease out."[54]

Doby and Robinson versus Satchel Paige

Doby's feeling may have been stronger than that. He and Jackie Robinson became close friends, often sharing notes and commiserating with each other. They conferred frequently by telephone. "Jackie detested Satch, strongly." Robinson openly expressed his disdain. "I don't see how you could stay with a guy like Paige. I just couldn't take it," Robinson told Doby.[55] Those conferences and the feelings expressed must have rubbed off on Doby.

Satch was funny. He was an outstanding athlete. He had the age thing and the Stepin Fetchit thing. He was black. "Jackie and I wouldn't tell jokes. We weren't humorists. We tried to show that we were intelligent, and that's not what white folks expect from blacks," Doby concluded years later, reflecting back on 1948–49. More pejoratively, Doby added: "Satch gave whites what they wanted" and what they expected of black baseball players.[56] An older, more experienced black roommate and companion "would have been a great help to me. I could have forgotten about a great many things I took home at night. [But] going with Satch wasn't my thing."[57]

The Strength of the Satchel Paige Legend

In 1948, the year the Indians won the American League pennant and the World Series, again, Larry Doby batted .301 and hit 14 home runs, in 489 at bats. In the six-game World Series, won by Cleveland four games to two, Doby batted .318, in 22 at bats.[58] His defensive play in center field was nothing short of acrobatic.

In that season, Paige, on the other hand, pitched seventy-three innings, winning six games. Yet according to a 2010 biography, Satchel Paige "was the hottest story in baseball that summer and the hottest draw at box offices nationwide."[59] Doby and his feats were not mentioned by the admiring Satchel Paige biographer.

The backward take on Paige's brief foray into the Major Leagues, written sixty-two years later, shows the strength and longevity of the Paige legend, as do other sound bites:

"Satchel's fairy-tale story [captured] the imagination of Americans."[60]

Paige was "one of the greatest pitchers of any hue in baseball history."[61]

Paige's pitching performances were "transcendent."[62]

Reportedly, Joe DiMaggio called Satchel Paige "the greatest pitcher I ever faced."[63]

That the Paige legend has incredible strength and longevity today illustrates how strong that legend must have been back when Larry Doby labored in its shadow. Part of the reason it endures now and was so powerful even back then was its breadth.

Satchel Paige claimed to have pitched for 250 baseball teams, all over the United States and in seventeen foreign countries (Brazil, Columbia, Cuba, Dominican Republic, Mexico, Trinidad, Venezuela, and several countries of the West Indies, to name a few). He pitched in Hawaii, Alaska, and Puerto Rico at the time when all three were possessions of the United States.

Also, "no player barnstormed as wide, or as far, for as long, as Satchel Paige."[64] Many of the Major League greats—Babe Ruth, Dizzy Dean, Bob Feller—did it, playing with and against the great stars of the Negro leagues—Josh Gibson, Cool Papa Bell, Buck O'Neil, Satchel Paige. Big leaguers could make as much or more barnstorming than playing in the World Series. They traveled by bus, bringing big league baseball to jerkwater towns across America. For example, the 1944 Bob Feller All-Stars, whose day-in-and-day-out opponent were the Satchel Paige All-Stars, played thirty-four games, in seventeen states, after the regular season had concluded. Feller even formed a corporation, RoFel, Inc., which employed the players.

Paige barnstormed for the money. Given his extravagant lifestyle, his expenditures always exceeded his income, which for many years included revenue from barnstorming. He was thought to be the highest-paid player in organized baseball, major leagues included. Barnstorming also help spread the stories, the antics, the humor, and the reputation of Satchel far and wide.

Final Notes on the Paige Legend

One more story is worth noting in conclusion. In a workout Satchel popped one fastball after another into the catcher's mitt. "Do you throw that fast consistently?" asked the manager. "No sir," Satchel answered. "I do it all the time." That may have been Paige doublespeak, which formed part of the legend.

Paige, however, could back it up with achievements. *Denver Post* sports columnist Leonard Cohn called Paige "the greatest Negro pitcher in the world."[65] Others made similar over-the-top statements and assessments. "He was the most proficient pitching machine ever."[66] "None (of the mythic greats such as Cy Young, Jim Thorpe or Joe Lewis) was as titanic as Satchel Paige. He was a comic, and preacher, a warrior, and a student of human nature. He could weave a brilliant tale, then reweave it again."[67] Woody Allen, the Academy Award–winning move producer, named his now-estranged son "Satchel."

Satchel Paige was inducted into the Hall of Fame in 1971, six years after his last game and in the second year in which he was eligible. He is the only pitcher in the Hall of Fame with a losing record lifetime (28-31, ERA 3.29 in the Major Leagues), but the Satchel Paige legend and the shadow it casts resoundingly trump that.

11

Should Paige Have Been the First?

That was my right [to be first]. I should have been there. I got those boys thinking about having Negros in the majors.

—SATCHEL PAIGE, in Ribowsky, *Don't Look Back*

[For Negro League old timers] it was Satchel Paige rather than Jackie Robinson on center stage. . . . Jackie opened the door to the new racial reality . . . but it was Satchel who inserted the keys.

—LARRY TYE, *Satchel*

Satchel Paige always thought he should have been the first black in the major leagues, ahead of Jackie Robinson and ahead of Larry Doby, and as the quotations show, he was emphatic about it. He was "embittered by not being selected as the pioneer."[1] When Bill Veeck signed Doby in July 1947, Satchel Paige sent Veeck a telegram, "IS IT TIME FOR ME TO COME?"[2] Veeck declined, at least until a year later.

So, too, have many of the Paige biographers and baseball historians maintained that, by all rights, Satch should have the first. To them over the years, Paige has become a praying mantis encased in amber: a lanky figure whose legend and alleged exploits have become untouchable.

Even when not maintaining that he should have been the first, Paige went to pains to tear Robinson down, denigrating Jackie's baseball skills. Based on the short time that Robinson and Paige were teammates on the Kansas City Monarchs, according to Satchel, Robinson was "an untested rookie who could not hit a curve, gun a throw to first, or land the job as the Monarch's second baseman. . . . Satchel had little use for Jackie and he was not alone."[3] Others stated that Robinson "was mainly a novelty act to everyone." He was "an unspectacular fielder and a hard guy to be with."[4]

To answer the question, could or should Satchel Paige have been the first black player to break the color line? It could never have been. Paige should never have been the first, for a number of reasons:

Satchel Paige was not a veteran. With the titanic, all-pervading struggle of World War II fresh in every fan's consciousness, the first blacks had to be veterans, if not of combat, at least of military service. Robinson (U.S. Army) and Doby (U.S. Navy) were veterans, while Satchel Paige was not. Although Paige was on the cusp of being too old (thirty-five) for military service when the Japanese bombed Pearl Harbor (December 7, 1941) and later claimed that he had flat feet, he might have served or at least tried to volunteer. He did not.

At age thirty-three, Ted Williams flew as a Marine Corp pilot in the Korean War, and previously he had flown in Second World War. In World War I, Branch Rickey enlisted at age thirty-six and served in combat, alongside Ty Cobb and Christy Mathewson.[5] Of approximately 400 men on Major League rosters at any given time during the World War II years, 219 served in the wartime military in 1942, increasing to 242 in 1943, and peaking at 385 in 1944.[6] Nearly 100 Major Leaguers enlisted and fought in the First World War.[7] Of those veterans it was said "they gave up parts of their tomorrows so that the rest of us could have our todays," which was doubly true of baseball players whose career windows were greatly truncated. Those feelings were especially strong in 1947–49 and on into the Korean War years, the time in which Paige and his biographers claim that he should have been the first.

Paige was roughhewn and uneducated. Robinson had attended UCLA and been an officer in the army. Before the war broke out, Doby had been a student and a basketball player at Long Island

University, playing under Clair Bee. After a brief interlude at Virginia Union, Doby left the university to enlist in the navy. Satchel had only six years of schooling, many days of which he skipped.

Pro baseball player turned author (and cynic), Jim Bouton describes the distillation of his Major League years: "The best way to get through professional baseball is never to let on that you have an education."[8] The truth or falsity of that observation aside, the first African Americans who broke the color barrier (Doby and Robinson) were helped immensely by having been well educated.

Robinson and Doby were products of integrated schools and societies, Robinson in Pasadena, California and Doby in Patterson, New Jersey. They were used to playing on and against integrated teams. Paige grew up "across the tracks" in the segregated South (Mobile, Alabama). After being arrested for shoplifting, he spent ages twelve through seventeen in reform school (Mount Meigs farm in Alabama).

Satch was too old and in many respects immature to boot. The first players to integrate baseball had to have the maturity and the presence of mind that comes with it to be able to withstand the brickbats, taunts, name calling, and discrimination that were likely to come their way and to refrain from reacting to those things. In 1947, when they broke in, Doby was twenty-four, Robinson twenty-six. Both would have met that requirement, as would have the older Satchel Paige, at age forty-one in 1947.

On the other hand, though, the first black players had to have been young enough to have the prospect of a career before them. Doby ended up playing thirteen years plus a year in Japan. Robinson played ten years for the Brooklyn Dodgers. Paige, too, played Major League Baseball until 1955 and Minor League Baseball after that.

But all of that is in retrospect. When in 1947 Major League general managers would have been considering Satchel Paige prospectively as a candidate for integration, those GMs would have been looking at a forty-one-year-old, likely to be approaching the end of his career. The latter appraisal turned out to be wrong but would not have been apparent at the time.

The Likely Effect of No Wartime Military Service

Mickey Mantle, the Hall of Fame center fielder of the New York Yankees, broke into Major League Baseball a few years after Robinson and Doby, in 1951. In 1949 he had flunked his draft physical. His left ankle was diagnosed as weakened by osteomyelitis, which in turn resulted from a high school football injury. Mantle's draft board declared him 4F (physically unfit for service of any kind, including limited duty).[9]

Contrary to being a "big break," allowing Mantle to pursue his baseball career uninterrupted, the "[4F] classification would bring him so much public scorn that he would wonder if it had been a break at all."[10] In those days, with the Korean War in the daily newspaper headlines and in fans' consciousness, hecklers hounded Mantle for ten years or more, labeling him a bum, a chicken, and a "commie rat." He was subject to constant "boos, catcalls and curses. . . . 'Go Back to Oklahoma!' The draft dodger label just wouldn't go away."[11]

One wonders if Satchel Paige would have been subject to at least some of the same scorn had a Major League club chosen Paige as the first black in baseball. A fair guess is that Paige's lack of veteran status alone would have eliminated him from consideration as the first African American player, especially in those post–World War II years.

From 1942 onward the "biggest big leaguers were swept into military bases around the world."[12] Many went willingly. Bob Feller, a twenty-five-game winner in 1941, enlisted in the navy the day after Pearl Harbor. "In 1942 the majors lost . . . a .359 hitter, the Senators' Cecil Travis." In the following year, 1943, "they lost Joe DiMaggio, Ted Williams, Bob Lemon, Big Cat Mize, and Country Slaughter, all future Hall of Famers. Luke Appling would go in 1944 and Billy Herman for 1944 and 1945; Duke Snider, Stan Musial and Bobby Doerr all missed the 1945 season."[13]

Paige and his biographers allege that, in addition to having been too old for service, Satch had flat feet that kept him out of the service, but there is no documentation to that effect. Instead, they say, "Satch committed himself to pitching in frequent exhi-

bitions to sell war bonds and raise money for war-related char-
ities."[14] But if that were the case, and the efforts Satch expended
truly were significant, Satchel Paige's income would have stayed
flat, or even declined, during the World War II years. Instead,
Paige's income mushroomed, to $40,000 or more annually, by
one measure worth $1.7 million today and by another worth $4.2
million in 2015.[15] During the Second World War Satchel Paige
became "easily the highest-paid athlete in the world."[16]

So in addition to the risk that fans or a sportswriter might have
labeled Satchel Paige a draft dodger, a disgruntled onlooker also
could have labeled Satchel Paige a "war profiteer," albeit a small-
time one. Hard evidence exists that during the war years, time
and time again Satch made efforts to, in the words of the *Chicago Defender*, "stuff his pockets." At the last minute he routinely
would *threaten* not to take the field unless, in addition to the salary he had agreed upon, game or tour promoters agreed to pay
him a percentage of the gate.[17] The raw material existed with which
the allegation of war profiteer could have been made. Perhaps in
1946–47, looking back over the previous years, Branch Rickey, or
Bill Veeck, or both, saw that possibility. Instead, the Satchel Paige
apologists assert Paige's nobility: "Satch was becoming a palpable
symbol of continuity on the home front for millions of blacks."[18]
Such is the strength of the Paige legend.

A Mixed Bag of On-Field Performance

Major League teams, and their pitchers, play a long, 162-game
(back then 154-game) season that grates on teams and players,
grinding them down, especially as the season stretches on after
the All-Star Game break, through the heat of July, the dog days
of August, and the bone-wearying days of September. Many a
Major League pitcher has begun well enough only to underper-
form later in the season and then often buckle under all together
against big league competition. The pace is relentless ("Spahn
and Sain, and pray for rain," over and over again; or if Sain were
injured, "Spahn and rain and pray for a hurricane"). A pitcher
in a four-person rotation may start thirty-seven, thirty-eight, or
thirty-nine games in a season. A five-person rotation is still tough,

taking its toll, with over thirty-one or thirty-two starts for each pitcher per season.

In his prime, in the National Negro League, Paige seldom made more than thirteen or fourteen starts per season, and often less. He pitched only on Sundays and made limited, showcase appearances in neighboring semipro leagues during the week, earning an extra $500 or more per appearance. Said teammate Jimmy Crutchfield, "He'd pitch on Sunday and then we wouldn't see him again until the next Sunday. Very seldom did he travel with us."[19] He would sometimes take the money and be a no-show at the scheduled exhibition; on other occasions he would keep the assembled fans waiting for an hour or more.[20]

The National Negro League season also was a short one, usually consisting of 90, 100, or 110 rather than 154 games. And Satch's record, while okay, was nowhere near the spectacular performance his gullible biographers attribute to him. Satchel Paige was 103-61 over seventeen years in the Negro Leagues, for an average of 6-4 per season.[21] What's the hullabaloo about?

Paige biographer Mark Ribowsky, who labels Satchel Paige "the greatest pitcher ever" and "the most perfect pitching specimen ever created," calls Satchel's 1931–37 stint with the Pittsburgh Crawfords "the high water mark" of Paige's career.[22] So let's linger there for a minute. Satch's record in those years was thirty-four wins with fourteen losses—over seven years, that's a little less than five wins per year, even less than his overall Negro League record of six wins per year. If you include the first half of the 1931 season, spent with the Cleveland Cubs, the record does not change much, increasing only to 35-16, still yielding only a paltry five wins season. A highlight-reel performance? Hardly.

Paige's best years with the Crawfords were 1932 (10-4) and 1934 (14-2) but sandwiched in between was a mediocre, or down, year (5-7). Most ballyhooed of all is the season in which, according to biographer Mark Ribowsky, Paige "went 31-4 for the Crawfords."[23] Except Paige never won more than fourteen in any one year for the Crawfords, and that was in 1934, not 1933. He also won ten games in 1932.[24] He certainly never won twenty, let alone thirty-one, in the Negro Leagues.

The Uneven Nature of the Competition Satchel Paige Faced

Paige did have some spectacular years pitching against third- and fourth-rate, but not Negro League, competition. He piled up numbers when he walked away from his obligations to the Crawfords, gallivanting off to spend August pitching in Wichita or Bismarck. When throwing for the North Dakota Bismarck "Bismarcks," Paige went a jaw-dropping 29-2, against the likes of the Jamestown Red Sox; the Sioux Falls Canaries; the Grand Forks, North Dakota, and the Waseca, Minnesota, teams; and Russell, Langenberg, Virden, and Portage la Prairie in the Canadian prairie provinces.

Negro League competition was several cuts above that. Batters such as Josh Gibson, Buck Leonard, Cool Papa Bell, Oscar Charleston, Ted Radcliffe, Judy Johnson, and others were Major League– and Hall of Fame–caliber hitters. But Negro League teams could not maintain that caliber through the entire heart of their lineups. "There never were enough good black players to seriously challenge big league sovereignty . . . even though some historians . . . have blithely claimed superiority for these men."[25] Pitching in the Negro Leagues at best was a very imperfect substitute for performing in the lengthy, big league grind, against Major League competition.

Most days, months, seasons, and decades, though, Satchel Paige faced off against teams such as the Club Azules and the Charos de Junta (Mexico), or the Estrellas Orientales, the Aguilas Cibaenas, Los Indios, the Santuce Cangreeros, or the San Juan Senadores (Puerto Rico). In no particular order clubs Satchel Paige faced in the United States included the Devil's Lake Satans; the Wichita Watermen; the Hillsdale Club of Darby, Pennsylvania; the Denver Fuelers; the Halliburton Cementers (Duncan, Oklahoma); the Reidsville, North Carolina, Phillies; the Greensboro, North Carolina, Patriots; the Shreveport Acme Giants; the Mineola, Texas, Black Spiders; and the Ethiopian Clowns (Indianapolis, Indiana). Against many, or even most, of these teams, Paige pitched three innings or less, depending on what his freelancing arrangement provided and what he felt like doing.

Nine seasons Paige pitched in Joe Pircone's California Winter League, compiling an overall 56-7 record. In his first five seasons, 1931–36, he went an amazing 46-2. Yet the California Winter League was a grab bag, filled with Minor League, semipro, and even high school players. The few Major League players who went west to play soon dropped out after they had seen the uneven level of playing personnel in the league.

The Satchel Paige legend trumps all these facts about his actual career, including the very mixed level of competition he faced, and does so in each and every treatment of the great pitcher's life. Much of his greatness may radiate from his possession of a rubber pitching arm, together with his clownish demeanor and buffoon antics, and not his greatness in the traditional sense, although one would be hard pressed to convince the Paige biographers of that.

Paige's Personal Life and Professional Relationships

"Don't Look Back" emanated from Paige's lack of any hesitation whatsoever to move on if he could obtain better money elsewhere, or had a girl friend to visit, or a good fishing opportunity, contract, handshake, or word be damned. True, player contracts were broken quite often in the Negro Leagues, especially in the early days. "Players jumping contracts was a common occurrence in Negro ball," but Satchel Paige carried it to the highest heights ever, and beyond, "bouncing like a pinball from one offer to another."[26] Don't look back, and he didn't.

Married or not, Paige was a womanizer. He never let baseball get in the way of chasing women. For example, while on the Kansas City Monarchs roster, he did not show up for the last three games against the Newark Eagles, in the 1946 Negro World Series no less. Paige and outfielder Ted Strong had hooked up with "two wild women" in Chicago, spending three days holed up in a hotel rather than at the ballpark.[27]

Bill Veeck reported that even when Paige made the Majors, with the Cleveland Indians in 1948–49, he would leave tickets at the "will-call" window for "Mrs. Paige." Each day a different Paige girlfriend would pick up the ticket, while the real Mrs. Paige remained in Kansas City, where she and the children made their home.[28] Throughout his career Satch continued his "casual adultery" and lechery, considered an "open secret" and, later in his career, "at the peril of big league ostracism."[29] His continued actions were seen by many as "intolerable."[30] The open secret of his adultery alone would have forestalled any choice of Satchel Paige as the first black player to integrate the Major Leagues.

But there is more. Besides adultery and woman chasing, and besides not showing up for games, which he did even after he made the Majors (he did not show up for a game at Yankee Stadium, claiming that his arthritic toe had told him the game would be rained out), Paige showed up late, missed trains, and missed airplanes. Many of the reported instances came after he made the big leagues, but they evince a pattern of conduct that permeated his entire career. His record of and utter lack of reliability also would have prevented a choice as "the first."

In Paige's earlier days promoters would hire him for freelancing and barnstorming appearances during the regular season. The promoters would then wire Paige the $500 or $800 appearance fee; he would then pocket the money and not bother to show up for the game.[31] After he had made the Majors, "Satch's blasé attitude offended [Cleveland player-manager Lou] Boudreau. . . . Satch missed or delayed trains, broke curfew, and showed up just in time at the park—and as many times as he was fined—not one time did he seem contrite."[32]

One reason Paige was never contrite is that he would never feel the sting of the fine. Bill Veeck, the owner of the team and a pioneer in the integration of big league baseball, reimbursed Paige the amount after the field manager had assessed a fine against him and Paige had paid it. Fellow Cleveland pitcher Steve Gromek looked back: "Satch had his own rules. . . . Lou [Boudreau] was disgusted by the stuff Satchel pulled off. And it was a lot of stuff. Everything did not come out in the papers."[33]

Later Paige's track record for his utter and complete lack of professionalism may have caught up with him. When in 1959 Bill Veeck acquired a controlling interest in the Chicago White Sox, he asked field manager Al Lopez to consider adding Paige to the Sox roster. Lopez would not hear of it: "Al wants players who catch every plane and meet every roll call and Satch [isn't] a particularly good bet to catch the next street car."[34]

Paige's irresponsibility and lack of professionalism may well have had another, earlier result. His negatives, including those from his Minor League days, were well known. They made him a very poor candidate for breaking the color line. His continued irresponsibility would have caused fans and fellow players to think, if not mouth, "See, I told you so."

In contrast the supreme professionalism of Jackie Robinson and Larry Doby was evident. They showed up every day, swallowed any outward sign of resentment, and played hard and well, proving that they were the ideal candidates to be the first African Americans to play Major League Baseball.

Nonetheless, the Paige Legend Rolls On, and On

In a 1953 feature story in *Collier's*, a leading weekly of that era, author Richard Donovan penned "The Fabulous Satchel Paige," pronouncing him fit for one hundred more seasons.[35] For *Time*, in a 1948 feature, he was "Satchel the Great."[36] Biographer Mark Ribowsky laments that "the toll of depriving Satchel Paige of twenty or more years in the sunlight [has] cost American baseball heavily."[37] In the thirties and forties, according to Ribowsky, Paige "was the best ball player not in the major leagues."[38] In 1936 Paige was flat out "baseball's best pitcher."[39] Once he had been signed by a Major League club, the Cleveland Indians, Paige "was arguably the best pitcher in a staff that would count two twenty game winners," according to biographer Ribowsky.[40] Satchel Paige was 6-1 that year, pitching seventy-three innings.

Gene Bearden, a twenty-game winner for the 1948 Indians, pitched 229.2 innings that year, and was 20-7. Bob Lemon, the other twenty-game winner, also a future Hall of Famer, pitched 293.3 innings that year, and was 20-11. A third starting pitcher, Bob Feller, also a future Hall of Famer, pitched 280 innings and was 19-15. The assertion that Paige was the best pitcher on staff is patently absurd—but the all-pervading Satchel Paige legend allows the assertion to be made.

Bolstering the Paige legend still further, Paige biographers denigrate the other black players who integrated baseball, other than Paige and perhaps Jackie Robinson, and those players on-field performances: "Unlike the spasms of excitement that awaited Jackie Robinson, these lesser known players . . . generated barely a twitch. . . . Unimpressive on the field, they settled into the background of their teams."[41]

Unimpressive? Background players? In 1948 Larry Doby played center field for the Indians in 121 games, with 439 at-bats, 132 hits, 9 stolen bases, and 15 home runs. For the regular season, he hit .301. In the six-game World Series, he played all 6 games, hitting .318. His fielding percentage was .975. Satchel Paige won 6 games and lost 1, pitching 73 innings. In 1949 Doby played center field in 147 games, with 547 at-bats, 153 hits, 10 stolen bases, and 24 home runs. He hit .280 and was named to the American League All-Star team. His fielding percentage was .980. Satchel Paige won 4 games and lost 7, pitching 83 innings.

So who was the more everyday player? Who was more in the shadows? Was Paige truly Cleveland's and Major League Baseball's best pitcher, as Paige's starstruck biographers have maintained? Paige's legend seems like an inverted cone: his wide-ranging fame seems balanced on a small platform of actual achievement. Based on performance Doby was there every day, piling up first-rank performance numbers, and Paige was mostly in the shadows.

According to the Paige legend, the opposite holds "true." Doby was the bit-part, unimpressive player, who made "barely a twitch" and faded "into the background," while Paige was "arguably the best pitcher" on one of the better pitching staffs of all time. Larry Doby was in the shadows, then and in many of the succeeding years, while Satchel Paige then and now remains in the limelight, the "Great Satchel Paige."

Go figure.

12

The Mantle Shadow?

*Mickey, Mantle Boulevard, Mantle Museum,
Mick Lit, Mick Legend, The Mick*

Like Ruth, Mickey hits towering line drives. Like Ted Williams, he smacks
crackling line drives. Like DiMaggio, he beats out hot-to-handle ground-
ers . . . Ruth, Williams, DiMaggio.

—"Young Man from Olympus," *Time*, 1953 (cover story)

There will never be another like him. Never.

—BUZZ BISSINGER, *The Classic Mantle*

There never has been a purer baseball talent than Mickey Mantle.

—MAURY ALLEN, *You Could Look It Up*

It was like watching a young, blonde god.

—GIL MCDOUGALD, New York Yankees, 1951–60

Larry Doby and his integration of the American League were as
much shadowed by the achievements and the legend of Mickey
Mantle as they were by the shadow of Jackie Robinson and his
integration of the National League. An Amazon search produces
citation to fifty-eight books by or about Mickey Mantle, surpass-
ing even the number written about Jackie Robinson (fifty-five) and
certainly the number written about Larry Doby and his integration of the American League (one). Many of the treatments and
phrasings in the "Mick lit" are beyond superlative, beyond over-
the-top products of checkout-counter journalism: one of "the great-

est players of all time"; one of the "most naturally talented players of all time"; or "the greatest centerfielder of all time."[1]

Mantle batted .298 lifetime, with 536 home runs and 1,509 RBIs, over an eighteen-year career. He won the Triple Crown in 1956 (batting average, home runs, and runs batted in), becoming only the fourth player to do so. He was the American League Most Valuable Player (MVP) three times (1956, 1957, 1962). He possessed blazing speed, both in the outfield and on the base paths, stealing sixteen bases in 1957, eighteen in 1958, and twenty-one (his peak) in 1959 (they did not steal as many bases then as they do today). So there is quite a bit of reality backing the legend—but not completely.

Take the matter of Mantle's injuries. What the reality was is far from clear. In the second game of the 1951 World Series, Mantle, while in right field chasing a blooper (hit by Willie Mays), caught his rear cleat on a drain or drain cover. He tore ligaments, putting him out for the remainder of the series and requiring a five-day hospitalization.

Later, though, at the conclusion of the hospitalization, the Yankees doctor pronounced Mantle fully healed, which medical staff at Johns Hopkins corroborated: "Examination reveals that the cartilage was not damaged and that the torn ligament on the inner side of his right leg has completely healed" (December 1951).[2] Surgery was not required until two years later, occasioned by another injury to the knee, this time to the cartilage rather than ligaments.[3]

Since that 1951–53 time frame, though, the biographers have never stopped passing out the purple hearts. "That October [1951] was the last time Mantle set foot on a baseball field without pain," or "It seemed incredible that he could play through such pain every day."[4] The 1969 New York Times headline announcing Mantle's retirement was "18 years of Pain, Misery and Frustration."[5] Mickey Mantle's 1951 injury "alter[ed] the entire course of his career."[6]

Mantle undoubtedly was injured then and injured again many times in his career, especially because he always played all out. For the rest of his career, before each game Mantle wrapped that right leg with so many ace bandages that he looked like a "mummy." The Mick was the "Man of Mishaps," "a tragic figure," "the champion hard luck guy," "the most famous invalid in the long history of sport."[7]

Then, too, any professional athlete whose career spans any length of time has injuries, playing through greater pain for longer durations later in their careers. Mantle's injuries and the pain they caused him may not be appreciably different from those that other professional iron men have endured. If it had not happened to Mantle then, the odds are great that it or some other severe injury would have happened to him later, as it invariably does to most athletes playing a sport at the highest level.

The principal difference, then, is that Mantle's injury, at least the one to which so much pain is attributed, came in his very first season, and not in the middle of or later in his career. "He would play the next seventeen years struggling to be as good as he could be."[8] Playing with extreme and excruciating pain is part of the Mick legend. In his playing days Mickey Mantle early on became a martyr. He remained a martyr throughout his career.

Beginnings of the Legend

Any retrospective on the Mantle legend should emphasize the stellar achievements of a baseball player called "a hero all his life," "the Natural," "the All-American boy."[9] "It was Mantle and Mantle alone who did things in the baseball field that were not simply spectacular but crossed the line into the world of the surreal, the unfathomable."[10]

Mantle made his first marks playing semipro baseball for the Whizzes in Oklahoma, where he hit two home runs out of the park into the Spring River. He was then "discovered in the middle of nowhere by the legendary Yankee scout Tom Greenwade."[11] Known throughout the Missouri-Oklahoma-Kansas territory, Greenwade was noted for his three-piece suits, felt hats, and black Cadillacs. But he did not merely discover Mantle; rather he swindled Mantle and his family and bamboozled many others as well.

Scouts for other teams such as the Indians had heard of Mantle. Greenwade conspired with Mantle's high school principal to put other scouts off the scent. During a storm and a rain delay in a game Mantle was playing, Greenwade corralled Mantle and his father, Mutt, putting them in the backseat of his Cadillac. He told Mutt that his son "was a marginal prospect. He might make it, he might not," remarking, "Kid is kind of small." He persuaded Mantle and his father to sign for $1,150 when other, less promising Major League prospects in the region were signing for bonuses of $25,000 or $50,000. Moreover, $750 of that amount was contingent upon Mantle sticking with the Yankees' Independence, Missouri, farm team beyond June 30.[12] "Greenwade did not become a legend until he discovered Mickey Mantle."[13] He achieved that only by being deceitful.

In his fifty-plus-year Major League Baseball career, Branch Rickey saw every aspect of it, as a player, a field manager, and a general manager of the Cardinals, the Dodgers, and the Pirates. He developed the first true farm system at St. Louis and reprised the act at Brooklyn for the Dodgers. One salient truth he learned from his vast experience was that "there is more room for the twilight zone double cross in scouting than in any other phase of the baseball business."[14] Mickey Mantle learned that lesson early in his baseball career.

After spending the summers of 1949 and 1950 in the minor leagues, Mantle reported to Yankee spring training at Phoenix, Arizona, in 1951. Ordinarily, the Yankees trained in Florida, but at that time Del Web, an Arizona real-estate developer, and the father of Sun City, owned half of the Yankee baseball club. He wanted to showcase "his" team in his home city.

In 1950, the previous year, Mantle had hit .383, with 26 HR, 136 RBIS, and 141 runs scored, being named Most Valuable Player in the Western League.[15] Soon, in his first year with the big club, Mantle merited superlatives. He had hit .402, with 9 HRs in spring training 1951. "He has more speed than any slugger and more slug than any speedster—and nobody has ever had more of both of 'em together. The kid ain't logical. He's too good," said Yankee manager Casey Stengel.[16] "The kid runs so fast that he doesn't bend the grass when he steps on it."[17] Sportswriters termed him "the Commerce Comet," after his home town of Commerce, Oklahoma; "the Colossal Kid"; and "the Wonder Boy."[18] Others termed Mantle "the Yankee Oakie Doakie"; "Rookie of the Eons"; "Magnificent Mantle"; "Mighty Mickey"; the "One-Man Platoon"; and "the Future of Baseball."[19] The press coverage "bordered on the hysterical. No matter what paper you read, on what day, you [would] get Mickey Mantle, more Mickey Mantle, and still more Mickey Mantle."[20] He was heralded as a "phenom" before he had even arrived in New York.[21]

Not all of Mantle's instant fame was based on performance on the field. There was a cosmetic fillip as well: "Blond and blue-eyed, with a coast-to-coast smile [and] with his limitless potential, Mantle was America incarnate."[22] Fast-forwarding a bit, here is one hero-worshipping biographer's description of Mantle in a 1952 Yankee clubhouse photo: "The smile on his face was soft and serene. You could see the perfect alignment of white teeth and the soft eyes and the bull neck of someone who was all of twenty years old. He was as all-American as apple and pecan and cherry pie put together under one crust. He was boyish and beautiful. The legend had only just begun."[23]

Storm Clouds Impinge on the Budding Legend

Few competitors, especially black ones like Larry Doby, Jackie Robinson, Don Newcombe, or Monte Irvin, African American players then in the major leagues, could compete with Mantle's boyish good looks, blond hair, and muscular physique. Without fault whatsoever on Mantle's part, there was a certain racial tinge to the near-instantaneous rise of the Mantle legend. But for Mantle not all was blue sky either.

The DiMaggio Cloud. The Mickey Mantle legend was not without storm clouds scudding over the horizon. First to be confronted were the legend of Joe DiMaggio and the long shadow it cast; second came the demotion of Mantle to the Yankees A A A farm team, the Kansas City Blues, in July, 1951, for forty games; third came the death of Mickey Mantle's father, Mutt, in May 1952; and fourth, Mantle had to endure the continued criticism of his 4F draft classification and failure to serve during the Korean War, accompanied by catcalls and taunts of "commie rat," "draft dodger," and worse. Another storm cloud, the injury to his right knee in game 2 of the 1951 World Series, has already been described.

Joe DiMaggio, christened Giuseppe Paolo in the Fishermen's Wharf area of San Francisco, was the incumbent center fielder for the Yankees, known as "Joltin' Joe" or the "Yankee Clipper." DiMaggio burst on the scene in his rookie year, 1936, when Mantle was only five years old, hitting .323 with 125 RBIS in his first season. His 1941 string of base hits in fifty-six consecutive games is a record that has endured to the present day.

Oblivious to his humble roots, DiMaggio exuded an "intimidating frostiness" to fans and teammates alike. Second baseman Billy Martin thought that DiMaggio "looked like a senator or president" rather than a baseball player.[24] Mantle's impression was that "you needed an invitation to approach him."[25] DiMaggio could be reserved even with his family and closest friends and even in the best of times. "If he said hello to you," DiMaggio's contemporary Hank Greenburg said, "that was a long conversation."[26] On road trips DiMaggio spurned a bus ride with his teammates from hotel to stadium. He rode alone, in a taxi.[27]

Every day, in the clubhouse, Mantle would go by DiMaggio's locker, "just looking for word of encouragement . . . but DiMaggio never said a word. It crushed Mickey."[28] Mantle had hoped that Joe DiMaggio would assist him in his transition to the outfield from shortstop, where Mantle had played throughout his Minor League career. Not only did DiMaggio not help; no one else in the Yankees' spring-training clubhouse befriended or spoke to Mantle, other than Yogi Berra.[29] The Yankees made no effort to provide Mantle with a mentor or a surrogate uncle to guide him in his first several weeks with the club, as other teams had done.[30]

When Mantle came up in 1951, "instantaneous pressure and expectations [were] placed upon him as a worthy successor to the great DiMaggio."[31] A 1951 *New York Times* profile of Mantle summed it up: "Not even Jesus could have met all the expectations" put upon the newest Yankee.[32] The New York press characterized Mantle as the "inheritor of the Babe Ruth–Lou Gehrig–Joe DiMaggio legend."[33]

Mantle's boyhood hero had been Stan Musial of the St. Louis Cardinals. The Yankees' front office immediately corrected Mantle's "misconception [about] the story line he was expected to follow—

Joe D was his hero."[34] But Joe would not deign to speak to him: "No one spoke to Joe. Teammates, reporters and clubhouse attendants seemed to part in front of him . . . . Mantle was even more terrified at the thought of talking to the Yankee Clipper than to a reporter. He needn't have worried; Joe DiMaggio scarcely knew that Mickey Mantle existed."[35] DiMaggio, "perhaps resentful that a nineteen-year-old rookie had been anointed as his successor, said and did nothing to encourage the painfully shy rookie."[36]

By mid-July of his first Major League season, Mantle was hitting only .260. Casey Stengel informed him that in order "to get his swing back," the Yankees were sending him down to the Kansas City affiliate. Stengel worried that Mantle struck out too often, as with many others in baseball back then, not realizing that with an increase in power and home run production comes an automatic increase in the number of swings and misses. Mantle, though, did strike out often, too much by the standard of the stars of that day. For instance, DiMaggio struck out twenty-four times in 1946 and thirty-two times in 1947. "In contrast . . . Mantle would strike out that many times *per month*."[37]

It worked. In forty Minor League games with the Blues, Mantle hit .351. He was called back up to the big league club, with the bonus that he received uniform "7," the number he wore the rest of his career and which he made famous.[38]

The third storm cloud passed over Mantle early in the 1952 season when his father, Mutt, died from non-Hodgkin's lymphoma at age forty on May 6 of that year. Mutt had named Mickey after Mickey Cochran, an All-Star catcher of the twenties and thirties (Philadelphia Athletics and Detroit Tigers). Mutt rolled baseballs to the infant Mickey before he was old enough to play catch. In third and fourth grade, Mantle converted into a switch hitter, at his father's insistence. Mutt raised son Mickey from the cradle to be a Major Leaguer. Mutt's death "was the defining moment of his son's life." Without Mutt, Mantle "was adrift. . . . Free to make his own decisions, he made bad ones. He wasn't under anyone's finger anymore."[39] Mickey Mantle's leading biographer, Jane Leavy, concludes that "Mutt's ghost would remain the animating force in his life for the next forty years."[40]

Chapter 11's discussion of why Satchel Paige should not have been the first black in the major leagues projects onto Paige some of the scorn later heaped on Mickey Mantle for avoiding military service and possibly the Korean War. Satch had served neither in the United States' massive, global effort in World War II nor in the military at all. We can get an idea of the scorn that fans and the media might (hypothetically) have heaped on Paige by revisiting the scorn they actually did heap on Mantle.

Mantle's Oklahoma draft board had, of course, exempted Mantle from the draft and possible service in the Korean War. The ensuing draft dodger "stigma would [nonetheless] plague [Mantle] through the entire decade and result in more hate mail, booing and bad feelings than had ever been directed at an athlete."[41] Boos, catcalls, and curses followed Mantle every time he took the field.[42] "The backlash was so severe that the Yankees asked the draft board to reexamine [Mantle's] case."[43] In one Mantle biographer's estimation, there merely were "nagging questions as to why [Mantle] had been declared 4F and therefore exempt from the draft during the Korean War."[44] More unbiased accounts describe the toll more accurately as lasting and significant. For instance, biographer Allen Barra concludes that "Mickey's rejection by the draft board would stain his reputation for a decade."[45] Along with his rejection by Joe DiMaggio, his demotion to the minor leagues, and the death of his father, criticism of Mickey Mantle's draft status and his failure to serve clouded the early years, and more, of his Major League playing career.

The First Tape-Measure Home Run

Mickey Mantle moved from a question mark to an exclamation point before he had played his first regular-season baseball game. The Yankees left their spring-training facility in Phoenix to play a series of exhibition games up and down the West Coast. Several of those games were in Los Angeles. The finale was to be a doubleheader against the University of Southern California (USC) on the USC campus.

Rookie-to-be Mantle hit a towering home run that landed in the middle of the adjacent Trojan football practice facility, at a spot estimated to be six hundred feet from home plate. "Six days earlier he had been mere background in some Hollywood flack's snapshot," but after reports of that home run had circulated, Mantle "moved to center stage, where he would remain the rest of his life."[46] "Who is this Mickey Mantle who knocked my Yogi off the front page?"[47] Carmen Berra asked.

Thus was born a central ingredient of the Mantle legend, the tape-measure home run, a score of which Mantle hit throughout his career. As developed in the chapter that follows, reality did not always square with the legend, including the tape-measure home run part of it, but before he had even set foot in New York City, Mantle had become Oklahoma's most famous export, at least since Will Rogers.[48]

Year-In and Year-Out Performance

Mickey Mantle's tumultuous rookie year has already been described. He hit a respectable .267, with thirteen home runs, but this performance did not meet expectations for the Oklahoma Kid, the Rookie of the Eons, the Phenom, of whom most had anticipated much more.

In 1952, his sophomore season, Mantle began to string together performances that guaranteed him a subsequent position in the Hall of Fame, a string that lasted until 1965. His batting averages were .311 (1952), .295 (1953), .300 (1954), and .306 (1955). His performance then escalated to .353 (1956) and .365 (1957), as if the blood in his veins had been replaced by high-octane jet fuel. For a few years in the midst of the string, Mantle's performance trailed off a bit, to a mere mortal star's pace of .304 (1958), .285 (1959), and .275 (1960). In 1961 Mantle found his second wind, hitting .317 that year, .321 (1962), .314 (1963), and .303 (1964). In that stretch the Yankees appeared in twelve of fourteen World Series, winning seven of them. With a couple of exceptions, Mantle's home run totals ranged from thirty to thirty-one to as high as fifty-two and fifty-four. He was among the fastest players in the major leagues, timed from home plate to first base in 2.9 seconds. As a center fielder he won several Gold Glove awards. He became the "most sought after endorser in American sports: Wheaties, Camels, Gem Razor

Blades, Esquire socks, Van Heusen shirts, Haggar slacks, Louisville Slugger baseball bats"; the manufacturers of these and other products paid him to appear in their commercials.[49]

Beginning in 1965 both Mantle and the Yankees began to taper off, at first gradually and then suddenly, as Hemingway described bankruptcy. His playing career ended in 1968. By then the once-proud Yankees had fallen to last place in the American League. Mantle, though, had earned his place in the record books, giving a solid basis for growth of a legend that already existed.

The Peck's Bad Boy Persona Augments the Legend

The first images the public viewed were of the young, blond baseball player chewing gum and blowing bubbles in center field, a tad bit irreverent but nothing as naughty as, say, Hollywood actors and starlets partying in Las Vegas. In the clubhouse the Mick became known for squirt-gun fights and other forms of boyish, raucous behavior.

His partners in crime became well known too. Casey Stengel called pitcher Whitey Ford, infielder Billy Martin, and Mantle his "three musketeers." The first episodes were away from New York, thus hidden somewhat from public view. For instance, Mantle wrecked his new Lincoln Continental while drag racing with Billy Martin racing his new Cadillac.[50] Both were drunk, but it was the off-season and in Oklahoma, away from the New York press.

As Mantle's celebrity status grew, a certain innocence radiated outward from the ballpark. "Night club stars were thrilled to be in the company of America's most celebrated young baseball star: Joey Bishop, Larry Storch, Buddy Hackett and other [stars] flabbergasted Mickey by asking for his autograph."[51] His celebrity status, though, whetted Mantle's appetite for the big, flashy New York clubs, the limelight, and the booze. His own fatalistic attitude toward life, based on the death of his father at such a young age, and a "reckless immaturity" fueled the mix.[52] The public image of Mantle, however, was still one of a proclivity for engaging in horseplay and pulling pranks, perhaps widening into whispered stories of "legendary carousing . . . with partners in crime Billy Martin and Whitey Ford and Hank Bauer."[53] Sportswriters in those days, though, refrained from commenting on players' lives away from the baseball diamond or on road trips.

Then came the "Copa Caper." In May 1957 Mantle, Yogi Berra, Hank Bauer, Whitey Ford, and their wives were celebrating Billy Martin's twenty-ninth birthday with a night out at the Copa Cabana nightclub. A large loudmouth at the next table recognized the Yankees and came over to them, not exactly picking a fight but saying things the Yankees found unpalatable. The group took it to the restroom, where later the loudmouth was found unconscious, bleeding on the floor with a broken jaw.[54] No one has ever determined what happened or who did what to whom, but educated guesses were made that night at the Copa Cabana. One newspaper's headline assumed things, reading "It Wasn't a No Hitter."[55] Criminal investigations but no prosecutions followed, although civil suits for damages were filed later. "The Copa kerfuffle was the first public intimation of Mantle's off-field embrace of *la vida loca* . . . . Whitey, Billy and Mickey: grown men with little boy's names."[56]

The Yankees traded Billy Martin that summer to Kansas City, not only because of the Copa caper but a mere day or two after the hot-headed Martin had picked a fight with Larry Doby, then playing for the White Sox. Martin's punching Doby was the last straw for Yankee management.

After the Yankees traded Martin, Ford and especially Mantle had New York all to themselves: "[Mantle] was the king of New York. Everybody loved Mickey. . . . Men wanted to be him. Women wanted to be with him. His domain was vast. . . . Wherever he went—Danny's Hideaway, the Latin Quarter, the '21' Club, the Stork Club, El Morocco, Toots Shor's—his preferred drink was poured as he walked through the door. Reporters waited by his locker. . . . Boys clustered by the players' gate, hoping to touch him."[57]

Jim Bouton was an ex-Yankees pitcher who had enjoyed some success in a medium-length career as a Yankee, 1962–68 (21-7 in 1963, 55-51 over seven years). In 1970 he published *Ball Four*, a book mostly about his season with the expansion team Seattle Pilots. The book though, included a tell-all about his years as a Yankee and about Major League Baseball. Bouton regaled readers with exposes of Yankee behavior—water guns, water balloons, whoopee cushions, hard drinking, fighting, and carousing, peeping Tom exploits extraordinaire—in which Mantle figured prominently.[58]

During Mantle's baseball career and shortly thereafter, baseball had moved from a cone of silence over player's off-field escapades, to selective reporting of incidents too big to cover up (the Copa Caper), to tell-all, mildly shocking (back then very shocking) no-holds-barred revelations. Mickey Mantle, "the last boy in the last decade ruled by boys," figured prominently in Bouton's and other tales.[59] Major League Baseball, as best it could, tried to discredit and even ban Bouton and his book from the game.

Some say that most people "hate the sin but love the sinner." So it was with Mickey Mantle. The counterintuitive upshot of all his peccadilloes and shenanigans was to augment and enhance, not deduct from, the Mantle legend, while it might have torpedoed a less highly regarded ball player. Mantle's All-American boyish looks, a "boys will be boys" forgiveness on the part of his fans, and his absolute toughness overrode any negative connotations. On the field Mantle played hard, and well, with superhuman performance in everything, playing through injuries, and hangovers as well.

Life after Baseball

Performance on the field acted as a counterweight to Mantle's drinking and carousing off the field. He announced his retirement in spring 1969. Without the counterweight of being on a team and playing regularly, Mantle drank more heavily. He played golf and made celebrity appearances throughout the United States. He did endorsements and commercials ("I want my Maypo" in 1967).

One thing he did not do was to resume a family life, in part because he never had a family life to resume. In 1958 his wife, Merlyn, and his four young sons, moved from New Jersey to the Preston Hollow section of Dallas, Texas. The Mantles had built a home there. Still tony Preston Hollow is where former president George W. Bush and his wife, Laura, now make their home. During his playing days Mantle stayed in New York, while, in pursuit of a more normal existence, the Mantle family moved to Texas.

Life in a prestigious section of Dallas did not save Mantle's family. All four of his sons and his wife ended up with severe alcohol and drug dependencies.

In the early 1980s Mantle faced numerous medical bills for treatment of his son, Billy, who had been diagnosed with cancer. In 1980 Bally's Atlantic City casino had hired former San Francisco Giants center fielder and Hall of Fame entrant Willie Mays as a public relations representative and official greeter of sorts. Bowie Kuhn, then commissioner of baseball, promptly banned Mays from all connections with Major League Baseball, invoking the no-tolerance rule that Commissioner Kenesaw Mountain Landis had implemented following the 1919 "Black Sox" scandal. Despite the potential of a lifetime ban like the one imposed on Mays, Mantle needed the money enough to take the risk. He accepted a job similar to Mays's for $100,000 per year, requiring him to "smooze with the high rollers" at Claridge's, the oldest, and what many considered the most downscale, the smallest, and the most threadbare of the Atlantic City casinos. "It was degrading and . . . Mantle knew it was degrading."[60] Predictably, Bowie Kuhn banned Mantle from baseball.

Then and there, at Claridge's, in Atlantic City, New Jersey, Mantle's really heavy, world-class drinking began. In the mornings he began his day with "the breakfast of champions": brandy, Kahlua liqueur, and half-and-half or cream. He would put two shots of vodka into a glass of wine before drinking it. Seeing an individual ordering a drink at the next table, Mantle would order ten or more of the same drink, polishing off all ten, or even twenty, one after the other.[61]

In 1985 Mantle met a Georgia schoolteacher named Greer Johnson. Soon thereafter he began cohabiting with Johnson in a townhouse in Greensboro, Georgia, outside Atlanta. His marriage with Merlyn of some twenty-five years, long over in many respects, was thus visibly rendered asunder. Greer Johnson became Mantle's lover, housemate, companion, handler, and employee.

The baseball memorabilia craze of the 1980s could have saved Mantle, and perhaps did for a few years. He was the number one attraction for all the card shows, signings, auctions, and other events that took the country by storm, rising very quickly to a $1.2 billion industry. Greer Johnson booked him, arranged his travel, accompanied him, banked the receipts, and kept the books. For his part, ever the loyal and faithful teammate, Mantle used his star power to persuade show and action promoters to include Yankees less prominent or less remembered than Mantle. After several years, however, the baseball memorabilia craze declined, swiftly returning to the $200 million level from whence it had come. Mantle continued his drinking. One of his favored hangouts became the Preston Trail Country Club, where he could be found, if not playing golf, drinking and allowing fellow members to bask in the Mantle aura.

Mickey Mantle entered the Betty Ford Clinic in Palm Springs, California, on January 7, 1994. He stayed thirty-two days and remained sober thereafter, which was not to be long. Later in 1994 Mantle's third son, Billy, died of a heart attack at age thirty-five, weakened by the bouts of chemotherapy and other treatments he had undergone to beat cancer.

A short time later, doctors diagnosed Mickey Mantle with cirrhosis and cancer of the liver, detecting a severe and prolonged decrease of liver function. They said his liver was "like a door stop." The Baylor Medical Regional Transplant Center put him on the liver transplant list. He cleared the list. In early June 1995, while transplanting the healthy liver into Mantle, surgeons saw what they had been unable to assess previously: cancer had metastasized from his liver to his pancreas. Mantle had a few weeks left. In August 1995 he reentered the hospital. He died early in the morning of August 13, 1995, at age fifty-three.

Mickey Mantle's tombstone reads "The most popular player of his era." His lawyer, Ray True, uttered a partial eulogy: "To me he was one of the saddest, loneliest people I have ever known. He had no place in the world."[62] Oscar Wilde said, "I drink to keep body and soul apart." So did Mantle. But another Mantle friend, Tony Molito, opined, "Mickey Mantle was not destroyed by alcohol. He was destroyed by celebrity," by his own legend.[63]

13

Conflation of the Mantle Legend

He was the brightest star, a talisman of the supernatural.

—BUZZ BISSINGER, *The Classic Mantle*

Mickey Mantle's star power was unchallenged by any other athlete . . .
not approached in American sports until Michael Jordan in the 1990s.

—ALLEN BARRA, *Mantle and Mays*

A sports book author penned that superlative not in the fifties or
sixties but fifty years later. The Mantle legend lives. Authors produce doorstop-sized biographies about him. Not only does the legend endure; with each passing year it is embellished and grows.
Much of the Mantle legend is justified, based on his performance
and his exploits. But here and there the Mantle legend seems to
grow beyond all bounds, obscuring from view the achievements
of Mantle's baseball contemporaries such as Larry Doby, Roger
Maris, Ernie Banks, or even Ted Williams.

Mighty Mouse

Mantle stood five feet eleven; he weighed 195 pounds.[1] He hit 536
home runs over an eighteen-year career. Mantle holds the record
for home runs in the World Series, at eighteen, having surpassed no
less than Babe Ruth (fifteen). Revisionists today term his achievements all the more remarkable because of his supposed small
stature: "His talent was unlike what anyone had ever seen, his
power an anomaly because of a diminutive frame of 5-11 and 190

pounds."[2] Even more remarkable yet was that "power hitters in the big leagues were big, hefty . . . all compaction."[3]

True, for his day, Babe Ruth was "big and hefty": six feet two, 215 pounds. But almost all the power hitters, in Mantle's time and subsequently, were *smaller*, not larger, than Mantle, contrary to what Mantle hagiographers would have you believe. A partial list would include

Henry Aaron, six feet, 180 pounds, 755 home runs

Willie Mays, five feet ten, 170 pounds, 660 home runs

Ernie Banks, six feet, 180 pounds, 512 home runs

Stan Musial, six feet, 175 pounds, 475 home runs

Willie Stargell, six feet two, 188 pounds, 475 home runs

Carl Yastrzemski, five feet eleven, 175 pounds, 452 home runs

Duke Snider, six feet, 179 pounds, 407 home runs

Roberto Clemente, five feet eleven, 280 home runs

With weight training many of the power hitters of the eighties and later decades became bigger, for instance, Frank "The Big Hurt" Thomas of the Chicago White Sox (521 home runs). The arrival of the steroid era in baseball brought even greater numbers of bigger power hitters: Barry Bonds, Mark McGuire, Rafael Palmeiro, Manny Ramirez, Alex Rodriguez, Gary Sheffield, Sammy Sosa, and Albert Pujols. In fact, seven of the last eight players to join the five-hundred-or-more-home-runs club have been proven users of banned performance-enhancing drugs (Pujols is the exception), which bulked them up to extraordinary size.[4] The steroid era, though, came in the mid-1990s and later, not in the era in which Mantle played.

Nonetheless, the legend overrides the reality. With his small college-fullback's build and his bull-like seventeen-and-a-half-inch neck, Mantle is celebrated not only for his accomplishments but as standing out all the more because of his compact, supposedly "smaller" size.

Tape-Measure Home Runs

Another Mantle legend began with his home runs in a 1951 exhibition game that the Yankees played against the University of Southern California baseball team, as recounted in the last chapter. The legend became lore, though, with the home run Mantle hit against the Washington Senators ("first in the hearts and minds of their county men, last in the American League") at Washington DC's Griffith Stadium in April 1953. With wind blowing at twenty miles per hour and gusts up to forty, Mantle hit what appeared to be a long pop-up. The baseball, however, cleared the stadium wall by a large margin, seeming to go on forever. Arthur "Red" Patterson, the Yankees public relations man, immediately saw the "entrepreneurial potential."[5]

Patterson exited the stadium and found the neighborhood youth who had retrieved the home run ball, who showed Patterson the spot in a back yard where supposedly the ball had landed. Without a tape measure, Patterson paced off the alleged flight of the baseball, then passed off as absolute truth that the ball had traveled 565 feet. "None of the intrepid residents of the press box ventured out of the stadium to interview the neighborhood boy" or verify Patterson's measurements. Without raising any question whatsoever, the *New York Daily News* reported that "the magnificent moppet of the Yankees today hit the longest home run in the history of baseball."[6] Mickey Mantle "exploded on the national scene in 1953 when he hit his first 'tape measure' home run," meaning the home run at Griffith Stadium that April.[7]

Experts have later determined that the ball probably traveled 506 feet, or 515 feet, but not 565 feet, or 600 feet, as later accounts embellished it. "The myth of the Tape Measure Home Run," though, became ensconced in Mantel mythology.[8] The myth then proceeded to grow. "Hondo [Frank Howard] and Boog Powell are two of the only people on the planet who know what it is like to hit a ball as hard as Mickey Mantle."[9] Mantle became "the Yankee mighty man of muscle."[10]

In his later career Mantle did hit some truly tape-measure home runs. He hit a ball out of Briggs Stadium, home of the Detroit

Tigers.[11] He hit two over the high Griffith Park center field wall, into an oak tree beyond.[12] Casey Stengel said, "They tell me that the only other fella to hit that tree was Babe Ruth."[13] Even Mantle himself, however, discounted the tape-measure home run from which the legend emanated: "The one I hit in Washington I had a 50 mile-per-hour tailwind," he told author Jane Leavy.[14]

Moreover, the Mantle legend masks completely from view the feats of others that equaled or exceeded Mantle's "historic" home run. Josh Gibson, a star of the Negro Leagues, hit one out of Griffith Stadium, at least as long as and long before Mickey Mantle did. In times close to Mantle's supposed feat, Larry Doby hit a ball over the thirty-one-foot wall bordering Griffith's right field, something no one had done before.[15] Nonetheless, the enhanced tape-measure home run legend, despite its dubious origin, seems to live on and obscure all that occurred before it.

Injuries and Pain

Mickey Mantle had numerous injuries throughout his career. Subsequently, Mantle followers have expanded the ambit of injury and pain longitudinally, back further in time, as well as latitudinally, broadening out through his playing career. An example of the former is the hint, of recent vintage, that the high school football injury that resulted in the osteomyelitis, which, in turn, kept him out of the army and the Korean War, can be traced to infections earlier in his youth.[16] It seems he had afflictions from an age earlier than we have thought. For example, even in the year (1956) in which Mantle won the triple crown, hitting .353, with 52 home runs and 130 RBIs, becoming only the fourth player in history to do so (after Ty Cobb, Roger Hornsby, and Ted Williams), the revisionist claim is that Mantle was hobbled by injuries and pain that year.[17]

Mantle had many injuries throughout his baseball career. It seems unnecessary to enhance and expand them, as recent biographers have done. Additionally, although one cannot question the incidence of his injuries, one can raise questions about the severity of the injuries, the pain they induced, and the effect on his playing career. Those questions may be inferred from his stellar playing performance; his longevity; what the physicians found and said at the time; and what he himself opined after his playing days had ended.

Performance. Mickey Mantle batted over .300 ten times in his career. He hit over fifty home runs twice, over forty four times, and over thirty nine times. The Yankees won the American League pennant twelve of the first fourteen years Mantle played, the exception being 1954 (Cleveland Indians) and 1959 (Chicago White Sox). The Yankees won seven of the twelve World Series in which they and Mantle appeared. Mantle won the triple crown in 1956. He was the American League Most Valuable Player three times (1956, 1957, and 1962). He was an All-Star sixteen times.

Further evidence, aside from his performance on the baseball field, that his injuries could not have hobbled him that badly comes from outside of baseball. Postseason in 1953, after he had injured his right knee in 1951 (the uncovered-drain incident), and after, in 1953, he had undergone open knee surgery to trim his medial meniscus, he organized a basketball team, Mickey Mantle's Southwest Chat All Stars, to barnstorm through Missouri and Oklahoma. Not only did the Mick coach the team; he played point guard.[18] One cannot play competitive basketball at that level, or at any level, with the injuries and pain that the sportswriters and biographers have always ascribed to Mantle. Mantle worshippers ignore this evidence perhaps because it is strongly contrary to what they wish their audiences to believe.

Longevity. Mantle played for eighteen seasons. He played in over 2,400 Major League games, 2,401 to be exact, the all-time Yankee record until Derek Jeter surpassed it in 2011. It would have been a herculean effort to have done so with the injuries and pain ascribed to him. Perhaps it was, that is, a herculean effort, but the length of his career, as well as his productivity, constitute evidence on the other side of the ledger.

Medical opinions. In October 1951, after the uncovered-drain field incident, Mantle was hospitalized for five days at Lenox Hill Hospital in New York City. Doctors there diagnosed no lasting injury to his knee and also determined that surgery was unnecessary. They released him with a prescription for rest.

In December 1951, at the Yankees' request, Mantle journeyed to Johns Hopkins Hospital in Baltimore to get a second opinion. The knee did not bother him, but the Yankees wanted to assure themselves that nothing was amiss. Orthopedists at Johns Hopkins examined him and gave him a clean bill of health. He returned home to Oklahoma.

Then, on August 8, 1953, Mantle injured, or reinjured, his right knee while chasing down a fly ball in center field at Yankee Stadium. Thereafter, Mantle experienced "swelling, locking and buckling of his right knee," symptoms common to those who have torn cartilage in the knee.[19] Dr. Dan Yancey performed open knee surgery in Springfield, Missouri. He found only "a bucket handle tear of the medial meniscus," the most common injury of the knee, which affects many athletes, amateur as well as professional, including this author and several of his friends.[20] Dr. Yancey found the surgery "unremarkable, the post-operative course smooth, and the future unimpeded."[21] "It's a fairly common thing," the orthopedic surgeon continued. "If you had to have something wrong with the knee, you'd want this to be it."[22]

Undoubtedly something else went on inside Mantle's knee. An educated theoretical diagnosis was made by Dr. Stephan Haas, medical director for the National Football League Players' Association. His guess? "It appears that the most likely critical event was an acute combination of torn medial and anterior cruciate ligaments [ACLs] and medial meniscus tear."[23] That verdict, however, was a guess made only many years later, without the benefit of a physical examination, or X-rays, or an MRI. The several doctors who physically examined Mantle previously found no such injuries, at least at the time.

The legend and the lore, though, continue to endure and to expand. Mantle's 1951 injury "alter[ed] the entire course of his career," asserts author Allen Barra, writing in 2013.[24] "Mickey caught his cleat on the open drainpipe . . . forever destroying the possibility that he would be the greatest baseball had ever seen."[25] Mantle won MVP Awards and the triple crowns playing "in terrible pain."[26] Buzz Bissinger introduces Mantle's Yankee career with the preview that "he always played hard despite constant and unimaginable pain."[27] Later on the 2010 Mantle biography adds: "That October [1951] afternoon was the last time Mantle set foot on a baseball field without pain."[28]

What Mick himself said. Mantle himself did not see it the way many of his biographers do. In response to author Jane Leavy's question, "What about the injuries? The knees, the hamstrings, the shoulder, the spike caught in the drain?" Mantle told her, "That was overplayed. A lot of times I felt great. I wasn't always a one legged guy who looked like a mummy. I never had any problems from the waist up. I didn't hurt as bad as everyone thought I did. I still ran down to first faster than anyone. I played twenty-four hundred games . . . eighteen years."[29]

Something does not add up with respect to the received wisdom about Mickey Mantle's pain and injuries. At least the issue bears reexamination.

The Most Valuable Player Forever Hype

Yankee Roger Maris won the American League Most Valuable Player award in 1960 and again in 1961. Yogi Berra won the MVP award in both 1954 and 1955 (Cleveland Indian Larry Doby finished second in the 1954 voting). In between, occasionally, other players from other teams won (Jackie Jensen, Red Sox, in 1958; Nellie Fox, White Sox, in 1959). Yet to author Allen Barra, Mantle "should have won [MVP] award[s] for eight straight seasons from 1954 to 1961."[30] By a single stroke of the pen, Barra dismisses, or attempts to erase altogether, Maris's, Berra's, Jensen's, Fox's, or anybody else's achievements and their value to their teams.

Matching Mantle up against another legend, Barra, a contemporary Mantle biographer, purports to find that "Mantle was not only better [than Ted Williams] but by a significant margin."[31] For the year in question, 1957, Williams won the numbers race hands-down, .388 versus .365 in batting average, 38 to 34 home runs. The Mantle worshipper explains away the difference by finding that Williams played in the more hitter-friendly Fenway Park, so his superior numbers do not really count. In particular author Barra trashes Roger Maris, who played right field next to Mantle and who, in 1961, broke Babe Ruth's single season of sixty home runs, a record that had stood for thirty-four years. He mentions Larry Doby only to note that he was "a fine centerfielder."[32]

In 1960 Roger Maris hit .283; Mickey Mantle hit .275. In home runs they were about the same: Maris 39, Mantle 40. Maris drove in quite a few more runs than Mantle, 112 to 94. The baseball writers voted Maris the M V P. Yet to Barra, "Mickey was the better player."[33]

The following year began the quest for which Maris is famous, the run at Babe Ruth's sixty-home-run record. On October 1, 1961, Maris hit home run number sixty-one, breaking a record that many thought might never be broken. The journey there was beyond arduous: "Maris lost gobs of hair; the circles under his eyes appeared etched in charcoal."[34] His smoking habit ratcheted up to three packs a day. When Maris opened up to sportswriters, acknowledging, "I can't make it, not even in 162 games [versus the 154-game season in which Ruth played]," rather than sympathizing with Maris, sportswriters turned on him, accusing him of the "big sulk."[35]

The background to all of this was that until early September it had been a Maris-Mantle race, "The Bronx Bomber Thrill Show."[36] Mantle injured himself, dropping out of the race with a fifty-four-home-run total. But Mantle, the loser, was the winner; Maris, the winner, was the loser. The reason? Even back then Mickey Mantle was the darling of the fans and the sportswriters. He could do no wrong. "He [Maris] beat Babe Ruth and he beat me, so the [Yankee fans] hated him. Everywhere we'd go I got a standing ovation," Mantle acknowledged. [37] Editors judiciously selected the photos to appear in newspapers: "The pictures of Ruth and Maris looked like mug shots. Mantle looks[ed] like a choir boy."[38] Roger Hornsby called Maris a "punk baseball player"; Jimmy Cannon called him "a whiner."[39] Immediately after he had hit sixty-one, Maris was asked by a radio announcer: "As you were running around the bases, were you thinking about Mickey Mantle?"[40] Even back then it was all Mickey, all the time.

It continues, unabated, to the present day. Mantle biographer Allen Barra concludes with another over-the-top assessment: "In 1961, Mickey Mantle was better than Roger Maris . . . or any other player in baseball by a wide margin." "Mantle was by far the superior ballplayer" and should have been named the MVP.[41]

Maris broke a long-standing, almost sacred record and helped his team to a 4-1 World Series victory over the Cincinnati Reds, a series in which Mantle played well. The sport writers elected Maris, not Mantle, the MVP, and the vote was supported, amply so, by the record. Remember that it is for the player most valuable to his team, not necessarily the one with the best numbers or superior athletic ability. Poke through the fog of Mantlemania— give Maris, other players of the time, and the sportswriters who voted for MVPs other than Mantle, their due.

Deflation rather than Conflation

My wish is not to negate Mantle's skills and accomplishments; Mickey Mantle played hard every day. He played with injuries and with "absolute toughness." He was the ultimate "gamer." He never bragged. He sublimated his ego in the clubhouse and elsewhere. He was the most popular among his teammates and considerate of them, the opposite of a Satchel Paige. After his playing days had ended, Mantle never forgot the other Yankees with whom he had played and shared a clubhouse, keeping in contact with them and benefiting them in many ways. This is an aspect of the Mantle lore that, if anything, is downplayed, deflated rather than conflated. For that reason this seldom-seen aspect of the Mantle legend bears further examination.

The Gamer. In 1961 Mantle had gone for injections by the "feel good doctor," whose methods were less than sanitary. Mantle had to have an infected mass the size of a golf ball removed from his right buttock. In the World Series against the Reds, he hit a single, and while he was running to first base, the stitches gave way, the wound opened, and blood gushed out. Mantle shielded the bloody patch on his uniform pants from view, using his glove as he ran to and from center field. In the fourth inning Mantle hit a ball into the gap in right-center, a possible double. Running, he had to stop at first, and his leg was a bloody mess. Everybody could see how badly he was hurting. Manager Ralph Houck lifted Mantle for a pinch runner. Limping back to the dugout, Mantle received a standing ovation from his Yankee teammates. The incident demonstrates "his absolute toughness. Teammate after teammate attested to it, the acceptance of pain, however severe."[42]

He was the ultimate gamer. "The one thing he always did was try," Yankee second baseman Jerry Coleman said. "Mickey never, ever stopped doing the best he could."[43] "He was a hero in the clubhouse because of the respect the other players had for the way he played the game—not just his ability but the intensity he played it with."[44]

Humble and Modest. Another "thing other players, teammates and opponents, admired" was Mantle's humility: "No ego," said Gil McDougal. "Great control of his ego," said Reggie Jackson. "Wasn't no individual," said Jim Coates.[45] With all his home runs, Mantle always ran the bases with his eyes and head down, neither taunting the pitcher nor celebrating his own prowess and superiority, as many modern athletes do. He "never showed anyone up, never called anyone out, never blamed anyone but himself."[46] Longtime teammate Tony Kubeck appreciated Mantle off the field as well as on it: "He [Mantle] didn't want to be exempted as one of the great players. He just wanted to be with his boys." He was seen as "the best teammate ever. . . . He didn't phony up anything."[47]

Loyal Forever. Mantle gave, not loaned, money to ex-teammates when they were out of luck even if Mantle could ill afford to do so. When the sports memorabilia craze escalated in the 1980s, Mantle was among the biggest draws at card shows and signing events. He used his star power to drag along lesser-known former Yankees, often several at a time. In the years he ran fantasy camps, for which middle-aged men paid $5,000.00 or more for a week of "spring training," Mantle hired all his former teammates as counselors.[48] His generosity and loyalty to his boys knew few bounds.

Back to Conflation

The hype and exaggeration seem to crescendo at higher and higher points each year. One 2010 baseball biography ratchets upward Mantle's torn medical meniscus, suffered in the 1951 World Series. "[Mantle's] spikes of his right shoe caught the rubber cover of a sprinkler. His knee collapsed and he lay motionless, a bone sticking out of his right leg."[49] So with the passage of time, Mantle's cartilage tear, which necessitated surgery only two years later and was followed by a winter of basketball barnstorming, has become a compound fracture, possibly with Mantle's blood spurting out onto the field.

At the height of the card-show craze, actor Billy Crystal paid $239,000 for a baseball glove Mickey Mantle once wore. "Crystal says the glove is more valuable to him than the Picasso hanging in his home."[50] The Topps Bubblegum Mickey Mantle baseball card "went from $600 to $3,000 practically overnight."[51] So the conflation has continued and, in some instances, cannot be quantified and monetized.

Mickey Mantle was a great athlete and baseball player. The onrushing legend and the shadow it casts, or most of it, are justified. The human tragedy that his life as a whole, including his self-destruction, exemplifies makes the Mantle story all the more poignant. In the words of Daniel Defoe's Robinson Crusoe, "He was born but to be his own destroyer."

The downside of the Mantle legend is that the ever-burgeoning legend masks from view the athletic accomplishments and milestones others in baseball achieved, which should not be forgotten. In the context of this book, the accomplishments of outfielder Larry Doby of the Cleveland Indians, a contemporary and a competitor of Mantle's, and the man who broke the color barrier in the American League, have been largely blocked from view by, among other things, the Mickey Mantle legend and its aura.

14

Willie Mays and "The Catch"

He's a once in a lifetime ballplayer, and we may never see his equal again. . . .
Whatever he does, he does to perfection.

—LES BIEDERMAN, sportswriter, *Pittsburgh Press*, 1930–69

Willie Mays is the greatest player ever to put on a uniform, greater than Ted
Williams, Stan Musial or Mickey Mantle.

—ALVIN DARK, shortstop (1950–55) and manager (1960–62), San Francisco Giants

You're the best ballplayer I ever saw. Having you on my team made everything worthwhile. . . . I'll always be looking out for you.

—LEO DUROCHER, manager of the New York Giants, 1947–55

Mays is the greatest thing I have seen in my life. And there's not one guy in
the major leagues who thinks different.

—LEN GABRIELSON, first base, San Francisco Giants, 1965–66

The exaggeration and hyperbole surrounding Mickey Mantle
seem to know few bounds, although without it Mantle would
rate as one of the game's all-time greats nonetheless. The hype
about Satchel Paige as possibly "the greatest pitcher of all time,
any color, any league," is beyond the pale, for much of Paige's
fame is due to his extraordinary longevity, consisting largely of
three-inning appearances against no-name players and teams.[1]
William Howard Mays Jr. is another story. Mays is the real deal,
top to bottom, side to side, through and through, without hype
or with it.

Mays hit 660 home runs in a twenty-two-year career, at one point the second highest in history, behind Ruth, and third all time at the conclusion of Mays's career. Hank Aaron passed Mays on the all-time list when both Mays and Aaron were still active, in 1972. Seemingly, Mays's record would have been eclipsed in the steroid era of Mark McGuire, Sammy Sosa, Barry Bonds, and Alex Rodriguez. Yet Mays still ranks fifth all time (Bonds, Aaron, Ruth, Rodriguez, Mays).

After being National League Rookie of the Year in 1951, Mays played in twenty All-Star games. He batted .302 lifetime. In the outfield he made legendary circus catches. Once the Golden Glove Awards were initiated, in 1957, Mays won twelve of them consecutively. He was a daring base runner, taunting pitchers and stealing bases. His signature trademark was his baseball hat flying off as he rounded the bases pell-mell, or as he turned to make a rocket throw from center field after making yet another fantastic catch.

Movie actress Tallulah Bankhead, a Giants fan and a Mays aficionado, in an interview in *Look*, a popular magazine of that time, stated: "There are two geniuses, Willie Mays and Willie Shakespeare."[2] Frank Robinson, himself a star and a Hall of Fame player, thought that "Mays was the greatest player of all time, who could hit, run and field with amazing grace, while seemingly always having fun."[3] Baseball writers voted Mays into the Hall of Fame the first year he was eligible, only the eighth time in baseball history the writers did so.

Larry Doby was not so much overshadowed by Willie Mays because Mays himself and his achievements were masked from view, at least partially, by Mays's own demons, so to speak. First was "The Catch," Mays's dead-run, over-the-shoulder fielding of Vic Wertz's fly ball in the first game of the 1954 World Series (Giants versus Indians). Entire books have been written solely about the game in which "The Catch" occurred.[4] For decades and even today, many baseball fans remember Mays more for his catch than his career achievements and the joy and exuberance with which he played the game. Many regard "The Catch" as celebratory of Mays's feats and career, according to author Allen Barra, "the most famous catch in World Series and probably baseball history," but one can contend that his great 1954 World Series catch actually had unforeseen and possibly negative consequences for Mays.[5]

Second, once the Giants moved to San Francisco, Mays fell more squarely under the shadow cast by the hometown hero, Joe DiMaggio, the Yankee Clipper. Once in the Bay Area, Mays met racial and other forms of discrimination one never would have expected in the city of Haight-Ashbury and the flower children. The press defamed him; Giants' followers booed him; and the same fans voted inferior, less-deserving players MVP as well as other awards over him.[6]

In 1959 Mays and his wife actually sold their San Francisco house, bought a house in New Rochelle, New York, and moved back there. A racist had thrown a Coke bottle through the living-room picture window of their San Francisco house. "I didn't know any of my neighbors," Margherite Mays said of the upscale neighborhood where she and Mays had lived. From then on, during the season Willie would live in a rented house or apartment in San Francisco.[7]

Mays did not emerge from those shadows until the conclusion of the 1962 season, when the Giants beat the other West Coast Major League team, the Los Angeles Dodgers, in a playoff for the National League pennant.

Other Clouds

There were a number of smaller demons as well. Early in his career Mays played in the shadow of Mickey Mantle and the New York Yankees, a stone's throw across the Harlem River from the Giants (the New York Gothams until 1895) and the Polo Grounds but a quantum leap ahead of the Giants in media coverage and in the hearts and minds of many New Yorkers. Mays also was but one of a trio of Hall of Fame center fielders, all in New York. Mickey Mantle played for the Yankees; Duke Snider played for the Brooklyn Dodgers; and Mays played for the New York Giants, all at the same time. The other two were white, lending at least a tinge of racism to the competition among the three.

After the Giants' World Series win in 1954, management let the team age without infusing new blood. From 1956 onward Mays played on successively worse Giants teams. Attendance fell, from over 1.5 million in 1954 to 629,000 in 1957. Suburbanites, fed up with the lack of parking at Giants games and content to watch the ever-increasing number of televised baseball games, stayed at home.[8] The Milwaukee Braves, with Warren Spahn, Lew Burdette, Eddie Matthews, Joe Adcock, and Hank Aaron, eclipsed the Giants and every other National League team, winning pennants in 1957 and 1958.

Mays also came under the cloud of a vocal Jackie Robinson, who had become not only the paragon of integration in professional sports but a leading civil rights activist overall. Robinson criticized Mays for his lack of involvement in the civil rights movement.[9] Robinson went so far as to single Mays out in a 1968 nationally televised interview, calling Mays a "do-nothing Negro," who should have become more active especially after the way Mays had been denied housing when he first moved to San Francisco.[10]

Mays had his own clouds whose shadows overlaid his achievements on the field and with which he had to deal, including the long-lasting hostility he encountered in California, the image of the young, blond superhero Mantle, a rapidly deteriorating Giants team, and Jackie Robinson labeling Mays as an "'Uncle Tom' for refusing actively to support civil rights."[11]

Mays and Doby

Willie Mays and Larry Doby were friends. They barnstormed together in the early fifties, with Mays forming Mays All-Stars following the 1955 season but barnstorming with other team leaders before then. Before Mays the organizers had been, first, Jackie Robinson and second, for a year, Roy Campanella. Mays's 1955 team had an outfield of four black future Hall of Famers: Willie Mays, Larry Doby, Henry Aaron, and Monte Irvin.[12] Think of that!

Until suddenly eclipsed by national and then local televised broadcasts of baseball games and the presence of television sets in a growing number of American homes, barnstorming was a valuable source of extra income for Major Leaguers, whose presence on a traveling team could draw fans to the ballpark. Mays and Doby were teammates for twenty-plus games following several Major League seasons, traveling together through smaller cities and into Mexico.

The Giants and the Indians were two of the first teams to relocate spring training on a permanent basis to Arizona. Bill Veeck relocated Indians spring training there because he thought Tucson attitudes and establishments would be more receptive to a black player (Doby) than would be Florida's, an assumption that proved to be erroneous.[13] For much the same reason, Branch Rickey had moved the 1947 Brooklyn Dodgers and the Montreal Royals, then with Jackie Robinson on the roster, to Havana, Cuba.[14] Indeed, Veeck's calculation proved to be doubly or triply erroneous. Each spring, and not merely the initial one in 1948, Tucson's Hotel Santa Rita insisted that Larry Doby, and later Larry Doby and his young family, seek separate accommodations.

By contrast Horace Stoneham, Leo Durocher, and the Giants would not tolerate the Hotel Adams's initial attempts in Phoenix to segregate Mays. The Hotel Adams had previously (pre-Mays) allowed the first black players with the Giants to room there and quickly capitulated on other points as well.[15]

Today the Cactus League (Arizona) far outstrips the Grapefruit League (Florida) in the number of Major League teams training there but not back then. At that time the Giants and the Indians, the pioneers of spring training in Arizona, had few choices other than playing each other. So for practice the Giants (Phoenix), with Mays, and the Indians (Tucson), with Doby, played each other. They played as many as twenty or twenty-one Giants-Indians exhibition games each spring.

Also, along with the Dodgers, the Indians and the Giants were the first Major League teams to integrate. By the time of Mays's elevation to the big leagues, in 1951, the two teams combined had eight black ballplayers. The presence of more than just tokens reinforced the respect for and the friendship with one another that the Indians players, including Doby, had, and the Giants, including Mays, had as well.[16]

Discrimination in Baseball: Mays versus Robinson and Doby

Seeking to inject a bit of drama into their books, Mays's biographers describe Mays as having been subject to the same sorts of taunts and discrimination that Jackie Robinson and Larry Doby had faced several years earlier when they began the process of integrating the major leagues. They recount Mays as having to stay in separate hotels, apart from his teammates, while he played in the minor leagues.[17] None of that is true to the facts.

First, in the Minors Mays played for the Chattanooga Choo-Choos and then the Birmingham Barons. These were black teams. All the players roomed together—there was no separation. Second, the biographers lead you to believe that two evils of segregation were inferior accommodations and inedible meals. That was not true. Black ballplayers of that era recall rooming-house home-cooked food as far superior to hotel fare of the time. Instead, a real evil of segregation was isolation from the team, from someone with whom you might discuss today's and tomorrow's games, from someone with whom you could just hang out. Mays did not experience any of the singling out or isolation such as Doby and Robinson recalled. While Mays played in the minor leagues, by and large he was in the mainstream, with his teammates.

Once Mays signed with the Giants, the club assigned him to the Trenton, New Jersey, Giants of the Class B Interstate League. Because Mays was the first black on the team, the Giants assigned a Cuban from the New York Cubans Minor League franchise to Trenton, where he could be Mays's roommate.[18] No evidence exists that Mays and his Cuban roommate had to stay in boardinghouses or hotels separate from the team.

Trenton did have to play the Hagerstown, Maryland, team, also in the Interstate League. Maryland, of course, is below the Mason-Dixon Line. In some respects, then, Maryland is more southern than northern. On Mays's first night on the field in Hagerstown, he was subjected to some brickbats and slurs, but the abuse did not last for long. By the third night of the series, the Hagerstown fans were cheering him and his spectacular exploits on the playing field.

Mays then played for the Giants A A A franchise, the Millers in Minneapolis, Minnesota. He became an instant celebrity. "[He] drew a round of applause seldom accorded to any player. The local media swooned as well."[19] In thirty-five games he hit .477, made acrobatic catches, and ran bases with abandon. "The fans loved him. He was everything they heard about and more."[20] Mays also was in a town where little or no racial prejudice seemed to exist. "It would have been hard to imagine a city on the United States in 1951 that had less racial tension than Minneapolis."[21] Mays had the run of the city.

After only thirty-five games in Minnesota, the Giants called Mays up to the big club. Mays did not want to leave. Leo Durocher, the Giants manager, had Mays paged in a movie theater where Mays was enjoying one of his favorite pastimes, watching motion pictures, especially cowboy movies and other westerns. "I'm not ready to go yet. I'm not coming," Mays told his would-be boss. "What are you hitting now?" Durocher asked. Willie told him, "Four seventy seven." "Well, do you think you can hit two-fucking-fifty for me?"[22] That did not seem so bad, so Mays went to join the Giants, then playing in Philadelphia. Stoneham and the Giants felt constrained to take out a large newspaper ad in the Minneapolis newspaper, apologizing to the public for so suddenly taking their fan favorite away from them.

So, no, it is not accurate to say that Willie Mays endured segregated dining, housing, or travel, or that he was subjected to hooting, slurs, taunts, and threats in baseball, either in the minor or major leagues. There are no hints of such rough treatment. Instead, Willie Mays was pampered, coddled, and protected, from the age he was a toddler, through the Minors, and on into the Majors, probably equal to or in excess of what any other Major League baseball player ever has experienced.

The Pampering of Willie Mays

As with Mickey Mantle and his father, Mutt, Mays was a project that his father, Cat, undertook almost from the day of Mays's birth, May 6, 1931: "Make no mistake, Cat [Mays] wanted his son to play baseball and to play better than anyone else. He exposed

Willie to the sport as early as possible. . . . Even before Willie could walk, Cat gave him a two-foot long stick and a rubber ball, and the future home run champion, sitting on his diapered butt, whacked the ball and crawled after it."[23]

Doby, of course, had no fatherly guidance as he grew up. When he was still small, Doby was sent north to Patterson, New Jersey, to live with aunts. His father bounced between Camden, South Carolina, and Saratoga Springs, New York, never again having much contact with his gifted son. He died by drowning at the age of thirty-seven in an upstate New York lake.

Cat played on the same industrial league teams as did his son, the teenaged Willie. It is interesting to note that all three, Mays, Mantle, and Doby, began their baseball careers as shortstops and later were converted to center fielders (Doby not until he reached the major leagues). Both positions, more than others on the field, require a strong throwing arm, which all three had in abundance.[24]

In addition to his father, Mays was fortunate always to have had older teammates as well as managers who were in awe of his talents and protective of him. "He was the most exciting young player you have ever seen," said a teammate and mentor on the Birmingham Black Barons, James Zapp, as early as 1948.[25]

Contrary to most players, for whom protection and paternalism lessen, if not disappear, when they reach the major leagues, for Mays they escalated. First, the Giants assigned him a "handler," or chaperone, who became ubiquitous in Mays's life. Frank Forbes was an older Harlem resident, given to wearing bow ties and spouting erudite sayings. Mays could not go anywhere—a dinner, a menswear shop, a picture show—without Forbes accompanying him. When the army discharged Mays in May 1953, the Giants sent Forbes to Fort Eustis, Virginia, to fetch their new center fielder. Mays was "coddled, even patronized, by the Giants."[26]

Jackie Robinson too had a chaperone, or a companion at least, for Branch Rickey hired Wendell Smith, the *Pittsburgh Courier* sportswriter, and an activist in the integration of baseball, to be a chauffeur and friend to Robinson. Perhaps because he was parachuted into the major leagues, with little in the way of advance planning or preparation, Doby had none of these aids for his transition.

Second, the Giants assigned Monte Irvin, a future Hall of Famer, also black, and twelve years Mays's senior, to be Mays's room-mate.[27] Leo Durocher, the Giants manager, told Irvin, "'Tell him what to do and how to do it.' Irvin positioned Mays in the out-field, advised him on what pitchers threw, how well they held base runners, and which catchers had good arms."[28] "Look after him," Durocher commanded, "watch who he talks to, make sure he gets to the ballpark on time, make sure he doesn't have too many hang-ers-on, make sure he talks to the right people."[29]

Third, manager Leo Durocher became a second father to Mays. "Leo made other players nervous with his style, but he made Mays feel comfortable right away. He simply buttered up the big rookie."[30] At practices Durocher played pepper games with Mays, fast-paced, short-range hitting and fielding drills, which Mays later remembered as "one of his fondest memo-ries."[31] Mays called Durocher "Mr. Leo"; Durocher called Mays "son" or "kid." When Durocher and Mays first met, in spring training 1951, Durocher began the dialogue with, "Hey, kid, what are you going to show me today?"[32] Russ Hodges, Mays's team-mate, expressed wonder: "Mays was the only player I ever saw who could do no wrong in Durocher's eyes. Everyone else felt the lash of Leo's tongue, sooner or later, but Willie never did."[33] "With Willie," Durocher openly said, "you have to just keep pat-ting him, keep rubbing him."[34]

The "paternalistic way that Durocher treated Willie Mays" never would have worked with the fiery Jackie Robinson. "The pair hated each other," despite Durocher's intervention on Rob-inson's behalf in order to quell player dissatisfaction with inte-gration of the Dodgers.[35]

Fourth, from the get-go, the fans at the Polo Grounds, where the Giants played, loved Mays and cheered for him without res-ervation. New York papers "heralded Mays [and Mantle as well] as pheenoms when they arrived in New York in 1951."[36] The Polo Grounds center field fence was 505 feet from home plate, "giv-ing Mays a sprawling pasture for his skills, the quick jumps, the pell-mell running style, the rocket arm."[37] He was a "savvy show-man," fixing his Giants baseball cap so it "would fly off when he rounded the bases or chased fly balls, a pulsating flourish turned into pure theater."[38] The crowds loved it.

Today Mays is "revered for capturing the joy and innocence of a bygone era."[39] But back then, in the early 1950s, it was evident to all that "a love of life just flowed out of him."[40] Giants first baseman Whitey Lockman saw every day that Mays "just bubbled over with excitement and enthusiasm."[41] "Willie's exuberance was his immortality," author Roger Kahn wrote of those early years.[42]

Mays's exuberance stood out all the more because prior to his breaking into the lineup, one unnamed sportswriter had described the Giants' pre-Mays outfield "as a trio of morticians."[43] "Mays introduced a new aesthetic, a combination of drama and athleticism that broke fresh ground on the playing field. His crowd appeal was immense."[44] Mays also met and rubbed shoulders with the celebrities of his day, at least the black ones: Joe Lewis, Duke Ellington, Billy Eckstine, and Dizzy Gillespie, to name a few.[45]

Fifth, "his teammates, black and white, loved him, his joy in playing the game was contagious, a quality they much appreciated during those tense late-summer weeks of the pennant race. The press loved him too."[46]

In his rookie season the Giants trailed the Dodgers by thirteen and a half games in August. By season's end the Giants had made up all of it, forcing a playoff. In the "shot heard 'round the world," Giants infielder Bobby Thompson hit a home run off Dodgers reliever Ralph Branca to win the NL pennant. Mays hit .270, with 20 homers, 68 RBIs, and 7 stolen bases, in 121 games that season, a showing that won him Rookie of the Year honors. In the ensuing World Series against the Yankees, the Giants folded, possibly exhausted from their regular-season herculean effort. In the Series Mays hit .247, slightly lower than the minimum .250 Durocher earlier had prescribed for him.

The Negatives

All was not a bed of roses, however. After Mays's arrival in the big show, he went 1 for 25 at the plate, nearly despairing. After a game manager Leo Durocher emerged from his office. "I saw Willie crying and I put my arm around him."

"What's the matter, son?"

"Mister Leo." Mays replied, "I can't hit up here . . ."

Leo pointed to Mays's uniform and told him, "Willie, see this across [your] uniform? It says 'Giants.' A long as I am manager of the Giants you're my centerfielder." And he was.[47]

Application of stereotypes to Mays, mostly by sportswriters, necessitated a larger adjustment than did a temporary inability to hit a Major League curveball. "Most of Willie's early profiles were condescending, portraying him as an adolescent, or at least . . . with an adolescent's mentality. [Readers] never knew of his mental problems, his anxiety over money, the desire to succeed that so often resulted in fainting spells."[48] The press labeled him the "say hey kid"; none of his teammates or friends called him that, leading a sports columnist to wonder if as Mays matured the time had come to call him William.[49] The say-hey nickname continued to stick long after outliving its usefulness, adding to the Stepin Fetchit flavor and image many had of Mays.

"Journalists were using Mays to perpetuate negative stereotypes about Negroes . . . as having an 'innate gaiety of soul' [living] a lifetime of laughs and thrills, excitement and fun . . . unburdened by unnatural inhibitions."[50] This was the Stepin Fetchit image, "servile and simplified."[51] Manager Leo Durocher contributed to the unfavorable perceptions "with Mays calling him 'Mr. Leo,' and Durocher responding with 'boy.'"[52]

Mays's own behavior contradicted these images that sportswriters succeeded in promulgating about the early Willie Mays. Early in his career Mays told his father of racial epithets he encountered in Hagerstown, Maryland, when Mays played for the Trenton Giants against Hagerstown. A racist fan had hollered, "Who's that n——r walking out on the field?" Cat Mays told the young Willie to "turn the other cheek." "Willie told him he had no intention of turning the other cheek."[53] The attitude displayed is the opposite of the simple, servile image the press portrayed.

That substance and resolve became more apparent as Mays matured. He was not active in the civil rights movement, and Jackie Robinson went to extremes to castigate him for it, but Mays was introspective about his position: "I wasn't much for controversy. Not then. Not now either, I guess. Never."[54] But he had a long, little-noted devotion to children's causes, visiting hospitals and parties for needy kids throughout his career.

In those early Major League years, Willie Mays led a charmed life. "Whenever an obstacle appeared in his path, it magically seemed to vanish . . . . [He] signed with exactly the right organization in exactly the right city that could shield him from the still powerful influence of Jim Crow."[55] He was on a roll. "His teammates liked him, the fans adored him, and to the veteran New York sportswriters, he was the black son they never had."[56]

Larry Doby encountered obstacles that Mays never had to think about. Without preparation or planning, Doby was parachuted into the major leagues as the first black in the American League. Growing up he had no father or other mentor to school him, advise him, or help him improve as a baseball player, as Mays and Mantle did. When he got to the big leagues, Doby had neither chaperone nor handler nor companion, as Mays and Robinson did.

Cleveland manager Lou Boudreau was the antithesis of Leo Durocher. Even Boudreau describes the early Doby-Boudreau relationship as "awkward." Midway through his first full season, Doby did acquire a black roommate, Satchel Paige, but he was no Monte Irvin. The self-centered, woman-chasing, wild Paige turned out to be a liability rather than an asset to the young Indians center fielder. The question that arises is whether Doby, had he had all the pampering and coddling Mays received, would have put up numbers even greater than those he did achieve and if instead of thirteen years his career would have stretched out toward Mays's twenty-two or Mantle's eighteen seasons? We will never know.

The Catch

In the first game of the 1954 World Series (Indians versus Giants), played in New York's spacious Polo Grounds, the Indians jumped out to a 2–0 lead. The Giants tied the score in the third. There the score stood, 2–2, until the top of the ninth inning, when the Indians put Larry Doby and Al Rosen aboard at second and at first, respectively. Next up was the powerful Vic Wertz, the Indians' slugging first baseman, recently acquired from Baltimore.

On defense in center field, Willie Mays was playing shallow, hopefully to prevent Doby, who was an extremely fast runner, from scoring from second on a Wertz single. Wertz crushed the first pitch from Giant relief pitcher Don Liddle. The hit was variously described as a "long low fly ball" or a "high liner . . . not terribly high."[57] Arnold Hano, who authored an entire book about the game that day, *A Day at the Bleachers*, describes Wertz's hit "as hard as I have ever seen a ball hit, on a high line to center-field."[58] "I have seen hitters such as Babe Ruth, Lou Gehrig, Ted Williams, Jimmy Foxx, Ralph Kiner, Hack Williams [and] Johnny Mize. . . . None, that I recall, ever hit a ball harder than the one hit by Wertz."[59]

Mays turned and made a dead run toward the Polo Ground's center-field wall, at that point 483 feet from home plate. At the last second, an estimated twenty feet from the outfield wall, Mays looked over his shoulder and took the ball over his head. "He put his hands up in a cup-like fashion, over his left shoulder, and caught the ball much like a football player catching leading passes in the end zone."[60] In one motion Mays whirled and threw toward the infield.

"I saw [Larry] Doby, too, hesitating, the only man, I think, on the diamond who conceived that Mays might catch the ball. Doby is a centerfielder and a fine one, and very fast himself, so he knows what a centerfielder can do," Hano recounts.[61] Doby, who at first had run toward third base, recognized that the ball would be caught. He returned to second, tagged up, and ran to third. Al Rosen, the Indians third baseman, began to advance to second but thought better and returned to first.

Mays's catch and throw prevented a run (Doby) from scoring. The game went into extra innings, with reserve Giants outfielder Dusty Rhodes hitting a walk-off pinch-hit home run, breaking the tie and winning the game for the Giants.

The Mays catch and throw have become legendary. The throw was, according to Hano, "the throw of a giant, the throw of a howitzer made human, arriving at second base as Doby was pulling into third and Rosen was scampering back to first."[62] "What a throw, what an astonishing throw."[63]

Few remember the "stupendous hitting" by Vic Wertz in the 1954 World Series, when he hit 8 for 16. "All they remember is his out. . . . The catch made the 1954 World Series. Five decades later few people can even name the teams, say, in the 1957 World Series. But fans know that the Giants won in 54 because of Mays's mad dash to straightaway center. The catch became Willie Mays's brand."[64]

Even at that time The Catch was accorded a great deal of hype, some deserved, some not. *Sporting News* appraised The Catch as "sports' greatest thrill" for the year 1954, ranking it ahead of Roger Bannister's breaking the four-minute barrier for the mile.[65] For posterity Mays's catch has been said to be "the greatest event that ever happened" in the long history of New York's Polo Grounds.[66] By virtue of Mays's "incredible catch," one hyped-up scenario goes, "the Indians became demoralized" and lost the entire World Series.[67]

Other Views on the "Catch"

Author Arnold Hano's view is that "no one else could have made that catch."[68] But there are other views, coming from players and managers in baseball, rather than from sportswriters, given as the latter are to hyperbole, or from sycophantic biographers, given as they are to hero worship. For instance Bob Feller, the Indians' Hall of Fame pitcher, remembers "a spectacular running catch to snare a long drive off Vic Wertz's bat." Biographer John Sickels reports: "It was a great play, etched in baseball memory forever by constant replays ever since on television and film, though some observers, [Indians manager] Al Lopez and Feller included, felt they had seen better plays, even from Willie. Feller especially pointed out a tremendous catch earlier in the year by Larry Doby as a superior play."[69]

Throughout his career Doby made a number of highlight-reel catches. In one, earlier in 1954, Doby climbed the outfield fence at Cleveland's Municipal Stadium, made the catch high in the air over the fence, fell to the awning over the bullpen bench, and rolled off the awning onto the ground, where he lay unconscious. Right fielder Al Smith pried the baseball from Doby's glove hand and threw it into the infield.[70]

Mays describes his catch in more prosaic terms than do the sportswriters or the biographers:

> Wertz hit the first pitch. I saw it clearly. As soon as I picked it out of the sky, I knew I had to get to [deep] center field. I turned and ran full speed toward center with my back to the plate. [I] knew I had to be in full stride to catch it, so about 450 feet from the plate, I looked over my left shoulder and could see the ball. I timed it perfectly and it dropped into my glove maybe 10 to 15 feet from the bleacher wall. At the same moment, I wheeled and threw in one motion and fell to the ground. I must have looked like a corkscrew. I could feel my hat flying off, but I saw the ball heading straight for Davy Williams on second. Davy grabbed the relay and threw home. Doby had tagged up at second after the catch. That held Doby to third base.[71]

The Basket Catch

Willie Mays, though, is famous for another type of catch besides his 1954 catch made famous by being in the World Series and on nationwide television. While he was in the army, a teammate, whose name Mays did not recall, taught Willie the basket catch, which Mays used forever after and which also became a Mays trademark.

An outfielder catching a fly ball holds his glove hand next to his face. With his eyes he tracks the flight of the ball, arcing downward and into his glove. In a Mays basket catch, the outfielder holds his gloved hand flat, palm up at the waist, making a basket like receptacle for the ball. The maneuver is only for those possessing superb hand-eye coordination. Willie Mays equaled the best hand-eye coordination ever, so the basket catch was easy for him, augmenting the showman image he cultivated, flying hat and all.

A Willie Mays biographer contends that "the [1954] catch became Willie Mays's brand. . . . To this day, when a kid on a sandlot, or a big leaguer under the lights, reaches over his shoulder for a ball on the fly, the cry is heard, 'A Willie Mays catch!'"[72] Undoubtedly that is true, but it tells only half the story. The basket catch also is a "Willie Mays catch," as probably are many other spectacular plays in the outfield.

The question, though, has to be asked: did The Catch," the 1954 one, mask from view the durability, longevity, exuberance, and even more spectacular events and statistics of Mays's baseball career? Mays was one of the greatest if not the greatest player of baseball's golden years. One senses, though, that Mays's achievements, upstaged to a degree by The Catch, do not loom as large as they should. Many baseball history buffs remember Mays more for the 1954 catch than his career-long achievements.

The other side of the coin is that Mays's achievements also do not cast the shadow over what Larry Doby achieved and the hardships he endured in integrating the American League, at least not as much as do the auras surrounding Jackie Robinson, Mickey Mantle, or Satchel Paige.

The Joe DiMaggio Cloud

"To the chauvinistic residents of the Bay Area [where the Giants moved in 1958] Mays was the embodiment of New York. He had the temerity to play centerfield at Seals Stadium where the native born DiMaggio had played . . . . Also Mays was black."[73] For the first time in his professional career, in San Francisco Mays heard boos from the stands. "For whatever reasons, San Francisco fans went out of their way to show Willie Mays how little he was appreciated."[74]

One principal reason was that, as Mickey Mantle had felt with the Yankees in New York, where DiMaggio had preceded him, in San Francisco Mays felt the backlash of not being Joe DiMaggio. "Proud and provincial [San Francisco] didn't need East Coast writers to designate their heroes, and the only player in San Francisco history who'd ever post the kind of numbers . . . projected [for Mays] was Joe DiMaggio, playing for the Seals. . . . The town wasn't big enough for two baseball legends."[75]

As well as the boos and the hostility of the sportswriters, Mays was troubled by the racism that he and his wife encountered in finding a house in supposedly enlightened San Francisco; the racism inherent in the Coke bottle flying through their picture window; and the beginning deterioration of the marriage to his glamorous wife, Margherite.

The San Francisco sportswriters were especially vicious. One wrote, "As we figure it, Mays has to play about $50,000 more baseball to earn his [$70,000] salary."[76] And racist: "Willie's trouble is that he needs to be driven. Anybody got a whip?"[77] Fan mail referred to "Rig's jigs" (after manager Bill Rigney, who had followed Leo Durocher) and "Sheehan's Shines" (after successor manager Bill Sheehan). In 1960 a *Sports Illustrated* baseball columnist actually wrote, "There are several dozen players, coaches, managers, writers and executives who will tell you that what is really wrong with the Giants: too many Negroes. . . . 'That's' the real reason the Giants are losing."[78] Mays, of course, was the most prominent of the African Americans on the San Francisco roster.

There was and is no excuse for racism. Mays never should have had to endure a single iota of it. Some of the other clouds over Mays's head, though, especially including the prolongation of the DiMaggio cloud, Mays brought on himself. Mays always was a reluctant interview, opening up only to journalists he knew and trusted. So even though he was now in San Francisco, Mays let down his guard only with East Coast journalists visiting San Francisco with other National League teams. This very much irritated West Coast journalists, who had a chip on their shoulder anyway, located as they were far out of the East Coast mainstream.

Friends advised Mays about possible reasons for press hostility. Mays still did not "get it," at least completely: "Do they [sportswriters] want me to talk to them like I would to old friends? Well, first they have to become friends."[79]

Broadcasters, sportswriters and columnists criticized Mays for his high salary, the Giant's losses, and—most of all—for not being Joe DiMaggio. These often-harsh critiques continued until the Giants beat their in-state rivals, the Los Angeles Dodgers, in a playoff for the 1962 National League pennant. Mays was the hero of that encounter and only thereafter received his due from San Francisco and its baseball fans, who finally embraced him as one of the greatest players of all time, the equal at least of the Yankee Clipper.

In the meantime it must have been galling to Willie Mays, in sharp contrast to the reception he received upon his return to the Polo Grounds for the 1960 All-Star game. As Mays came out of the National League dugout, "an unbroken, throat-swelling peal of adulation sprang from the hearts of the Giants-starved New Yorkers. It rolled and volleyed off the giant tiering of this triple-decked palace and against the vague outline of the Bronx County Courthouse. . . . They rocked and shouted and stamped and sang. It was joy and love and welcome, and you never heard a cascade of sound quite like it."[80]

The Willie Mays Shadow

Willie Mays was "the greatest centerfielder of all time."[81] At his prime Mays had "the distinction of easily being the best player in baseball."[82] He was better fielder and hitter than was Larry Doby.

Former Major Leaguer Jim Bouton writes that "there are several kinds of athletes. First, there's the guy who does everything instinctively and does it right in the first place," Bouton begins. "I think Willie Mays is that kind of guy, and so was Mickey Mantle." But so too was Larry Doby. "They just know what to do and how to do it."[83]

Willie Mays, however, was not "the first black five tool player to reach the major leagues," as his biographer maintains.[84] Larry Doby was. Doby could hit for average, hit with power, run the bases, patrol center field, and had a throwing arm, to quote Arnold Hano, "like a howitzer made human."[85] Doby did those things instinctively.

Doby began his career in 1947, four years and fifteen other black players before Mays (Robinson was the first, Doby the second, and Mays the seventeenth), and brought those skills to bear over a thirteen-year, war-shortened career. Doby's achievements, on the playing field and in integrating the American League, should neither be forgotten nor overshadowed by Willie Mays's outsized achievements.

And, to a certain degree, they are not. By the time Willie Mays began being universally recognized for his skills and joie de vivre, Larry Doby had retired, although he continued in baseball as a coach and, for a short time, as manager of the Chicago White Sox. While both men were active players, in the 1950s, and for a time after Doby had retired as a player, Mays's achievements were themselves to an extent overshadowed—by The Catch, by the rough landing a few years later in San Francisco, and by other demons that plagued him. Perhaps the best that may be said is that Mays and Doby were different men, with different achievements, but they both were "the real deal."

15

Casting Their Own Shadows

Robinson, Doby, and the News Media

Larry's not very controversial. He doesn't run his mouth a lot . . . . He says
what's on his mind, and that's it. If he doesn't have anything to say, he
doesn't say anything.

—DUSTY BAKER to Joseph Thomas Moore, June 11, 1980

I believe I would have made Larry one of the greatest players who ever
lived. . . . There were a whole lot of rough spots he had to face. He's a beautiful person, but few people know him.

—Negro League legend JOHN "BUCK" O'NEIL, June 24, 1980

Two diametrically opposed views swirled around Larry Doby.
For example, *Cleveland Press* writer Franklin Lewis's opinion of
Doby was the opposite of those expressed in the epigraphs; fellow
writer Gordon Cobbledick joined in Lewis's assessment in a piece
he penned for *Sport* in February 1952: "Larry Doby is a mixed-
up guy . . . a badly mixed-up guy . . . a friendless loner." Why the
diametrically opposed views?

Entering the major leagues, Larry Doby had a three-year hon-
eymoon (1948, 1949, and 1950). In 1950 he had had a banner year,
hitting .326, 25 home runs, and 102 RBIS, after seasons in which
he hit .301 and .285. The following season, 1951, Doby slipped, to
twenty home runs and a .295 batting average, still laudatory season totals.

In that year, 1951, the Indians finished their season in second
place in the American League, five games behind the New York

Yankees. Undoubtedly frustrated, the sportswriters for Cleveland's three dailies (*Cleveland Plain Dealer, Cleveland Press, Cleveland News*) blamed Doby, unfairly, because in their view Doby had gone flat in the stretch run at season's end. The sports reporters were on Doby like a pack of wolves, then and in the baseball seasons that followed, without letup until manager Al Lopez and general manager Hank Greenberg managed to get Doby traded to the White Sox after the 1955 season.

The Cleveland sportswriters were vicious, by today's standards as well as by the supposedly more-genteel mores of those days. Under today's standards, of course, nothing is sacred, and all is fair game for reporters: "The new sports writing . . . has become more ironic, cynical. Warts and all has become warts and warts." By contrast, older generations of sports writers "wrote with elegance and wit mostly about what went on between the lines."[1]

Not so in Cleveland, Ohio; there was seemingly little elegance or wit in Cleveland sports writing even back then. Upon the Indians' trade of Doby to Chicago, one Cleveland columnist wrote: "Larry Doby whose opportunities for immortality in baseball ended where his complexes began—at the neckline—was in a new green pasture today [with the White Sox]. . . . The Indians got the worst of the bargain, though this does not mean that I consider the departure of Doby a calamity. . . . He has been a controversial athlete. Highly gifted, he was frequently morose, sullen and upon occasion, downright surly to his teammates and his public."[2]

Cleveland sportswriters criticized Doby for being too close to and taking directions from Helyn, his wife. Inferentially, they faulted him for being too much of a family man, overinvolved in the lives of his two, three, four, and finally five children, retreating to them in New Jersey every off-season.

No one pointed out that, despite his established star status, Doby was still forced to live much of the time, including in spring training, in segregated facilities, apart from the team on which he was a star. Doby himself mildly protested that because he neither smoked cigarettes nor drank alcohol, it was difficult for him to "hang" with the other ballplayers, for whom smoking and drinking were principal occupations, at least when on the road. Doby, "the friendless loner," was in fact a good friend and sometimes companion to Al Rosen, Bob Lemon, Jim Hegan, Early Wynn, Bob Feller, Lou Boudreau, Joe Gordon, Steve Gromek, and others on the Cleveland team. All those men and other players were on record as saying so.[3]

Three, or perhaps four, observations come from examination of the evidence. One, all the negative commentary comes from the Cleveland press, whose reporters seem to have collaborated and fed upon one another. All the negativity swirling around Doby comes from them as well as the duo of Al Lopez, field manager, and Hank Greenberg, the Indians' general manager, who may have been influenced by the Cleveland press.

Second, none of Doby's teammates ever came forward with anything remotely resembling the pot shots the pundits took at him, repeatedly after the 1951 season.

Third, of the existing reports by those who knew Doby well, all are superlative, revealing a dignified, classy, and taciturn man, just the type of person a pack of print journalists might identify as vulnerable because he was either unable or unwilling to defend himself.

Fourth, perhaps the notion that journalists can change the course of human events is not merely their conceit; particularly in sports, they actually do. As author Jim Bouton writes of Johnny Sain, then a Major League coach: "Believe it or not, . . . sportswriters actually play a part in deciding who's going to make the team. Sain said that he sat in on meetings where the performance of the individual player hadn't changed, but there had been two or three articles written about him and the coaches and management tended to look at him in a new light."[4]

African Americans as Players and the Press

Negative commentary by Doby's teammates was nonexistent, or nearly so. Late in his career, while with the Chicago White Sox, Doby was referred to as a "J & J player," short for Johnson & Johnson player. The reference was to the copious amounts of tape he used on his injured shoulder and legs. Similarly, Mickey Mantle's teammates described Mantle as a "mummy," because of the amount of gauze and tape he applied to his legs and shoulder before a game (see chapter 13).

The only known teammate criticism of Jackie Robinson came early, rather than late as with Doby, in his career. Widespread doubt existed about the strength of Robinson's throwing arm, so the Dodgers had him play first base for a very short while, before he settled in at second base, where a strong throwing arm is not required.[5] He played there for the heart of his Major League career. The last three years of his career, though, Robinson did duty at third base, where a strong throwing arm is needed. Evidently, Robinson had overcome whatever deficiency had existed in his throwing, for his error rate is not by any means over-the-moon (50 games at third and 7 errors in 1954, for a .952 fielding percentage; 84 games and 9 errors in 1955, for .966; and 72 games and 15 errors in 1956, for .967). Of course, the statistics do not indicate which of Robinson's errors at third base were fielding and which were throwing errors.

Robinson's third base fielding statistics are in line with those of other third basemen of that era. Al Rosen of the Indians played 154 games in 1953, with 19 errors, for a fielding percentage of .964; 87 games in 1954, with 11 errors, .959; and in 1955, 106 games, with 18 errors, .945. Over in the National League, Don Hoak of the Pittsburgh Pirates had similar numbers:

1959	155 games	20 errors	.966
1960	155	25	.948
1961	143	20	.953
1962	106	10	.969

The comparisons could go on, say, comparing Robinson to Andy Carey, third baseman for the New York Yankees, or Ray Jablonski, third baseman for the Cincinnati Reds, but those comparisons would reveal no surprises.[6]

Willie Mays enjoyed and suffered a bit of both the positive and the negative at the hands of the media. He was the darling of the New York sportswriters, "the black son they never had," while the Giants were in New York. Precisely the opposite occurred when Mays and the Giants moved to San Francisco. There, as chapter

14 recounts, Mays encountered distrust, disbelief (he wasn't Joe DiMaggio), and racism (he had difficulty finding a house) in his first years in the Golden State. Mays and his wife actually moved their principal residence back to New York, principally because of the treatment he had received from the West Coast press and the treatment he and Margherite had experienced at the hands of San Francisco realtors, homeowners, potential neighbors and, last of all, Giants fans.

Quiet and Somber, with a Seriousness of Purpose

Bill White, who had a stellar career as a Major League baseball player and as president of the National League, grew up in Cleveland, where Larry Doby was a hero to him. Meeting Doby for the first time, White was "impressed by his humility."[7] Doby himself stated that throughout his career the attitude he tried to maintain was one of balance, "combining humility with pride, of feeling proud but remaining 'plain me.'"[8]

We will never know of all the stresses that came with being the first black player in the American League. We do know of the isolation and the loneliness; the discrimination against Doby by hotels and other team lodgings and the "whites only" taxicabs in the South; the insult of being denied entrance to ballparks because of the color of his skin, (even when he was suited in his Indians uniform); the taunts, threats, and other visible abuses Doby repeatedly endured—without the partly compensating limelight that Jackie Robinson enjoyed.

Doby labored in the shadows. Perhaps those stresses added to his natural persona, which was to speak out only when called to do so, a facet of his personality with which Cleveland sportswriters found grievous fault. Adding to his taciturnity was the pressure Doby felt, much of which he put upon himself. Doby was fully aware of the historic nature of his inaugural into the major leagues. He knew what a role model, for good or for bad, he would be, not only for other African American baseball players who might follow in his footsteps but for all blacks and the entire society.

Chapters 10 and 11 recount Doby's feeling about Satchel Paige, who spent half of the 1948 and all of the 1949 seasons with the Indians. Doby felt that Paige projected exactly the Stepin Fetchit image that would ill-serve Doby, Robinson, blacks, and well-meaning people in general—the opposite of the image that Doby tried to and did portray.

Pressures of Being First

In 1950 the Indians opened the season with Luke Easter at first base, a large, powerful man (six feet four, 240 pounds), a power hitter (28 homers in 1950, 27 in 1951, 31 in 1952, sent to the minor leagues in 1953), and black.[9] Amazingly enough, "Doby and Easter were the only black players in the American League, four years after Doby's [1947] debut."[10] The Indians had discarded Satchel Paige, not renewing his contract after the 1949 season, in which Paige had pitched poorly.

Luke Easter, like Satchel Paige, did little to provide Doby with the companionship and feeling of solidarity that Paige was supposed to provide. Doby and Easter "were as different from each other as Doby and Paige had been. While Doby was totally serious on the field, Easter relaxed and enjoyed his status, at age 35, as a big leaguer."[11] Third baseman Al Rosen described Easter: "Luke was a great guy, easy going, devil-may-care, jolly, hail fellow well met kind of guy who took a ribbing and dished it out. Larry . . . [I think] may have looked at Luke like an Uncle Tom type."[12]

So rather than provide companionship and help to ease the pressure Doby felt, Easter added to it, just as Paige had done. Doby knew that he was a central figure in a crusade for racial equality, describing it as "a responsibility that called for all the dignity and diplomacy that had to be used, because I was involved in a historical and pioneering life. I could have been like an Easter or a Paige but that wasn't my role. I think that I have gained some dignity and respect from those who looked at me differently from what they were taught to expect from a black man. . . . It wasn't a matter of choice, though. That was the natural me."[13]

Allegedly, in 1953 Cleveland manager Al Lopez and Hank Greenberg got rid of Luke Easter, demoting him to the minor leagues despite excellent performance. It had gotten back to Lopez that Easter had been dating a white woman. Lopez did not approve.

Larry Doby tried to play baseball well and at the same time be a model for not only other baseball players but for all of us, then as well as in the years that followed. The Cleveland sportswriters of the time seemed lacking in an appreciation of the historic poignancy of what was occurring and for the courage and bravery of the man who was trying to do it.

Jackie Robinson's Experience

In New York Jackie Robinson seems never to have had to fly through the flak that Larry Doby had to navigate in Cleveland. Viewed in retrospect, the criticism of Doby for his quiet, unassuming ways seems unjustified. Why this glaring difference? After all, after the Rickey-imposed gag came off, Robinson was outspoken, opinionated, and always strident.

"Branch Rickey knew how much Robinson had taken in his first two years. The time had come [early in 1949] to let Jackie loose from the restraints Rickey had imposed upon him."[14] Robinson was "'unleashed' by Rickey to play and speak with abandon."[15] Robinson then became very much the public man, off the baseball field as well as on it, "with increased militancy, public stands, civil rights involvement, and assertiveness on the playing field."[16] "Jackie was a ball of fire. He was as fiery a person as I've ever seen. And he had the intelligence to know what things meant," Buck O'Neil offered.[17]

Most players thought that Jackie was "interjecting himself into situations where he shouldn't have been. He was not a politician. He was not a spokesman for anybody. He was assuming those roles," Monte Irvin, a racial pioneer with the New York Giants, observed from a close vantage point.[18] Teammates and opponents regarded Robinson as an interloper and an officious intermeddler. Nonetheless, "there was always an understanding between [Rickey and Robinson]. Jackie would go along with [turning the other cheek in silence] only for a limited time."[19]

As noted in chapter 8, at that time, in the early 1950s, New York had three Major League Baseball teams (the Dodgers, the Giants, and the Yankees). The city was the center of the fashion industry and the financial services industry, headquarters to more publicly held corporations than all other U.S. cities combined, the locale of Broadway, the theater district, the garment industry, and more. There was plenty of copy to be had, front page, local news, entertainment, business, or sports.

Perhaps, too, New York sportswriters felt intimidated by Robinson's fiery nature and high intelligence along with his near-mythic status after the first year of his career. They had a plethora of other things to write about. Compared to the Cleveland press's treatment of Larry Doby, the New York press never went negative on Jackie Robinson. New York sportswriters were either wholly laudatory, or they left Robinson alone.

The Benevolent Shadow Cast by Wendell Smith

In the 1930s Pittsburgh was an epicenter of African American culture and of Negro League baseball as well. Undoubtedly the city achieved that status because so many blacks of southern origins had come north for higher-paying jobs in the steel mills. They needed recreation, teams, and heroes after arduous days at the blast furnaces and the coke ovens. Thus the Steel City boasted of not one but two of the Negro League's most prominent teams: the Homestead Grays and the Pittsburgh Crawfords. Satchel Paige, Josh Gibson ("the black Babe Ruth"), Buck O'Neil, and other black Hall of Fame baseball players spent all or a major part of their careers in Pittsburgh.

The leading sportswriter of the time, Wendell Smith (1914–72), was also Pittsburgh based, writing for the *Pittsburgh Courier*, a leading African American paper of that period. Originally from Detroit, where his father was Henry Ford's personal chef, the younger Smith had journeyed south because he wanted to play college baseball, which he did as shortstop for West Virginia State University. WV State was the black state university from the *Plessy v. Ferguson* days, when separate but equal was regarded as equivalent to equal. Immediately after college Smith journeyed to nearby Pittsburgh and joined the *Courier* sports staff.[20]

Soon Smith graduated to writing a regular column for the *Courier*, Sports Beat. He wrote about all sports in which African Americans participated, including boxing and track as well as about the

Negro League and its stars. More importantly from the perspective of this book, Smith carried on a regular correspondence with Branch Rickey, urging Rickey and the Dodgers to be the first to break the color line in Major League Baseball.[21] Wendell Smith also pointed Rickey to Jackie Robinson, then playing for the Kansas City Monarchs, as well as Robinson's Monarchs teammate Kenny Washington.[22] Smith is one of the unsung heroes in the run-up leading to integration of Major League Baseball.

When Robinson joined his first Dodgers' spring training, Rickey hired Wendell Smith to come to Florida, where Smith served as Robinson's roommate, chauffeur, and confidant.[23] Thereafter, Jackie Robinson became Smith's darling. Smith wrote copious amounts of copy concerning Robinson, all praiseworthy. He and Robinson carried on a private correspondence, too, well into the 1950s. Many of the "Dear Jack" and "Dear Wendell" handwritten letters are still preserved among the Wendell Smith papers at the Baseball Hall of Fame in Cooperstown, New York.

Larry Doby and Wendell Smith also were friends. Smith referred to Doby as a "brilliant player," along with Jackie Robinson, Roy Campanella, Don Newcombe, and Minnie Minoso.[24] In another column Smith discussed and compared the salaries of seven blacks in Major League Baseball at that time, featuring Larry Doby prominently but in a lesser light than Jackie Robinson.[25]

Clearly Doby was crowded out in Wendell Smith's mind by Jackie Robinson. The news copy Wendell Smith wrote praised Doby but devoted great amounts of attention to Jackie Robinson and the Dodgers. This focus cast a shadow over Doby and his achievements albeit a benevolent one compared to some of the other shadows that had rendered Doby and his achievements obscure. The devotion Wendell Smith demonstrated toward Robinson was understandable in terms of the roles Smith played in getting Robinson in particular to the major leagues, keeping him there especially through the turmoil of his early years, and acting as his friend and confidant.

Pittsburgh also was a National League city as was Brooklyn, home of the Dodgers, for whom Robinson played, while Doby played for Cleveland, in the American League, and never visited

Pittsburgh. Wendell Smith lived and wrote in Pittsburgh and to some extent was a "homer": "The Pittsburgh club was particularly hospitable and friendly to the player some sports writers have termed 'the loneliest man in baseball.' Just why the Pirates treated Robinson so humanely is hard to say. Robinson's teammate, Don Newcombe, reported that in his first season in major league baseball, Pittsburgh was the only National League city where the home team clubhouse men pressed his uniform and shined his baseball shoes. It may be that Pittsburghers were more understanding and reasonable."[26]

Wendell Smith's fervor and effort to achieve integration, though, cannot be underestimated. Later in his career Wendell Smith moved on to Chicago, where he wrote for the *Chicago Defender* and the *Chicago American*. In an epitaph for Wendell Smith, Jerome Holtzman, the dean of Chicago baseball writers, wrote: "Wendell vowed even if he never gained a position of influence, he would do what he could to break baseball's color line."[27] Wendell Smith certainly did that, and much more.

At Bill Veeck's funeral, many luminaries from the baseball and entertainment world attended. Larry Doby did too, but rather than sitting among and glad-handing the notables, he sat with Wyonella Smith, Wendell's widow.[28] "None of the reporters paid any attention to Doby as [he and Wyonella] passed by the gaggle of reporters surrounding [Minnie] Minoso," who attracted much of the press interest. "Larry was delighted. He didn't need the publicity." The Larry Doby/Wyonella Smith pairing seems good evidence that although Wendell's efforts in favor of Robinson cast a shadow that obscured Doby, Smith's efforts were unintentional and had little negative meaning for Doby. Doby regarded Wendell Smith as a key figure in beginning the integration of baseball.

Doby's Relations with the Press

As noted earlier, "the new sports writing has become more ironic, cynical. Warts and all became warts and warts."[29] Cleveland, Ohio, seems to have been far in advance in this regard. Hank Greenberg remembers that while he was general manager of the Indians, Cleveland sportswriters criticized him for having too many black players on the team (the Indians had five on the roster). "I hate to harp on the press but the [Cleveland Press] was miserable."[30] Other observers made stronger statements: "The Cleveland sports writing militia [is] perhaps the most vicious in the country," one southern editor wrote.[31]

In Cleveland the Indians were under a microscope, and the shadows and aspersions cast were anything but benevolent. Major League Baseball was the principal game in town. There was not a whole lot of other news to be had. To be sure, Cleveland was still growing (in the 1930s it had been the fastest-growing city and was the fifth largest in the United States). The city boasted Great Lakes shipping, iron ore and steel mills, the railroads (the Baltimore and Ohio, the Chesapeake and Ohio, the Erie Lackawanna, all were headquartered there), and prosperity seemingly everywhere.

That the Indians were the only game in town perhaps explains the attendance records the Indians set. In 1948, 2,620,627 paying spectators watched the Indians play, a record not eclipsed until 1962, by the Los Angeles Dodgers.[32] The fifth game of the 1948 World Series bought out 86,288 fans, setting a record as well.[33] By contrast only 33,957 fans had turned out for World Series Game 1, held in Boston, where the Braves played.[34]

Doby was not the intimidating presence that Robinson was. No doubt as intelligent, Doby kept much of what he felt and what he experienced inside. By comparison with Robinson, Doby then was much easier pickings for sportswriters bent on getting a story as they always were and on creating a controversy whether or not an actual one existed.

A Conclusion

"Although [Satchel] Paige and [Jackie] Robinson shared the stage with Doby during those early years of the integration of baseball . . . Paige and Robinson kept the spotlight almost entirely upon themselves. [Larry] Doby, using a third method of coping, stood in a dimmer light, away from center stage."[35] Those who had gotten to know him well, unlike the sportswriters, termed Doby a "beautiful, tough, intelligent human being."[36] Baltimore Oriole star Ken Singleton, who had been coached by Larry Doby, summed up his feelings by saying, "I just love the man. Every time I see him I realize what he's done for me."[37]

The Cleveland papers' news accounts of 1951–55 do not at all jibe with the accounts of those who knew Doby well and were sensitive to the added roles he felt he had to play and did play. In 1947 *Plain Dealer* sportswriter Gordon Cobbledick offered this prediction in a column about Doby's Major League debut: "He will be accepted by his teammates and customers if he proves to be a good ball player and a good human being, and will be rejected, by both if the opposite is true." Looking back, as both a player and a manager, Lou Boudreau (Indians 1946–1950), validated that prognosis: "Larry Doby was accepted because he was a good human being and became a good ball player—make that *a very good* ball player."[38]

For the most part, Doby's teammates lived up to the bargain they had struck. One manager (Boudreau) and one owner (Veeck) did, and two other managers (the duo of Al Lopez and Hank Greenberg) did not. Sportswriters and the media did not at all, with negative consequences for a great man, a great player, and a racial pioneer, who now because of his treatment then is overshadowed today, largely forgotten.

16

Doby's Later Years

It's kind of like a bale of cotton has been on your shoulders and now it's off.

—LARRY DOBY on news of his election to the National Baseball Hall of Fame, thirty-six years after Jackie Robinson, quoted by Hal Bodley, USA Today, March 1998

Bill Veeck thought Doby was art in motion, something rare to behold, and a human being and a ball player who was a model for all.

—GENE BUDIG, *Grasping the Ring*

Often there is less pain if you do something unpleasant quickly, like stripping off a Band-Aid. Some professional athletes do that; they hang it up (quit) while they are ahead—quickly, often suddenly, experiencing a sharp but short pain. Many more professional athletes do not. They hang around as they age and their physical prowess and skills attenuate. The demise of their career is not a pretty sight. They do not see that even if the window has not closed, the shade is coming down. Larry Doby was one of the latter. His playing career lasted too long. His last years did not add to his legacy.

Following the 1958 season, Cleveland Indians general manager Frank Lane ("Trader Frank," "Frantic Frank," "The Wheeler Dealer") shipped Doby a little bit west and a little bit north, to Detroit, Michigan, in exchange for Detroit Tigers first baseman Tito Francona. By a twist of fate, years later Tito Francona's son, Terry Francona, also called Tito, became the field manager of the

Cleveland Indians—after an extremely successful run as manager of the Boston Red Sox (2004–11).

Doby did not fare well with the Detroit Tigers. While at Cleveland the previous year, he had played in eighty-nine games (247 at bats or ABs); at Detroit Doby appeared in only eighteen contests (55 ABs). He fell from a .283 batting average to .218, from 13 home runs to none, and from 45 RBIS to 4. His skill seemed to have fallen off a cliff.

A funny thing happened, though, on the way to Briggs Stadium, where the Tigers played. Farther west Bill Veeck acquired a controlling interest in the Chicago White Sox, his third Major League team. One of his first moves was to reunite with his old friend Larry Doby. Veeck caused the White Sox to purchase Doby's contract from the Tigers.

It was not all Veeck. Al Lopez aside, memories of Doby in his previous Chicago incarnation (1956–57) were good. Early Wynn, Hall of Fame pitcher in Chicago from 1957 on, summed up those prior two years: "Doby did good work for the Sox" (24 HR, 102 RBIS in 1956; 14 HR, 79 RBIS and .288 BA in 1957).[1]

Now the year was 1959, the year of the Go-Go Sox, who wound up winning the American League pennant that year. As stated, Doby was reunited with his friend from Cleveland, Early Wynn, who led the White Sox pitching staff (22-10) and took home the Cy Young Award, judged to be the best pitcher in the major leagues (and also master of the brush back, an inside pitch to move hitters back away from home plate and to intimidate, known by some as "Wynn's Burma Shave" pitch).

Other White Sox players included Luis "Little Looie" Aparicio, who teamed up with Hall of Famer Nellie Fox as a double play combination. Sherm Lollar, another friend of Doby's from his earlier stint with the Sox, was behind home plate. Ex-football and Cincinnati Reds star Ted Kluszewski, famous for the cutoff sleeves on his baseball shirts, which showed off his massive biceps, played first base. Bill Veeck chipped in with his usual zany promotions: snake charmers, rock-and-roll bands, exploding scoreboards, and the rest.

As stated, the White Sox won the American League pennant

that year, winning ninety-four games and losing sixty. They finished five games ahead of the second-place Cleveland Indians. In the World Series the Go Sox met the Los Angeles Dodgers. They lost four games to two. Doby was not around to see it.

Doby was done in again, for the third time, by his nemesis, Al Lopez, who managed the Sox. Lopez was aided and abetted by general manager Hank Greenberg, whom Veeck had hired after Cleveland had dismissed Greenberg as its general manager. Of Lopez and Greenberg, then, it could be said that "black hearts seldom beat alone." The three of them (Lopez, Greenberg, and team owner Veeck) met. Injured and thirty-five years old, in 1959 Doby appeared in only twenty-one games for the Sox, seven of those only as a pinch hitter, with fifty-eight at bats. He hit .241, with no home runs and 9 RBIS.

Veeck begged his managers to keep Doby a while longer so that Doby could recover from his damaged shoulder. But Lopez and Greenberg outvoted Veeck 2–1. In one of the hardest things he ever had to do in his baseball management career, Veeck assented to Doby's demotion. "I hated to do it. I'm just as fond of him today as I was in Cleveland. . . . He's always had great talent and he's far from through."[2]

The White Sox shipped Doby to their California farm team, the San Diego Padres. Figuratively, Doby forked his fingers into his baseball glove, boarding the plane for the West Coast. It was here, though, in San Diego, that his career finally skidded into the ditch.

Not because San Diego and the Padres were shabby, in any sense of the word. The Pacific Coast League, in which the Padres played, was regarded by many as a third major league—an exaggeration, albeit a slight one. The Los Angeles Stars, the Los Angeles Angels, the San Francisco Seals, the Portland Beavers, the Seattle Rainiers, the Vancouver Mounties, and the Salt Lake City Bees, along with the Padres, were mainstays of the league, although over the years the lineup of teams changed now and then.

The West Coast weather generally was good; California especially was booming; and the Pacific League teams played an exciting game of West Coast baseball. Still, the Pacific Coast League compared to the major leagues was as checkers compared to chess, or at least it felt that way to an accomplished Major Leaguer like Doby.

Hope Springs Eternal

At San Diego Doby's injuries compounded themselves. Doby wore a body-length brace because of a bad back. The brace limited his flexibility. Sliding into third base, Doby was unable to rotate his body because of the brace. He tore ligaments in his ankle. His short stint in San Diego was over.

Nonetheless, Doby was invited to camp for the White Sox 1960 spring training. A small silver lining was that the Sox would no longer put up with discrimination for their African American players. Doby stayed in the hotel with the rest of the players. For Doby it was only the third spring training in a thirteen-year Major League career in which he did not have to live in segregated housing.[3]

Later still the White Sox took a page from the Dodgers' playbook. In 1949 the Dodgers acquired land and built Dodger Town in Vero Beach, Florida, so that Jackie Robinson and other black Dodgers players would not have to face discrimination. Twelve years later, tired of negotiating with Tampa, Florida, hotels, the White Sox imitated the Dodgers' playbook and acquired a hotel in Sarasota, Florida.[4]

For Doby that spring training and the stay (finally) in an integrated hotel were the end of the line, or nearly so. After a few weeks the White Sox assigned Doby's contract to the Toronto Maple Leafs of the International League, near where Jackie Robinson had begun his ascent with the Montreal Royals. The Maple Leafs soon released Doby. It was like putting the cloth over the canary's cage at night. All the noise suddenly stopped. Doby's prospects for continuing his Major League Baseball career were over.

Ko Ni Chi Wa

Or were they? Doby returned to northern New Jersey. His baseball friends Don Newcombe and Roy Campanella owned bars in Newark and in Harlem, respectively. So Doby and his wife, Helyn, bought a bar and liquor store (the Center Field Lounge) in Newark, then much more a thriving city than it has been in recent years. The venture proved to be a financial disappointment, if not a disaster, and the Dobys sold it in 1965.

Meanwhile, Don Newcombe, Doby's close friend dating from their days as teammates on the Newark Eagles, called Doby. Newcombe was going to Japan as one of the first postwar Americans to play baseball there. He would play for the Chunichi Dragons of Nagoya. Nagoya, Japan's fourth largest city, lies about two hundred kilometers west of Tokyo. It is a company town, home of Toyota as well as other automobile manufacturers, not then as substantial a presence as today but a presence nonetheless. Doby agreed to go, along with Newcombe, igniting the "foreigner boom" in Japanese baseball.[5] Newcombe, his family, and Doby shipped off to the Land of the Rising Sun for the 1962 season.

Doby played first base, Newcombe the outfield. Doby did not hit for average but could still awe the Japanese players and fans with prodigious home runs. Off the field he lived alone in a hotel but spent considerable time with the Newcombe family.

When Doby came home, his playing days finally were over. The canary no longer sang. The cover went back on the canary's cage for good. The singing days were finished.

Second at Being Second

The percentage of baseball players who were white fell from 88 percent in the fifties to 64 percent in the sixties. During that same period, the percentage of players who were African American rose from 7.6 percent to 22 percent. The difference, 14 percent, represented Latino and Hispanic players, who increasingly were entering the game.[6] Yet there were few black coaches and no black managers at all in baseball.

After he had returned from Japan, Doby wrote to the general manager of every Major League Baseball club inquiring about coaching jobs, to no avail. Then Bowie Kuhn, commissioner of baseball, took Doby and Monte Irvin, another former teammate from Newark Eagles days, to lunch in Manhattan at Toots Shor's. Kuhn offered Irvin a position as a special assistant to the commissioner. He offered Doby a position as coach with the newest

Major League expansion team, the Montreal Expos, whose general manager agreed to go along with Kuhn.

Doby spent five years as a coach for the Expos, much of that time as a batting instructor and first base coach under manager Gene Mauch. Players applauded Doby's laid-back coaching style. He did not approach players; he waited for them to seek his help. And help he did. Expo players credited Doby's instruction with increasing their batting average as much as twenty-five points.[7]

At the beginning of those five years, in 1969, Doby did service as a roving instructor at lower-level Expos farm clubs such as Class A at Palm Beach, Florida, and Rookie League, at Bradenton, Florida. In 1970 Doby moved up to higher-level Minor League teams (class AA Quebec City and class AAA Memphis). In 1971 he joined the big league club permanently.

Mauch and Doby had a special relationship in part because Mauch, who had been a player for the Dodgers, had witnessed firsthand what Doby and Robinson had gone through: "You have to be some kind of a special person to go through what Larry and Jackie went through. I'm not sure there's a player in the game today that could handle it."[8]

After the 1973 season, Cleveland Indians general manager Phil Segui sought permission from Montreal to talk with Doby. Cleveland ended up hiring Doby as a coach for the 1974 season. Doby left Montreal very reluctantly. "I was very happy working for Gene Mauch. I didn't just pick up and leave, believe me," he stated. But Doby knew that Cleveland's manager, Ken Aspromonte, was on probation, so to speak.

During his stint as a coach for the Indians, Doby's hope was to learn enough about the Cleveland players and the teams in the American League so that he might be first in line to get the Cleveland job. He would thus become the first African American Major League manager.[9]

Enter Another Robinson (Frank, Not Jackie)

Doby's competition for the Cleveland job, a rival who came seemingly from nowhere, was Frank Robinson. Former American League president (1996–2000) Gene Budig recited, with approval, that "there are those, in growing numbers, who argue that [Frank] Robinson was among the greatest ever to don a major league uniform. George Brett believes that [as others do]."[10] In twenty-one seasons, mostly with the Cincinnati Reds and the Baltimore Orioles, Frank Robinson batted .294, with 586 home runs. He led the Orioles to three consecutive American League pennants (1969–71), with a World Series championship in 1971. Robinson was the only individual to win the Most Valuable Player Award in both the National and the American League.[11]

Frank Robinson went on to manage five Major League teams (Indians, Giants, Orioles, Expos, and Nationals, as well as managing in the minor leagues). As a manager his record of 1,065 wins and 1,176 losses (47.5 percent) was not as stellar as it had been as a player.[12]

Robinson "also broke the color barrier in 1975 when he was named player-manager of the Cleveland Indians," his first managing job.[13] "The press played up the significance of the achievement," comparing it to Jackie Robinson's breakthrough in 1947.[14]

Yet no matter how diplomatic and self-effacing Robinson may have been in his subsequent managing career, his first promotion to Major League manager was not as gracious as it could have been. One of Robinson's first acts, in October 1974, was to fire his principal competitor for the Cleveland manager's position, Larry Doby, who had been an Indians coach. To top that Robinson went public with criticism of Doby, possibly to neutralize adverse press and fan reaction to his shabby treatment of Doby. Doby was immensely popular in Cleveland, having, among other things, led the Indians to the 1948 and 1954 World Series.

Robinson publicly accused Doby of having undermined Ken Aspromonte, Robinson's predecessor as manager. Never mind that Aspromonte himself did not agree. Robinson said further that Doby had captained or encouraged a cabal, especially among the black players, who would support Doby's aspirations and also Aspromonte's demotion.[15] "The Indians were a racially divided team, with Aspromonte and Doby on opposite sides," Robinson repeated shortly after firing Doby.[16]

It got even worse. Robinson claimed, "Shortly after I joined the

Indians . . . I realized that the ball club was in trouble. The dugout was virtually segregated. On one side was Ken Aspromonte, with all the white players. On the other side was Larry Doby, a black coach, with all the black players. Any ball club that's split along racial lines like that is in real trouble."[17] Finally, Robinson twisted the knife: "I didn't keep any of Aspromonte's coaches because I wanted to clear the air. In particular, I did not keep Larry Doby because he had shown me that he wasn't loyal to the manager. Doby wanted to be the first black manager but splitting the team racially wasn't the way to do it."[18]

Both black and white players (Oscar Gamble, Gaylord Perry, Jack Brohamer) disagreed with Robinson: "We didn't think we had a split."[19] Cleveland general manager Phil Segui spoke to the press: "I don't think we had a split." Segui also spoke for dismissed manager Ken Aspromonte: "Ken never said anything about disloyalty to me."[20] Ted Bonda, Indians executive vice president, voiced his view: "No, I don't think so," in answer to a question of whether the Indian players might have been divided along racial lines.[21]

Realizing that he had been bested, Doby was gracious: "The best thing I can do for Robinson is to wish him luck."[22] Once again out of baseball, Doby returned home to Montclair, New Jersey, and his family. Doby and Robinson never spoke to each other again.[23] In subsequent years, the few times they shared a dais together, they were like two pitchers of ice water on a conference table.

Why did Robinson go so much out of his way to single out and belittle Doby? Among other things, the comments he made and the attitude he evinced seemed out of character for him. Organizational behavior and business psychologists describe one type of stereotypical role they frequently encounter. They label it the "queen bee syndrome."[24] "Once some [managers] get a taste of power, they may be afraid to delegate or share it. . . . They stay aloof" and become judgmental of those who aspire to similar status.[25]

The first woman or the first minority-group member to reach a certain management level or the inner circle, within a work group, a division, a subsidiary, or the entire organization relishes not only being the first but also in being the only and staying that way. The queen bee is the first one up in the tree house. He or she pulls the rope ladder up after him or her. Queen bees can further cement their position as "the only" within the inner circle by "putting down," publicly denigrating, or placing in a false light any other pretenders for the loftier position they have attained. In his first steps as the new Cleveland Indians manager and the first black baseball manager overall, Frank Robinson, it seems, may well have illustrated the queen bee phenomenon.

Bill Veeck Again

In 1975, after the Cleveland dustup, Doby returned to the Montreal Expos. He worked with hitters at Montreal farm clubs in Quebec City and in West Palm Beach. For the second time the Expos organization promoted Doby to the Major League team for the 1976 season. There he developed a special relationship with Andre Dawson (Hall of Fame, 2010), who called Doby "a keen, quiet individual." Dawson elucidated: "I'm a quiet individual and around Larry I would open up more."[26]

In 1977 Bill Veeck acquired a controlling interest in the Chicago White Sox, for the second time. He hired the All-Star pitcher from his Cleveland days, Bob Lemon, as the Sox's field manager. Together Veeck and Lemon asked Doby to come over from Montreal to be a coach with the White Sox.

Veeck's second tenure as owner of the White Sox and Doby's return to Chicago were complicated, and perhaps done in, by the arrival in baseball of free agency. Unable to come to contract renewal terms with the California Angels, pitcher Andy Messersmith had gone to arbitration. In the process he had become the "reserve clause's conqueror," convincing arbitrator Peter Seitz to void the reserve clause that would have bound Messersmith to the Angels for the 1977 season.[27] The age of free agency in baseball had begun. The era of larger and larger salaries, sale of player services to the highest bidder, and the demise of any notion of loyalty to a particular team or city had arrived.

Prior to the 1978 season, then, the White Sox lost six star players to free agency, among them Richie Zisk and Oscar Gamble.[28] Veeck had neither the personal wealth nor access to financial resources sufficient to replace the players whom the Sox had lost with anything near their equivalents. Once the season began, the Sox began losing games with regularity.

Bik Veeck fired manager Bob Lemon at the end of June 1978. He replaced him as manager with Larry Doby. Doby thus became the second African American again: second as a player in 1947 and second as a Major League manager in 1978, both times second to a Robinson. It was bittersweet for Doby. Bob Lemon was one of several Indians who in 1947 had welcomed Doby to the Cleveland club. They had remained friends. Doby remarked, "I was surprised and somewhat saddened. Bob Lemon and I have been friends since 1947."[29]

Following Veeck's announcement of the new manager, Doby and Lemon had a long talk. "Don't feel saddened. We're still friends and these things happen in baseball," Lemon cautioned Doby. Lemon, of course, went on to skipper the New York Yankees to a World Series championship, the first of several with Lemon at the Yankees helm. Doby took the extraordinary step of having Lemon speak to the team the following day, delivering a short farewell address. Doby then announced to the press: "I don't necessarily intend to run a 'tighter' ship. Let's call it a different ship."[30]

Doby and the different ship did not have a good start. Over the first six weeks of Doby's tenure, the team lost thirty and won only thirteen games.[31] But then, evidently, Doby succeeded in turning the ship around. Down the stretch, the Sox won twenty-four games while losing only twenty. Shortly after the 1978 season had ended, though, Bill Veeck fired Larry Doby as manager. In Doby's place Veeck hired the popular Don Kessinger, a former University of Mississippi basketball player who had spent twelve years (1964–76) as shortstop for the Chicago Cubs, on Chicago's North Side.

Low on funds, with his health failing, and with White Sox attendance continuing to fall, Veeck adopted sort of a whack-the-mole approach to managing the White Sox. Veeck truly had faith in Larry Doby, but the press had characterized Doby's hiring as "little more than a play for increased black attendance."[32] The newspaper criticism contained more than a kernel of truth. The White Sox home, Comiskey Park, was on Chicago's South Side, proximate to many of the city's oldest and most established African American neighborhoods. The increased attendance, however, never materialized following Doby's promotion to manager.

Desperate to increase gate receipts, Veeck switched horses. He hoped that Kessinger's hiring would bring white fans from Chicago's North Side and suburbs. Veeck's new ploy to raise ticket sales by the hiring of Kessinger worked no better than had his aborted plan in promoting Doby. Veeck was contrite: "I took a man [Doby] away from doing what he does best—instructing hitters—and asked him to manage. I don't deny that [Kessinger's] popularity in Chicago was a factor in his hiring."[33]

Back to His Baseball Past

Doby appeared to harbor no hard feeling, although he must have felt them. He went back to permanently living out of a suitcase, visiting the towns and cities where the White Sox had farm teams (Appleton, Wisconsin; Des Moines, Iowa; Memphis, Tennessee). Once again he was a roving hitting instructor for a Major League team.

After a season of roving, Doby was fifty-six years old. He had been in organized baseball for thirty-four years, since 1946. He went back to Montclair, his wife, Helyn, and his five children in New Jersey.

During the 1980s, Doby became the director of community relations for the NBA New Jersey (now Brooklyn) Nets. He always compared Nets' owner Joe Taub to Bill Veeck, finding them very much alike. Doby roamed the state and surrounding areas, giving speeches, handing out awards, and promoting the Nets.

A Last Baseball Incarnation

In 1996 Gene Budig, former president of West Virginia University and former chancellor of the University of Kansas, became president of the American League. He hired Larry Doby and former St. Louis pitching great Bob Gibson as his "on-field assistants." In that capacity Doby visited many Major League teams and ballparks. He also had the ear of President Budig, who later called Doby "an American Original."[34] "Both [Doby and Gibson] had strong views on matters of substance and no reluctance to express those views. They rarely disagreed on baseball matters such as player discipline."[35]

In the 1990s "many old-timers believe[d] the blinding focus on [Jackie] Robinson had delayed Doby's entry into the Hall of Fame." Among others Yankees great Yogi Berra and Red Sox great Ted Williams were on the Veterans Committee, which finally picked Doby for induction in 1998, thirty-six years after Jackie Robinson and seven years after Bill Veeck. In particular "Ted Williams was apologetic that it took so do long . . . believing that [Doby] was the ultimate gentleman, a distinct credit to the game, and 'one helluva ball player.'"[36]

At Doby's induction ceremony, Ted Williams, Yogi Berra, Joe Morgan, and others "went out of their way to underscore the greatness of Doby, on and off the playing field."[37] Berra said, "Truth is, he was a wonderful guy and an exceptional ballplayer. All his years, on and off the field all he meant was goodness and hope."[38] Bob Lemon "said that in case of war he would want Doby in his foxhole."[39] Pitching great Joe Black, an African American teammate of Jackie Robinson in Brooklyn, called Doby "a gentle soul who wanted nothing taken away from Robinson."[40] Doby himself told AL president Budig, who attended the 1998 induction ceremony, "that he and Robinson had the same goals—winning and opening the doors of opportunity for other deserving minority athletes."[41] So it finally happened. Earlier Doby had told Murray Chase of the *New York Times*, "I can't quite believe it. My whole working life was in baseball. Baseball was great to me and to my family."[42]

Doby's plaque at Cooperstown reads:

Exceptional athletic prowess and a staunch constitution led to a successful playing career after integrating the American League in 1947. A seven-time All-Star who batted .283 with 253 home runs and 970 RBI in 14 major league seasons. The power-hitting center field paced the A.L. in home runs twice and collected 100 RBI five times whole leading the Indians to pennants in 1948 and 1954. Appointed manager of the White Sox in 1978. The second African-American to lead a major league club. Played four seasons with Newark in the Negro

National League. Following baseball career worked as a scout and major league baseball executive.[43]

Larry Doby fought a long battle against kidney and then colon cancer. He died on June 18, 2003. His wife of fifty-two years, Helyn, had predeceased him in 2001. A flood of eulogies followed. Many greats of baseball attended his funeral at Trinity Presbyterian Church in Montclair, New Jersey. Baseball commissioner Bud Selig summed up the feelings of those who had attended and of the baseball world: "He was a force for good everywhere."[44]

17

Doby, Robinson, Baseball, and Racism

I just don't care to play for him.

—LARRY DOBY, accusing manager Al Lopez of racism (1957)

Doby suffered as much—if not more—than Robinson . . . but it took Doby 36
years to join Robinson in the Hall of Fame.

—PAUL DICKSON, introduction to Moore, *Larry Doby*

In his biography of Al Lopez, author Wes Singletary seeks to excuse
any racism on Lopez's part as "aversive" rather than intentional
or malicious.[1] The racism evident in the actions of managers such
as Casey Stengel (Yankees), Al Lopez (Indians and White Sox),
Solly Hemus (Cardinals), or other baseball men of the post–World
War II era is deemed the product of the circumstances and attitudes existing at the time those men grew into adulthood, in the
1930s, 1920s, or earlier.

"Aversive racism . . . refers to those who believe that they are
not prejudiced or discriminatory toward minorities, yet exhibit,
perhaps unconsciously, racist tendencies." New York Yankees
manager Casey Stengel, who used the N-word, and called black
players jungle bunnies, "was racist only in the casual, unthink-
ing way that most of his generation of Americans were," according to his biographer.[2] Less fault, or no fault, should be attached
to the aversive racism then pandemic in big league baseball, or
so the argument goes.

To the contrary, any racism, whatever its source, is nefarious, violating the most fundamental principle of our nation, that all men are created equal, as well as the moral precept most of us, religious or not, hold, that we are all God's children. I suppose a distinction between intentional and unintentional forms of racism might have been made back then, but today, and for several decades now, each and every form of racism, intentional or not, is deserving of and should receive the same level of opprobrium. After all, the target of racial name calling, taunts, slurs, or other discriminatory actions tends to feel the same sting, whether the source of these racist or discriminatory acts intends to wound or not.

No one should have to endure what Jackie Robinson or Larry Doby faced as the pioneers who broke the color barrier blocking African Americans from Major League Baseball. The experiences, the obstacles he faced, and the courage with which Jackie Robinson confronted them, are well documented. What Larry Doby endured, which was similar to, or indeed of greater amplitude than, what Robinson faced, has not been so well documented. In fact, most or all of it has been lost with the passage of time. More closely describing, examining, and comparing what Doby and Robinson faced makes the foregoing points evident while also reminding us that we should never again permit such actions to take place in our midst.

Conditioning for Robinson's Introduction

Jackie Robinson lettered in four sports at UCLA. In 1939 he was the leading rusher in college football, averaging twelve yards per carry. He was a legend in Southern California. Sportswriters called him "the Jim Thorpe of his age."[3] He played on All-Star baseball teams with Ted Williams from San Diego and Bob Lemon from Long Beach. While at Pasadena City College, Robinson was elected the Southern California Junior College Most Valuable Player after hitting .417 and stealing twenty-five bases in a twenty-four-game season. In California blacks had played football with whites, both at the high school and the university level, going back at least as far as the 1920s.[4] Robinson had teamed with and played against whites as well as blacks. He thought little of it.

Robinson also had a thick skin, at least on the sports field. When fabled sports reporter Red Smith asked Robinson whether, in Robinson's first years with the Dodgers, he had been on the receiving end of excessive amounts of taunting and razzing, Robinson shot back: "It hasn't been worse than anything I heard in college football."[5]

Robinson could be out-spoken, capable of defending himself when he had to. In the army as a lieutenant, he refused a direction to go to the rear of a bus. When he also refused to follow the directions of a responding military policeman, a captain, which by the way were directly contrary to what the secretary of the army had decreed, the captain wrote Robinson up, resulting in a court marital. Jackie spoke in his defense and was acquitted.[6] Branch Rickey thought Jackie Robinson "not only an exceptional athlete but a disciplined, strong willed person," based on Jackie's experiences in the army and in sports.[7]

Nonetheless, Rickey asked Robinson to suppress his self-assuredness and his sometimes combative instincts, sublimating them to the greater goal of breaking the color line:

> "I know you're a good ballplayer. What I don't know is whether you have the guts," Rickey told Robinson in their three-hour introductory meeting.
>
> "I'm not afraid of anyone," Robinson said as he started to take the bait.
>
> "I'm looking for a ballplayer with the guts not to fight back," said Rickey as a prelude to describing and physically acting out the threats and abuse Robinson would face.
>
> "I have two cheeks. Is that it, Mr. Rickey?"[8]

At another point in their session, Rickey, who was capable of long flights of eloquence, turning every speech into the Gettysburg Address, exhorted Robinson: "I want to beg two things of you, Jackie. Give it all you have as a ballplayer. As a man, give continuing loyalty to your race and to the critical cause you are going to symbolize. Above all, do not fight. No matter how vile the abuse, you must ignore it. You are carrying the reputation of a race on your shoulders. Bear it well."[9]

After two years, however, the gag came off. Robinson resumed his outspoken ways, not taking guff from anyone, at any time, on the baseball diamond or off of it. "The code words used to describe him were 'hot-headed, crusader, troublemaker.'" "The mild-mannered, soft-spoken, self-effacing image was replaced by one that was determined, out-spoken [and] socially conscious."[10]

The Run-Up to Larry Doby's Debut

Doby's experience was different, in at least two ways: one, the gag was never put on, and, two, the gag never came off. The latter was unnecessary because, although dignified and articulate, Doby was a different kind of person than Robinson: somewhat quieter, more retiring, less prone to speaking out unless he had been challenged or mistreated in an extreme way.

The gag was never put on Doby in the first place because, contrary to Branch Rickey's orchestrated, multistep, multiyear conditioning of Robinson, Cleveland owner-manager Bill Veeck summoned Larry Doby to Chicago on July 5, 1947, and had him in uniform for a game against the White Sox soon thereafter. Doby parachuted into the major leagues, while Robinson inched his way.

Doby played high school and college sports in an integrated setting as well, the latter for a year until the winds of war blew shut the university portal. After entering the navy, he was first stationed at Great Lakes Naval Training Base as a physical education instructor and later on the Western Pacific island of Mog-Mog, in the Ulithi Atoll. While on Mog-Mog, Doby was mentored by Mickey Vernon, the star first baseman of the Washington Senators, who remained a friend for many years.[11]

Bill Veeck recalls an introduction to Doby, followed by a heart-to-heart, albeit a shorter one than that between Rickey and Robinson: "Lawrence, you are going to be part of history. No arguing with umpires. No dissertation with opposing players . . . no associating with female Caucasians . . . above all, act in the appropriate way, as people [will] be watching. . . . We're in this together, kid."[12]

Doby's and Robinson's Preparations Compared

That was it. By contrast Robinson had a year and a half to prepare for his introduction to the major leagues. First, Rickey paid Robinson a $6,500 signing bonus, assigning Robinson to one year with the Montreal Royals in the International League, whose fan base was extremely receptive to a black player. Next Robinson had a winter and a spring to prepare him for what he might encounter with the big club. Third, Rickey moved the Dodgers' and Royals' 1947 spring training to Havana, "with the hope that playing games in front of people of color would make his ballplayers more comfortable playing alongside Robinson."[13] Fourth, Rickey hired a public relations associate, Frank Graham, whose job it was to keep his ear to the ground and smooth the way for Robinson. Fifth, in Robinson's first spring with the Dodgers, Rickey hired Wendell Smith, an educated and articulate sportswriter for the *Pittsburgh Courier*, the nation's leading black newspaper, to act as a chauffeur, chaperone, and confidante to Robinson.

Finally, Rickey himself undertook a campaign in the black community, albeit one with a counterintuitive twist. In meetings with community leaders, Rickey cautioned *against* an outpouring in support of Robinson, one that could result in a white backlash against Robinson and the integration of baseball: "You must remember that white ballplayers are human beings, too. That old green-eyed monster, jealousy, also moves among them, and it is only natural that they will resent the heaping of praise and awards upon a Negro who has not been in the major leagues long enough to prove himself. We don't want what can be another milestone in the progress of American race relations turned into a national comedy and an ultimate tragedy."[14] Black leaders responded to Rickey's entreaties: signs exhorting "Don't Spoil Jackie's Chances" appeared all over Brooklyn.

Robinson did encounter some rough patches, as when in his Minor League year the Montreal Royals played the Louisville Colonels in the Little World Series. Louisville fans heckled Robinson, what he termed "the worst race baiting" he heard in that Minor League season, which is somewhat surprising.[15] Rather than

being a southern city, as sportswriters and others assume, Louisville is an old German river city. In fact, our first Jewish Supreme
Court justice, Louis Brandeis, was from a Louisville family and,
pursuant to his instructions, lies buried beneath the front steps
of University of Louisville law school. Nonetheless, racism raises
its ugly head in many and various places, especially back then,
and it undoubtedly did in Louisville.

Jackie Robinson finished his year in Montreal in bang-up fashion, hitting .349, stealing forty-eight bases, and being named Most
Valuable Player of the International League. Black sportswriters
voted Robinson "the number one athlete of 1946," before he even
played Major League Baseball and six votes ahead of heavyweight
boxing champion Joe Lewis (25–19).[16]

Did Doby regret the brevity of his preparation for integrating
the American League, with no preparation time in integrated baseball and having been parachuted into Chicago two days before
his Major League debut? Not at all. "I look at myself as more fortunate than Jack," Doby told his biographer, Joseph Moore. "If I
had gone through hell in the minors, then I'd have to go through
it again in the majors. Once was enough!"[17] Bill Veeck, the Indians owner, had a different view: "Rickey was smarter than me on
that. I tried to bring [Doby] along too fast."[18]

Major League Teammates

Both Doby and Robinson met obstacles when first they entered the
major leagues, but these obstacles, not surprisingly, quickly dissi-
pated. Any initial hostility seemed to vanish after each had proven
his worth on the playing field, and the team spirit trumped over
racism. In fact, after only his first season, Hollywood proposed a
movie about Jackie Robinson, titled *Courage*, in which Robinson
was to play a part. After Jackie's inaugural Major League season,
the Robinsons went to Hollywood for production of the movie.
In the end the movie *Courage* was never made, but two years later
The Jackie Robinson Story was filmed with Jackie Robinson himself
playing his part (after his first Major League season, Larry Doby
returned to Patterson, New Jersey, where he took a job coaching
the boys' freshman basketball team at Eastside High School).[19]

On the team in spring 1947, four Brooklyn Dodgers players discussed undertaking a team petition against promoting Jackie Robinson to the Major League club. In a scene acted out in the movie 42, field manager Leo Durocher clad in robe and pajamas, called the team together and read them the riot act.[20] At least one player, Edwin "Duke" Snider, actively opposed the idea of a petition: "That kind of prejudice was not part of my life in Southern California. [Besides] Jack's an idol of mine."[21]

Durocher seems to have been by and large colorblind. Asked in 1941 if he thought players from the Negro Leagues could help the Brooklyn Dodgers, Durocher shot back, "I'd sign them in a minute if I got permission from the big shots," only to be rebuked by baseball commissioner Kenesaw Mountain Landis ("It is not within the field manager's purview to make comments on overall baseball policy").[22]

Two southerners, reserve catcher Bobby Bragan (later manager of the Cleveland Indians when Larry Doby stopped back there in 1958) and Fred "Dixie" Walker, asked to be traded rather than being made to play with Robinson. Rickey obliged, trading the popular Walker to Pittsburgh even though Walker had retracted his request. Walker, a football All-American at Alabama, had been the National League batting champion in 1944, had hit .319 in 1946, and was very popular with the Brooklyn fans.

Robinson's performance on the field and his locker room persona quickly made him a Brooklyn Dodger. One famous episode of taunting involved the Philadelphia Phillies and their Alabama-bred manager, Ben Chapman ("Go back to the cotton field," "which one of those white boys' wives are you dating tonight?" "Get out of here and take your coon fans along," Phillies players and their manager shouted at Robinson). Dodgers second baseman Eddie Stanky confronted the Phillies bench: "What kind of men are you anyway? You're all yellow. Why in the hell don't you pick on someone who can fight back? You know Robinson can't fight back."[23] The scene in which Brooklyn shortstop Pee Wee Reese, himself a Kentucky boy, put an arm around Robinson's shoulder in a show of solidarity before thirty-four thousand Cincinnati fans is one of several indicia demonstrating how Robinson's teammates coalesced around him.

Opponents injected the race card into the mix. Hall of Famer Enos "Country" Slaughter tried to spike Robinson (Robinson played first base in his first Major League games).[24] Various pitchers tried to brush Robinson back, knock him down, or hit him with pitched balls ("Stick it in his ear," "Knock the black son-of-a-bitch down").[25] Robinson survived, hitting .297 and winning Rookie of the Year honors for 1947 but fizzled in the World Series against the Yankees (7 for 27, or .258). And the taunts and abuse Robinson endured on the field came from opposing fans and players, not from his teammates.

One other threatened action against Robinson from opposing players occurred in St. Louis. In early May 1947 several Cardinals players began organizing a boycott against the Dodgers. Were Jackie Robinson to be announced as playing when Brooklyn visited St. Louis, a group of Cardinals were taking a pledge that they would refuse to take the field. Catching wind of the budding conspiracy, National League president Ford Frick wrote to Cardinals owner Sam Breadon: "Any action by St. Louis players against Jackie Robinson will result in permanent suspension from major league baseball."[26]

Doby's Major League Introduction

As he integrated the American League, Larry Doby had no one running interference for him as had Jackie Robinson in the form of Leo Durocher, Ford Frick, and others. Doby went alone into such southern cities as Washington DC (much more southern than Louisville) and St. Louis (the Browns did not move to Baltimore until 1955) and racist bastions such as Detroit, with Briggs Stadium seating still segregated in 1947–48, and Boston, which did not begin integrating until 1959, last in the major leagues to do so. Doby played exhibitions in southern cities in which stadium ushers refused him admittance (for instance, Lubbock, Texas, or Texarkana, where ushers refused him entrance even though he was wearing his Cleveland Indians uniform).[27]

Even with his teammates things there were rocky too, at least at the start. In early July 1947, when Cleveland player-manager Lou Boudreau introduced Doby to his teammates, two of them (Les

Fleming and Eddie Robinson) refused to shake Doby's hand.[28] Later, when Boudreau penciled Doby's name into the lineup card for the second game of a doubleheader against the White Sox, he put Doby down at first base. Doby, though, did not have a first baseman's glove. Doby asked the team's traveling secretary, Spud Goldstein, to intercede for him. Goldstein asked Robinson, a first baseman, if he would lend his glove to Doby. "I won't lend my glove to no n——r," Robinson barked. Goldstein shifted gears: "Eddie, will you lend your glove to me?" Robinson tossed him the mitt, saying, "Here take the glove." Boudreau, though, hesitated to judge Robinson harshly: "He was upset maybe not as much with Larry as with me for replacing him at first base."[29]

With his circus catches in center field and his home run hitting, Doby won a place on the team and in the locker room, especially after his stellar 1948 season. The photograph of Doby, who had hit a home run, and Steve Gromek, the pitcher who had won the fourth game of the World Series, appeared throughout the nation, an exemplar of what sports and life should be. In the locker room after the game, a smiling Doby and a smiling Gromek, black and white respectively, smile, hug, and together savor the 2–1 victory over the Braves.

"Baseball became, for the first time, in Doby's mind, an 'All-American game.'"[30] Doby told Joseph Moore, his biographer: "The picture was more rewarding and happy for me than actually hitting the home run. It was such a scuffle for me until that picture. The picture finally showed a moment of a man showing his feelings for me. I think enlightenment can [result] from such a picture."[31]

In 1949 Early Wynn, later named to the Hall of Fame, came over from the Washington Senators to join the Cleveland Indians pitching staff. Early on he made it clear where he stood with respect to Doby as a man and as a teammate. A Detroit Tigers pitcher knocked down Doby twice during the same game with inside pitches. Wynn determined that this was no coincidence, so when the Detroit pitcher came to bat (pitchers in both major leagues batted then), Wynn knocked him down four straight times. Wynn put it simply: "Doby is on my team. If they hurt Larry, they hurt me."[32]

To be sure, a three-hundred-game winner lifetime, Wynn culti-vated a facade of being ornery and downright mean. He was known for his sharp breaking curve balls and his "Burma Shave" pitches. Mickey Mantle said, "That SOB is so mean he would f——ing knock you down in the dugout." Once Wynn threw a ball at Man-tle when Mantle was standing on first base—not to pick him but to hit him, or at least make him hit the dirt.[33]

Al Rosen came up at the tail end of 1947, becoming a regular in 1949 and an All-Star thereafter. One day in a southern city, Rosen, Doby, and another Cleveland teammate flagged a taxicab and got in. "The cabdriver made a comment [that] Larry would have to get another cab," Rosen recalled.

> I got out myself. I can't remember who else was with us, Lemon or whomever. While I was a southern born and bred [Spartanburg, South Carolina] . . . I am a Jew who has been victimized by petti-ness and anti-Semitic feelings. . . . I was a little pugnacious at that time, and I threatened to kick the driver's teeth in. I was pulled away.
>
> As a southerner, I knew those were the customs but I knew that it was wrong. Whatever the customs are, that doesn't make it right.[34]

Other Cleveland teammates were not such stand-up guys. "When the team bus picked up or dropped off Doby at his segregated hotel, none of them rose in protest. Nor did they express their sympathies when they saw him, often in uniform, standing on the street in front of his hotel, waiting for the bus."[35] The team also let things fester, as illustrated by the oft-told story of Tucson spring training and the Santa Rita Hotel. When Veeck signed Doby, he arranged to move Indians spring training from Florida to Ari-zona, on the grounds that the Arizona populace would be more tolerant of a black player on the team. The opposite turned out to be true. The team hotel, the Santa Rita, barred Doby from stay-ing there and kept the ban in place until 1954. Doby stayed at the home of Chester and Lucile Willis; Willis was a black business-man whose company did the hotel's laundry.

When the Benjamin Harrison hotel in Philadelphia barred Jackie Robinson from staying there, Branch Rickey arranged for Rob-inson to stay at another hotel, the Warwick. Not only did he do so for Robinson, but he also switched the entire Dodgers team to the new hotel. Thereafter the Warwick became the Dodgers' Philadelphia headquarters, which was significant because in the days of an eight-team league, each team played an opponent twenty-two times in a season.[36]

But at the Santa Rita in Tucson, for Doby it was worse than it had been for Robinson at the Benjamin Harrison. In 1950 Helyn Doby bought their firstborn, Cristina, to Tucson for spring training. Cristina was coughing. The wife of a Cleveland sportswriter, Aldona Jones, suggested that a drink of water might alleviate the situation. As the trio moved toward a drinking fountain in the Santa Rita, a zealous and vigilant hotel employee intervened, telling the trio that they could not use the water fountain and barring their way.[37] For Larry Doby, and to some extent his family, those sorts of things continued until 1954 or 1955, seven or eight years after Doby had become a big leaguer and six or seven years after he had become a star.

By contrast "the Giants' first black players, Monte Irvin and Hank Thompson [and later Willie Mays], could stay with their teammates at the Adams Hotel in Phoenix." It was progress but still with a significant doses of Jim Crow. Irvin and Thompson "were not allowed to linger in the lobby, use the swimming pool, or eat in the dining room."[38]

Baseball Coaches and Managers

Here again, Jackie Robinson was fortunate. His first professional manager, in Montreal, was Clay Hopper, who had been raised in Alabama. Contrary to predictions by some, Hopper shepherded Robinson to a season in which Jackie hit .349 and was the International League's MVP. Robinson encountered incidents, to be sure, but nothing untoward. Before Robinson departed for the Majors, Coach Hopper gave him his benediction: "You're a great ballplayer and a fine gentleman. You're the greatest competitor I ever saw. It's been wonderful having you on the team."[39]

The protection and equal treatment that Leo Durocher, as Brooklyn Dodgers manager, extended to Robinson are a matter of record. The monkey wrench in the works was that, prior to the 1947 baseball season, Commissioner Albert "Happy" Chandler suspended Durocher from baseball indefinitely for conduct "detrimental to Major League Baseball." Durocher had associated with known gamblers, dated movie starlets, lived the high life, and, most fatally, shot his mouth off, often offending the powers that were in the baseball establishment.[40] It was not for nothing that from very early on Durocher was known as "Leo the Lip."[41]

Thus only a week before the season was to begin, and with the first black player in Major League history about to be introduced, the Dodgers had no manager. Branch Rickey searched around and settled on Burt Shotton, an old Rickey friend and lifelong baseball man living in semiretirement in Florida. An astute baseball man, a teetotaler (which pleased Rickey, a teetotaler himself), and a team man, Shotton led the Dodgers to National League pennants in 1947 and 1949 and managed until 1955.[42] He treated Robinson fairly and with dignity, even though some New York writers regularly lampooned him as "KOBS" (Kindly Old Burt Shotton).

Doby had similar luck, but it did not last. His first manager was Lou Boudreau, who played shortstop for the Indians and managed. Player-managers have disappeared from baseball but were common back then. Besides Boudreau they included Ty Cobb (the Georgia Peach) at Detroit, Frankie Frisch (the Fordham Flash) at St. Louis, and Rogers Hornsby (the Rajah) also at St. Louis.[43] Even Branch Rickey had been a player-manager with the St. Louis Browns, as was Hall of Famer George Sisler many years later.

Growing up in the Chicago suburbs, Boudreau had played with black baseball players in high school and later in college at the University of Illinois. He took Doby around the Cleveland locker room, introducing him to team members. Previously Boudreau had some misgivings: "My first reaction was skepticism. Knowing Veeck as I did, and knowing his penchant for promotion, I immediately wondered if signing a black player was another publicity stunt, a gimmick, another way to sell tickets." Veeck responded, "Larry Doby will be a great player, you'll see."[44]

Boudreau accompanied Doby onto the field at Comiskey Park that day, and a few spectators applauded Doby's entrance. Doby and Boudreau played catch before batting practice. Doby then stepped into the batting cage, where he "hit pretty well. Every time he stepped to the plate virtually all the players on the field, including those in the White Sox dugout, stopped what they were doing and paid close attention to the new black kid, wearing an Indians uniform for the first time, number 14."[45]

Doby took infield practice at second base, with Joe Gordon, the Indians' All-Star second baseman, who took special pains to ease Doby into the big leagues. "Doby's nervousness was even more evident as he took infield practice alongside Gordon. . . . Joe was great with Larry, not just that day, but every day."[46]

Boudreau, though, trod carefully. He did not insert Doby into the lineup for the first game of a doubleheader. "I knew it had to be done with care. I couldn't just throw Doby into the lineup anywhere. I had to pick the right spot, not let the kid get in over his head."[47] He used Doby only in the second game. As a pinch hitter Doby struck out in his first Major League at bat.

In his autobiography manager Boudreau gives Doby high praise, calling him "one of the best outfielders in baseball for 12 years."[48] He was "a good base runner," who stole home against the Yankees in 1949.[49] By 1950 Larry Doby had become an "established star in center field."[50] "Doby was an introverted and sensitive youngster when he joined us in 1947," Boudreau recollects, "but in 1948 he blossomed into one of baseball's best players, serving notice with a .301 batting average and 14 homers that he would soon be one of the game's brightest stars."[51]

Al Lopez and Larry Doby

But as the English duo Chad and Jeremy remind us, "All good things must end someday, autumn leaves must fall." Such as they were, good times for Doby ended in 1949–50. In November 1949 Bill Veeck sold the Indians to Cleveland insurance executive Ellis Ryan. Shortly after the 1950 season had ended, Ellis fired Lou Boudreau as manager and on November 10, 1950, replaced him with Al Lopez, a former Major League catcher known for his defensive skills who had played for, among others, Brooklyn, Boston, Pittsburgh, and, for one year (1947), Cleveland. Doby was to play under Lopez for six and a half uneasy, up-and-down years, five and a half with the Indians and again for one year in Chicago. When in 1955 the Indians traded Doby to the White Sox in Chicago, Marty Marion was the manager. A year later Marion was to be succeeded by—you guessed it—Al Lopez, who Doby already considered to be his "nemesis."

Lopez, of Spanish extraction but raised in Tampa, Florida, may have rendered a true snapshot of his feelings at the time he was Doby's teammate in 1947. Lou Boudreau sent Doby up to pinch hit for the Cleveland relief pitcher, Bryan Stephens, in Doby's first big league appearance. To his teammates on the bench, Lopez said loudly, "I'm glad that he didn't hit for me."[52] The meaning of the comment seems inescapable: it was somehow a mark or badge of dishonor to have a black player pinch hit or substitute for you.

You are judged by the company you keep. For forty years or more, Lopez's best friend in baseball was Casey Stengel, going back to their days together in the 1930s. As a rookie manager of the Brooklyn Dodgers, in 1932 Stengel had named Lopez team captain.[53] The highlight of Casey Stengel's retirement was the annual investiture proceedings at Cooperstown, "where he could mingle with some of his oldest pals, Rube Marquard, Burleigh Grimes, Al Lopez and Waite Hoyt."[54]

Stengel was a racist. The Yankees did not begin integration until 1955, one of the last teams to do so. Stengel had been at the helm since 1949. When black players did come aboard, he routinely referred to the first one, Elston Howard, as my "eight ball" (the eight ball, of course, is black). Stengel referred to African American players as "n——rs." Of Elston Howard, Stengel told reporters, "When I finally got a nigger, I got one that can't run." Later when he coached the New York Mets, he was on record as referring to black players as "jungle bunnies."[55] He well may have used the term earlier.

So here was Elston Howard, "the perfect Yankee rookie, soft-spoken, well mannered, well-educated, dedicated to excellence, a proven team player [and] a black man," playing for a racist manager.[56] Howard must have felt the sting of Stengel's name calling, although Howard denied it. To his dying day Jackie Robinson insisted that Casey Stengel was a bigot. "He never gave black players an equal chance."[57] Howard Cosell, the leading broadcast journalist of those times, agreed with Robinson. "[Stengel] was a doddering old man and a racist who should have been retired twenty years before he was."[58]

Lopez, Spanish by birth and raised the United States, maintained, "I'm Spanish and proud of it."[59] His lifelong friend, Casey Stengel, perhaps in his clownish manner, always referred to Lopez as "the Mexican," or "that Mexican," intending use of the term to be mildly derogatory.[60] Insensitive perhaps to such abuses, Lopez is not on record as having remonstrated with Stengel or attempted to curb him in any way.

Wes Singletary, Lopez's biographer, attempts to excuse the behavior of both Stengel and Lopez by citing the example of Solly Hemus, the "abusive driven manager of the St. Louis Cardinals 1959–61." Singletary distinguishes such name-calling based on, first, its etymology and, second, its direction. First, he argues that "coming of age in baseball during the 1940s, Hemus [and Stengel and Lopez] became accustomed to the sharp ethnic epithets still being hurled about, such as 'dago and guinea, Polack, and kike.'"[61]

Second, Hemus and many other managers and players used such epithets as a form of razzing, directed at the other team and its players. "[Hemus] had been conditioned to believe that was how it was done in baseball. The fact that such overt displays might upset those black players on his team did not matter. Their concern . . . should be on winning ballgames, not the feelings of their opponents."[62]

But the hurling of or tolerance for racial and ethnic epithets, no matter the intention or purity of heart behind them, did sting players other than the opponents at whom derogatory labels were aimed. Two of Hemus's and the Cardinals' stars, Hall of Fame pitcher Bob Gibson and outfielder Curt Flood, considered Hemus a racist and called him out on it.[63]

Lopez did not use such language and race-baiting himself, although he seemed to have been insensitive to their use by others. It is evidence, and so-so evidence at that, against Al Lopez as Larry Doby's manager at the Indians and later at the Chicago Red Sox.

Player Doby on Manager Lopez

Once again Larry Doby considered Lopez a racist, a field manager who, more often than not, mistreated Doby and held him back from maximizing his potential as a baseball player. After his trade from the White Sox to Baltimore in late 1957—a move engineered by Al Lopez that Doby only learned about when his oldest daughter, Cristina heard it on television—Doby told *Jet* magazine that "Lopez's racism had affected his play with the White Sox." Doby argued that it was Lopez's lack of respect for black players that had resulted in Doby not meeting Lopez's expectations (Doby's batting average had fallen to .288 and his home run total from 24 [1956] to 14, in his year [1957] with the White Sox managed by Lopez). "I can't have any respect for a man who lacks regard for a man because he's in a minority and acts as if we're always wrong and he's always right. I just don't care to play for him [Al Lopez]."[64]

For his part Lopez admitted his insensitivity to minority ballplayers, including Doby, and what they had to go through in those early years, but excused it as his managerial style. Despite that assertion the record is explicit that every time Lopez had a chance, he engineered the trade of black ballplayers, including All-Stars such as Larry Doby (three times), Minnie Minoso (three times), and Al Smith (three times).[65] Fred Hatfield, a teammate of Minoso's and of Doby's at Cleveland, termed Lopez "a grudge holder not able to let things go easily."[66] (Lopez traded him too, in 1957.) Lopez also is on record of accusing Doby of being a "head case," not playing to his potential, and often being a liability rather than an asset, principally because Doby struck out a fair amount, a characteristic of power hitters such as Doby but one that Lopez did not seem to countenance.

At the beginning it seems very uncharacteristic of Doby to speak out as he did in 1957. For his entire career, although he was no wallflower, Doby was dignified and taciturn, a gentleman through and through ("a shy and subdued man," "possessed of grace and tolerance").[67] Early on, when confronted with a Washington DC demonstration for further integration of baseball, Doby turned to his friend and teammate Joe Gordon, saying "Gee, Joe, I don't want to be a symbol—I just want to be a big league player."[68] He hewed to that standard most of his professional career. That he departed from it in 1957 is evidence that something out of the ordinary must have been at work.

All during his career Doby demonstrated extreme loyalty to his teammates—Joe Gordon, Al Rosen, Jim Hegan, Bob Lemon, Early Wynn, and especially Bill Veeck ("I think of Bill Veeck as my second father").[69] Doby even refused to name his enemies. At Doby's funeral in 2003, Hall of Fame second baseman Joe Morgan included this aspect of Doby's character in his eulogy: "He never, ever told me who those guys were who would not shake his hand . . . because some were in the Hall of Fame. But he did tell me about Joe Gordon."[70] Sports writer Ian O'Connor added, "He mentioned Joe Gordon's gestures of kindness each and every time. But when I'd ask Doby to name the opponent who once spat in his face, he'd never budge."[71] That Doby then went public with his assessment of Al Lopez as a closet racist speaks volumes.

The Lopez Rejoinder

In response to accusations of racism, Lopez's stand was that he managed with blinders on: the only thing that mattered to him was on-field performance. "When questioned about the off-the-field discrimination that Larry Doby, Jackie Robinson, and other blacks endured, including death threats and the separate, substandard living accommodations . . . Lopez abruptly responded that he knew little of it. His concern was only on the field and, as such, he may have blinded himself to the many indignities that black players suffered."[72] Lopez "did not relate as closely to the plight of Doby and other black players as one might expect."[73] A stronger statement might be that a baseball manager is akin to the captain of a ship. Although he is not running a popularity contest, he must be aware of and look out for the welfare of his crew. Lopez did not do so. His failure was beyond negligence if it was not intentional—perhaps reckless, or perhaps even purposeful or calculated.

There was more to ground Doby's accusations. Lopez tolerated racial taunts and other abuses in his midst. "Perhaps racial slurs did not bother Lopez because he never considered himself a minority. 'I treated everybody the way I wanted to be treated . . . I never had this minority thing handicap or affect me in any way,'" said Lopez.[74] So why should such actions affect others around him if they did not affect him?

In 1954 Doby hit a league-leading thirty-two home runs and accounted for 126 RBIS, also an American League–leading total. At season's end, when he was asked to evaluate the importance of his players, Lopez pointed to Larry Doby. "There's the guy who makes the difference. Without him . . ." Lopez gestured with a thumbs-down motion.[75]

In 1955 Doby trailed off from thirty-two to twenty-four home runs but hit a respectable .291. Lopez traded him anyway, to the Chicago White Sox for shortstop Chico Carrasquel and outfielder Jim Busby. Lopez stated that "he simply tired of waiting for what he believed was Doby's Hall of Fame potential to mature."[76] That does not ring true, for but a year earlier Lopez had denominated Doby the offensive heart of the Cleveland team. Neither had Doby's performance sloughed off that much; indeed, his slugging percentage increased to .505 in 1955, up from .484 in the previous pennant-winning year.

With the active assistance of Hank Greenberg, Lopez traded Doby every opportunity he had. He engineered the first trade to the White Sox in 1955, which Doby took with diplomacy and grace, saying, "I have enjoyed playing for Cleveland. It is a wonderful organization. I only hope I can fill the bill for Chicago and I think I can."[77]

The Cleveland fans, especially the black ones, were not so sanguine. Some felt it was racist. Many other "colored persons believed that the Indians had been unfair to Doby."[78] For his part "Doby did good work with the Sox."[79] He was thirty-two when he joined manager Marty Marion and his team, who welcomed the addition: "The guy used to murder us when we played Cleveland. He'll make a big difference in the number of one-run and two-run decisions we might lose," Wynn commented.[80] At age thirty-two Doby hit 24 home runs with 102 RBIS (1956). The next year he hit 14 home runs with 79 RBIS. Nonetheless, Lopez, who had taken over for Marion, and Greenberg, who had become general manager, traded Doby a second time, to the Baltimore Orioles, with no consultation or notification whatsoever to Doby.

Before opening day in 1958, Baltimore traded Doby back to Cleveland, where he had begun his major league career. Doby played somewhat sparingly in Cleveland, appearing in only eighty-nine games but hitting thirteen home runs for a .283 average.

Cleveland traded Doby to Detroit for the 1959 season. Then, to paraphrase the musical, a funny thing happened on the way to the ballpark. In late 1958 Bill Veeck had acquired a majority interest in the Chicago White Sox. Once the season had begun, one of his first steps was to reacquire Doby from the Tigers for the Sox, after Doby had appeared in only eighteen games, with fifty-five at bats, in Detroit. Doby remarked, "I knew that Bill got me over Lopez's objections. But Bill thought I could help him."[81]

Lopez was persistent. Once again he and Greenberg did Doby in. Over Veeck's opposition and after only a brief tenure for Doby with the Sox, Lopez had Doby sent down to the San Diego Padres of the Pacific Coast League. That demotion marked the beginning of the end for Doby's playing career. Lopez and Greenberg had done him in for the third time.

There was a semblance of a pattern or a pattern itself in Lopez's actions. He traded away another star black player not once, not twice, but three times. At Cleveland he traded the popular Minnie Minoso, the first Latino Major Leaguer, the "Cuban Comet," who was also black, to the Chicago White Sox. When Lopez took the helm at Chicago, he engineered the trade of Minoso again, back to Cleveland, even though Minoso had batted .310 for the Sox. When later Minoso came back to Chicago, Lopez saw to it that the club released him. "It is remarkable that Minoso was traded or released from a Lopez managed club three times, the last after the 1964 season," according to Lopez biographer Wes Singletary. As with Doby the persistent shedding of African American players, All-Stars at that, was merely coincidental, not evidence of bias on Lopez's part, Singletary concludes.

It is worth noting that when Lopez made these trades, he shed any kid gloves he may have had as well. He traded these black players with "no soothing words, no warmth, no show of appreciation. Just, 'Minoso you've been traded.' That was it."[82] With Doby Lopez undertook no notification. As noted, Doby's daughter Christina heard of the trade to Baltimore on television.

Power Hitters and Strike Outs

When Lopez had completed the divestiture of Doby from the White Sox, he remarked, "We've just traded away 100 strikeouts."[83] Casey Stengel, possibly Lopez's closest friend in baseball, had a similar attitude. "Stengel attempted to restrain Mickey Mantle's constant pursuit of the home run. . . . He retained an appreciation of the more conservative batting approach of his time," that is, that high strikeout totals were to be avoided.[84]

Power hitters, though (and Doby was a power hitter), strike out much more often than those batters who view their primary task as putting the ball in play. Mickey Mantle, Doby's contemporary, rung up one hundred strikeouts eight times, and over ninety strikeouts twelve times, in an eighteen-year career.

In 1958 Mantle recorded 120 strikeouts but 42 home runs. In 1959 he struck out 126 times but hit 30 home runs. In 1960 he racked up 125 strikeouts but 41 home runs. Doby's numbers are slightly more modest. His strikeouts numbered over 100 four times and over 90 six times in a thirteen-year career. In 1952 Doby struck out 104 times but hit 32 home runs (aka tatters, aka dingers). The 1953 and 1954 numbers are 102 and 29 home runs, and 126 and 32 home runs, respectively. In his one year with the Sox, prior to Lopez's arrival, Doby struck out 102 times but hit 24 home runs.

All, or most all, of the power hitters of the postwar era put up similar strikeout records or, indeed, struck out more often. Taken at random, the numbers for five hitters are as follows:

Alex Rodriguez, Mariners/Rangers/Yankees, 654 home runs lifetime, struck out over 90 times in each of his twenty years in the Majors, with one exception (2011), and over 100 times in fifteen of twenty years, with highs of 139 in 2006 and 131 in 2001 and 2004.

Reggie Jackson, Athletics/Angels/Yankees, 563 home runs life-time, struck out over 90 times in each of twenty years in the Majors with one exception (1981) and over 100 times in eigh-teen of twenty years, with highs of 171 in 1968, 142 in 1969, 156 in 1982, 140 in 1983, and 141 in 1984.

Mike Schmidt, Philadelphia Phillies, 548 home runs lifetime, struck out over 100 times in twelve of his sixteen years in the Majors, including 180 in 1975, 149 in 1976, and 148 in 1983.

Jim Thome, Indians/White Sox/Phillies, 612 home runs life-time, struck out over 100 times for twelve consecutive years, with highs of 131 in 2003 and 127 in 1999.

Ken Griffey Jr., Mariners/Reds/Mariners, 630 home runs life-time, 104, 121, 121, 108, and 117 strikeouts in 1996–2001, in the heart of his career.

Lopez was out of step with baseball wisdom, which had become known at that time, the late 1950s. That he tried to put another bum rap on Larry Doby, a good power hitter, as a drag on the team because of strikeouts, is further evidence, perhaps indirect, that Lopez carried a grudge against Doby and that the grudge ema-nated from racism on Lopez's part.

Summing It Up

We will never know all the day-to-day discrimination, taunts, threats, abuses, and stresses that Jackie Robinson and Larry Doby went through as they began the process of integrating the National and American Leagues in baseball. So we cannot compare them, nor should we.

It is clear, however, that no person should have to go through what Doby and Robinson endured. Major League Baseball, along with baseball fans everywhere, owe Robinson and Doby, along with their legacies, a debt, to be repaid by respect and gratitude for those two men and what they accomplished. That said, a few salient points may be made.

Outside the baseball season per se, Jackie Robinson was able to shelter in the sanctuary of Dodgertown in Vero Beach, Florida, while in spring training each year. In contrast the Santa Rita Hotel, the Cleveland Indians' spring-training headquarters in Tucson, discriminated and demeaned Larry Doby and his family from 1948 to 1954. Even thereafter hotel staff made Doby and other black players use back stairs rather than the elevators to go to and from their rooms.

"Robinson had a two year drum roll, Doby just showed up."[85] Bill Veeck just parachuted Doby in, with scant preparation for his debut as the first black baseball player in the American League. Dodger president Branch Rickey did the opposite. He planned and carried out an eighteen-month program to acclimatize Jackie Robinson for what might lie ahead, eliminating many (but certainly not all) rough patches that Robinson might face in being the first black player in the National League. At every juncture of his career, Robinson played for understanding, nurturing managers (Hopper, Durocher, Shotton). Doby, on the other hand, played for a manager who may well have been a closet racist and one who certainly "had it in" for Doby.

A final point could be that Jackie Robinson began integration of a league, the National, more receptive to progress on the racial front. "For reasons unclear—but proven out by history—integration came harder to the American League."[86] Doby may have faced a more uphill struggle. That subject, however, the National League versus the American League, would be fodder for another book, or at least a chapter, about integration of our national pastime.

18

A Seldom-Remembered Pioneer

If Larry had come up just a little later, when things were a little better, he might very well have become one of the greatest players of all time.

—BILL VEECK, *Veeck as in Wreck*

[Bill Veeck] saw Larry Doby as a potential Joe DiMaggio, and he always wondered what Doby could have done had he not been under all the pressure, if he had just come along ten years later.

—TERRY PLUTO, *Our Tribe*

Whitey Ford, the Yankee pitching great, remembered Larry Doby as "one of the most formidable hitters he ever faced."[1] In 1952 *Total Baseball* rated Mickey Mantle as the player with the second highest rating (4.8) in the American League. Who did the magazine rank first? Larry Doby of the Cleveland Indians.[2] In 1954 Mantle ranked fourth—again behind the leader, Larry Doby, who led the American League in home runs (32) and RBIs (126) that year.[3] Although admittedly biased, a Cleveland teammate, Bob Feller, rated Doby as "one of the greatest stars of [his] time."[4]

Doby was not without recognition in his lifetime, especially later in his life, when nostalgia caused baseball fans and writers to look back at the days when integration of baseball first began. For a short time, mostly in the late 1990s, fans and historians also began to look beyond the achievements of Jackie Robinson to those of other pioneers such as Doby. In that time Doby received honorary degrees from four universities: Long Island University (1996) where he had played basketball; Montclair State University (1987) in his home city; Fairfield University (1997), a Jesuit University in Connecticut; and Princeton University (1997) in his home state.

Doby received other honors including the following:

Induction in the Cleveland Indians Hall of Fame

Permanent retirement of Cleveland uniform number 14

Induction into the Chicago White Sox Hall of Fame

Dedication of the Patterson, New Jersey, post office as "Larry Doby Post Office"

Congressional Larry Doby medal authorized (S 1519, 100th CONG., 1st Sess. [1987]) (twenty-two senator sponsors) and cast

Induction into the National Baseball Hall of Fame (1998)

Installation and dedication of a larger-than-life-size statue of Larry Doby outside Cleveland's Progressive Field (joining statues of Bob Feller and Jim Thome) (July 25, 2015)

The Hall of Fame induction seems to have been the high point. Since that time, Larry Doby and his achievements have slipped in and out of view, often relegated to the backwater formed behind the continued celebration of Jackie Robinson and his achievements.

In a similar way, Duke Snider, the Brooklyn and Los Angeles Dodgers great, and his achievements were eclipsed as well, playing as he did in the shadows cast by Jackie Robinson, Willie Mays, and Mickey Mantle. "It was his fate to be overlooked. He was the perfect hero for an underdog borough [Brooklyn]."[5] Doby was eclipsed even more. The extent might be illustrated by author James Hirsch's 2010 denomination of Willie Mays in 1951 as the first black five-tool player.[6] Larry Doby, a true five-tool player if ever there was one, had preceded Mays by several years. But Larry Doby has been forgotten by baseball historians and authors such as Hirsch.[7]

One More Possible Shadow

My thesis here is that Doby and his achievements may have been insufficiently recognized and lauded not only because other players, often playing for higher-profile teams, overshadowed Doby but also because his achievements occurred during the final days of radio baseball coverage. Moreover, his best days came before the dawn of serious television coverage. Doby thus fell into the crevice between radio and the then-new medium of television. The waning days of radio coincided with the immense postwar popularity of baseball, both in itself and as a symbol, indeed the paradigm, of a return to normalcy after the cataclysmic struggles of World War II.

David Halberstam writes in *The Summer of '49*:

> It was [Joe] DiMaggio's good fortune to play in an era when his better qualities, both athletic and personal, were amplified, and his lesser qualities simply did not exist. If he did something magnificent on the field, he was not on Johnny Carson the next night, awkward and unsure of himself, mumbling his answers as a modern athlete might. Rather, he had Mel Allen [and Jackie Robinson had Red Barber] to speak for him. It was the perfect combination: his deeds amplified by Mel Allen's [or Red Barber's] voice.[8]

In 1947, when Doby broke in, the DuMont Broadcasting Network, which no longer exists, carried the World Series on television for the first time. The broadcast was carried by five stations, reaching an audience of 3 million—in a nation whose population numbered 170 million. By 1948 the number of television sets still numbered only seventy-two thousand, and there were just twenty-eight broadcast stations in the entire country. By contrast sixteen hundred radio stations broadcast every day.[9]

This modest inroad by television was in a nation that was still baseball nuts. Professional football, which today has become America's sport, then was only "a minor league ticket."[10] Baseball reigned supreme. Yet the demise of radio was on the horizon, although only a few could clearly see that. Television's coverage of baseball began to expand. In the early fifties the baseball television audience grew greatly, from 3 million to over 10 million in just a few years. Television coverage, though, was different than radio coverage, especially for athletes such as Doby. "In the beginning, television seemed to bring [players] greater fame, but in time it became clearer that the fame was not so much greater than quicker" and more ephemeral.[11] Television coverage evaporated sooner. Part of the reason may have been the overkill to which television was then and still is prone. "It is no coincidence that Joe DiMaggio's fame has been so long lasting, and that he was the last hero of the radio era."[12]

Doby came into his own under the clouds created by Joe DiMaggio and other heroes of baseball's postwar radio days. The new medium, television, was then advancing beyond baby steps to a walk. When television coverage finally did hit something resembling full stride, the coverage was different, more ephemeral, and seemingly unaware of the profound historical developments reshaping the baseball world in which Larry Doby played a central role.[13]

Why Not Jackie Robinson?

If Larry Doby fell into the cracks between the world in which radio coverage of baseball dominated and the one in which television coverage came to the fore, why did Jackie Robinson not fall into a similar crevice? The answer is multifaceted. First of all, Robinson was the first African American to break the color barrier in Major League Baseball, while Doby was the second. Second, Robinson played in the epicenter of the baseball world, New York, while Doby played in distant Cleveland. Third, history has recorded Robinson as a great and superior athlete, although that is not completely true. By any objective standard, Doby was the better baseball player, except as a base runner, an area in which Robinson not only excelled but had no peers.

But by the 1960s Jackie Robinson, then as now very much a public figure, had become "increasingly bitter." "His efforts in banking, public relations, insurance, real estate and broadcasting met with limited success."[14] His son and namesake, Jackie Jr., developed a drug dependency. Jackie Jr. later died in an auto accident on Connecticut's Merritt Parkway. Jackie Robinson publicly criticized other African American sports stars such as Willie Mays for their lack of overt involvement in the civil rights movement, coming close to calling them out publicly as "Uncle Toms" (see chapter 14).

Half a generation later, another baseball star, Reggie Jackson, commented that "character flaws bring comparison and attention to all colors."[15] Whether flaws or character traits, or a bit of both, Jackie Robinson's outspoken and constant presence in the limelight kept alive his heroic accomplishment of 1947 and his exploits on the baseball field in the years that followed.

Could it be that Larry Doby has been lost in the shuffle because he had fewer, if any, character flaws (if flaw is the right word), or burrs under his saddle? After Doby left baseball, he settled into a life with his wife and five children in a New Jersey suburb that might seem humdrum compared with Robinson's. He was a quieter, more reserved person to begin with. And as we have seen, even when active as a player, Doby never had the visibility of Jackie Robinson or many other players.

A Final Scorecard

As a tribute to the wisdom of integration, soon after they broke in, four of the first five blacks to play Major League Baseball became All-Stars. Jackie Robinson, Don Newcombe, and Roy Campanella represented the National League and Larry Doby the American in the 1949 classic. The presence of those African American stars should have acted as a powerful recruiting sergeant for the integration of baseball. It did in the National League; it did not in the American, in which all the clubs, save Cleveland, continued their exclusionary ways. Larry Doby was, and for a number of years afterward continued to be, the American League's only African American All-Star.[16]

Of the eleven blacks who entered Major League Baseball in the beginning years of integration, 1947–50, Larry Doby was the last to hang up his spikes. He had survived them all, including Robinson, Newcombe, and Campanella.[17] He was the only one of the eleven to play in the American League.

Doby's achievements include the following:

First black player in the American League

Seven-time All-Star

Star of the 1948 World Series

First black to hit a home run in the World Series (1948)

First player to be on championship teams both in the Negro League (Newark) and in the Majors (Cleveland)

First black player to win a Major League home run title (1952), which he repeated two years later (1954)

First black player to win a runs-batted-in title (American League, 1954)

Second African American manager in major league baseball (Chicago White Sox 1978)[18]

Years after Doby's playing days were over, Bill Veeck "wondered in print what Doby might have become if he had come to baseball when black players were more common and hostility less common, if he had come along when he had a black confidant on the team instead of spending so much of his early time alone. Veeck wondered what Doby might have been if he didn't feel he had to bear the burden of being a trailblazer." Always an astute judge of baseball talent, as noted earlier, Veeck concluded, "If Larry had come up just a little later, when things were a little better, he might very well have become one of the greatest players of all time."[19] In his obituary of Larry Doby, former baseball commissioner Fay Vincent gave a more subjective appraisal: "In an age in which we struggle to identify true heroes, Larry Doby is one of mine. His decency, quiet courage, remarkable achievements, and lasting contribution to racial progress are permanent legacies. Well done, old friend. May you rest in peace."[20]

We are "in an age in which fame and celebrity are regularly confused with accomplishment."[21] Today fame and notoriety often precede accomplishment, if indeed ever there is any true accomplishment to follow. With Larry Doby, it has been the other way round. Doby's achievements on the playing field and his paramount achievement in beginning the integration of the American League constitute monumental accomplishments. They have not been accompanied by anything remotely resembling proportionate recognition. In some small part, this book attempts to add to recognition of Doby's accomplishment and to dispel, perhaps, the large void that has persisted in American baseball history.

Postscript on Baseball Statistics

A new wave of baseball statistics and the study of them, known as *sabermetrics*, has come to the fore in the last two decades or so. My familiarity with it, barely more than passing, dates from 2003. In that year Michael Lewis published his book *Moneyball: The Act of Winning an Unfair Game*.[1] The book chronicled the efforts of Oakland Athletics general manager Billy Beane and his assistant, Paul DePodesta, to assemble a low-payroll but winning team for Oakland. They succeeded in doing just that. Later a Beane follower, Theo Epstein, took similar learning and methods to Boston, using new-age statistics in helping assemble teams for the Red Sox. The movie *Moneyball* (2011, starring Brad Pitt and Jonah Hill) took Beane and DePodesta's efforts to the screen.

The progenitor of new ways of evaluating baseball players and teams is Bill James, who, beginning in the late 1970s, published numerous books (his "abstracts") outlining his approaches and the incomplete nature of traditional baseball performance measures. Early on James's annual abstracts appeared in mimeographed form and are the movement's oldest antecedents.[2]

Practitioners of these new arts are known in certain quarters as "sabermathematicians," after the Society of American Baseball Research (SABR). An inner circle of SABR members holds a sabermathematicians meeting each year. Practitioners of those somewhat arcane arts are denominated, often pejoratively, as "stat rats." Another more neutral moniker for the movement is *Rotisserie Baseball*, derived from the name of a Manhattan restaurant (La

Rotisserie Francaise) where *Sports Illustrated* writer Dan Okrent began convening study groups in the early 1980s.[3]

Some of the performance measures the new approach has generated include the following:

- Runs Created (RC); RC = total bases (hits + walks)
- Range Factor (RF); RF = assists + putouts
- WARP: wins above replacement player (i.e., next man up)
- OPS: on-base percentage (OBP) plus slugging percentage; a statistic giving insight into possession of the blend of attributes considered most desirable in a player[4]
- WHIP: walks plus hits per inning; shows a pitcher's propensity for allowing, or not allowing, runners on base

Rationale for the New Statistics

If you have ever attended a game in which marquee high school or college players are involved, you have probably seen the Major League scouts. Each scout carries four items: a folding aluminum lawn chair, a seat cushion for the chair, a thick briefcase filled with statistics and reports on every amateur player of note, and a handheld speed gun. The scouts position themselves behind the backstop, where they can begin clocking the speed of the teams' pitchers. At games in which one or two reputed "pheenoms" are scheduled to appear as many as seven or eight scouts hover.

All, or most all, of these scouts rely primarily on similar "sight based scouting prejudices: the scouting dislike of short right handed pitchers, or the distrust of skinny little guys who get on base, or the scouting distaste for fat catchers."[5] The scouts look for players with Major League looks: six feet three, 195 pounds, and Hollywood handsome. They look for young eighteen- and nineteen-year-old pitchers whose fastballs travel at ninety-five, ninety-six, or ninety-seven miles per hour. Twenty-three or twenty-four is already too old.

The junk ball pitcher Jamie Moyer, who successful pitched for many years at Seattle and then Philadelphia, had a fastball that clocked, at best, in the low eighties. Had the decision whether to introduce Moyer to organized baseball been left to the scouts, almost all of whom think alike, Moyer's career would have been as a high school teacher or an insurance salesman, rather than as a star pitcher.

Scouts actually carry checklists. "Tools is what they call the talents they [check] for in a kid. There [are] five tools; the abilities to run, throw, field, hit, and hit with power."[6] By contrast, to a sabermatrician, "foot speed, fielding ability, even raw power tend to be dramatically overpriced. The ability to control the strike zone [is] the greatest indicator of future success. The number of walks a hitter draws [may be] the best indicator of whether [the player] understands how to control the strike zone." Sacrifice bunts, long considered a valuable element in a "small ball" baseball offense, are not considered valuable at all because they result in one more out.

The logic of new approaches to evaluating baseball players' performance, which, for instance, results in severe downgrading of the sacrifice bunt as an offensive tool, is compelling, as practitioner Eric Walker once wrote:

> Far and away—far, far and away—the most crucial number in baseball is 3: the three outs that define an inning. Until the third out, anything is possible; after it, nothing is. Anything that increases the offense's chance of making an out is bad; anything that decreases it is good. And what is on-base percentage? Simply put, it is the probability that the batter will not make an out. When we state it that way, it becomes crystal clear that the most important isolated statistic is the on-base percentage.[7]

Every batter, then, should think and attempt to act like a lead-off man and adopt as his main goal getting on base. After that almost every batter should possess the power to hit home runs, in part because home run power forces opposing pitchers to pitch more cautiously, leading to walks and higher on-base percentages. And home runs will clear those bases that, ideally, will previously have become loaded with runners on them.

The most important *team* statistic, then, is runs scored. As far back as 1979, Bill James had written, "I find it remarkable that, in listing [teams'] offenses, [baseball leagues] will list first—meaning the best—not the team which scored the most runs but the team with the highest batting average." The Jamesean observation reflects that most of organized baseball—the owners, its managers, coaches, and players—remain "thoroughly inoculated against outside ideas."[8] Batting averages, sacrifice bunts, and hit-and-run plays remain lodestars. The baseball religious wars continue.

Defensive Statistics

The most ubiquitous and traditional measure is fielding percentage. If, for instance, over a season, an outfielder has five hundred chances, that is, baseballs hit his way, and he muffles twenty of these, his fielding percentage is .960. If he muffles one hundred of them, his fielding percentage drops to .800 (and he may well be demoted to the minor leagues, or worse).

On a wider basis, however, fielding percentage may not be very reliable at all as a measure of performance. The safest way to have a high fielding percentage, being perhaps error free, is to be too slow to reach the ball in the first place. Often the daring, fast fielder may have a fielding percentage the same as or even lower than the plodding defensive player with the circumscribed small range. So Bill James and those who follow his approach have substituted another statistic, "range factor," for fielding percentage. They compute the number of successful plays a player has made in the field per game, not the number of successful chances out of all chances for that player.

Evaluating Doby and Other Players of His Era

In this book I have used the traditional measures of a baseball player's performance. For hitters the relevant statistics include plate appearances (ABS), batting averages, runs-batted-in (RBIS), home runs, runs scored, strikeouts, and slugging percentages. In the field, for position players the relevant statistic has been, for me, the old-fashioned and outmoded fielding percentage. For pitchers the focus remains on the win-loss record, the earned run average (ERA), and the ratio of strikeouts to walks.

I do not use any of the newer—in almost all cases more accurate or useful statistical methods for several reasons. First, I simply do not fully understand many of the new measures of baseball performance. I have Michael Lewis's and Bill James's books on my bookshelf, but it would be presumptuous of me to purport to apply them to yesteryear's performances. I am a newbie, a neophyte in the area of sabermetrics.

Second, those statistics generally are not available for yesterday's baseball players. It would be hard work to compute them today. True, Web sites exist that claim to provide access to the box score of every Major League game ever played, or at least as far back as a book of this nature might require. But ferreting out game-by-game performances for Larry Doby and other players of that era and deriving new-age statistical comparisons from those statistics seems a prodigious, if not impossible, task.

Third, Doby played in a different era, when the game was more of a pitcher's than a hitter's or power hitter's game. So his numbers may be lower than they otherwise would be. A big difference between then and now was the height of the pitcher's mound. The pitcher's mound in the forties and fifties was supposed to be fifteen inches higher than home plate, but authorities rarely policed it. As a result the pitcher's mounds in some Major League parks were twenty or more inches higher than home plate. For instance, Shibe Park in Philadelphia was known for having a greatly elevated pitcher's mound. From a higher mound a pitcher's downward weight shift and momentum were much greater, enabling him to generate greater velocity on this pitches. In 1968, though, Major League Baseball lowered the pitcher's mound to no more than ten inches above home plate, where it remains today.[9] Major League officials also policed the requirement. The results were significant increases in the number of players hitting more than twenty or thirty home runs in a season.

Fourth, overall I am reminded of Bill Bryson's admonition in his book *One Summer: America, 1927*: "It is generally futile and foolish to compare athletic performances across decades."[10]

Acknowledgments

My position as a professor at a major university, the University of Pittsburgh, enabled me to begin and complete research on an efficient basis. One ace-in-the-hole at the university was the ready availability of interlibrary loan. It also so happened that our back-office librarian in charge of interlibrary loan, Nathan Taurig, had been a college baseball pitcher (Denison University). Nathan took a special interest in the book and its subject matter. He sought out and obtained for me scores of books, many esoteric or downright obscure.

Like me, the interim director of our law library, Marc Silverman, traces his roots to Ohio, where Larry Doby played. Marc tracked down sources, statistics, and newspaper accounts for me. He answered many off-the-wall inquiries that came to my sometimes overly fertile mind.

My assistant at the law school, Patty Blake, was helpful in getting out letters and packages to literary agents and potential publishers. As always, she went about everything I asked her to do in a cheerful and efficient way.

I made a trip to the National Baseball Hall of Fame and Museum in Cooperstown, New York. For three days, I worked in the Giamatti Research Center. The reference librarian there, Cassidy Lent, prepared in advance printouts of sources within her library's collection. She also culled from the Hall's photo collection files of baseball photographs that I might want to review for possible use in the book. The visual arts director, John Horne, enhanced resolution in the file photos I chose. He prepared and sent to me a CD of those pictures that I then was able to upload to the hard drive of my computer. Many of them appear in the book.

A second trip was to Cleveland, Ohio, with two purposes in mind: First was a review of the Doby and Doby-era photographs in the sports photo collection of the Cleveland State University Library. Librarian Vern Morrison was gracious and helpful in that regard. Second was a review of the sports pages of the *Cleveland Plain Dealer* from 1947 onward.

My daughter, Clare McAuliffe nee Branson, fulfilled a similar task for me in New York. She spent mornings and afternoons making notes on Larry Doby and Jackie Robinson accounts in the *New York Times* dating from that era.

My wife, Elizabeth Hurtt, read and red-penciled a draft of the entire manuscript, correcting my grammar. Sister Mary Alyce, my fifth- and sixth-grade teacher and the best instructor I ever had, would be proud at how few the necessary corrections were. My wife also pointed out to me instances in which my explanations of things were confusing or less than clear.

My editors, Sabrina Stellrecht at the University of Nebraska Press and freelancer Barbara Wojhoski, performed yeoman-like labors, putting up with my sometimes-quirky prose and notions regarding a format for the book. I owe them a debt of gratitude. My acquiring editor at the Press, Rob Taylor, was unfailingly polite and helpful. He answered my emails, some of which were undoubtedly off-the-wall, promptly and with courtesy.

This book is dedicated to two professors who write about baseball. First is my friend Rob Garratt, a professor of English as the University of Puget Sound. A native of San Francisco, Rob is writing about the Giants' 1958 move from New York to San Francisco, which has been obscured by all the publicity and attention given to the Dodgers' move in the same year from Brooklyn to Los Angeles. Rob's efforts inspired me to undertake this book. Along the way, his encouragement has spurred me onward.

The second is Joseph Thomas Moore, a professor emeritus at Montclair State University in New Jersey. In 1988 Moore authored the definitive, and only, comprehensive biography of Larry Doby, *Pride against Prejudice: The Biography of Larry Doby*. In 2011,

Dover Publications reissued the book in updated form with the more descriptive title *Larry Doby: The Struggle of the American League's First Black Player.* I have relied on Moore's work, along with other sources, in several chapters of my book. Moore and I have exchanged emails, and he also encouraged me to write this book.

Notes

Preface

1. Kentya Kennedy, *Sports Illustrated*, April 15, 2013, 14.

2. See Kahn, *Rickey and Robinson*. See also Leigh Montville, "Revolutionary Rookie," *Wall Street Journal*, September 20, 2014, c-8.

3. Rich Cohen, "Where Are They Now? Ernie Banks," *Sports Illustrated*, July 7, 2014.

4. See, e.g., Anthony Castrovince, "Doby: The Forgotten Trailblazer," MLB.com, July 5, 2007. Cohen, "Where Are They Now?"

5. Moore, *Larry Doby*.

6. See Bill Livingston, "Cleveland Indians' Legend Larry Doby Deserves His Own Statute," *Cleveland Plain Dealer*, July 11, 2012.

7. Donald Hunt, "Baseball Great Larry Doby Receives a Postage Stamp," *Philadelphia Tribune*, April 5, 2012.

8. David Anderson, "Sports of the Times: Has Baseball Forgotten Larry Doby?," *New York Times*, March 29, 1987 ("In glorifying those who are first, the second is often forgotten").

9. Claire Smith, "Larry Doby, Who Broke a Color Barrier, Dies at 79," *New York Times*, June 23, 2003 (obituary).

10. Jacobson, *Carrying Jackie's Torch*, 29.

11. Barra, *Mickey and Willie*, 184.

12. Ribowsky, *Don't Look Back*, 12.

13. See, e.g., Ken Berger, Associated Press, "Baseball's Forgotten Pioneer," *Fredericksburg (VA) Free Lance Star*, July 5, 1997; Ira Berkow, "Larry Doby: He Crossed the Color Barrier, Only He Was the Second," *New York Times*, February 23, 1997.

1. The Coolest of Them All?

1. Barra, *Mickey and Willie*, 435.

2. Barra, *Mickey and Willie*, 89 ("Larry Doby had become the first black player in the American League").

3. Halberstam, *Summer of '49*, 14.

4. The National World War II Museum, at http://www.nationalww2museum .org (accessed January 7, 2015).

5. Halberstam, *Summer of '49*, 11.

6. Halberstam, *Summer of '49*, 12.

7. The 1998 New York Yankees eclipsed the Indians' 1954 record with 114 victories. In turn, in 2001, the Seattle Mariners eclipsed the Yankee record with 116 regular season wins. These latter two accomplishments took place over a 162-game schedule compared with the Indians' 111 wins in a 154-game season.

8. Published earlier under the title *Pride against Prejudice: The Biography of Larry Doby* (New York: Greenwood Press, 1988).

2. The Rickey Yardstick

1. Lowenfish, *Branch Rickey*, 325.

2. Fromer, *Rickey and Robinson*, 6.

3. Lowenfish, *Branch Rickey*, 324.

4. Lowenfish, *Branch Rickey*, 7.

5. Lowenfish, *Branch Rickey*, 280. Landis is said to have had "a real hatred for Branch Rickey. Rickey was too smart for him." Fromer, *Rickey and Robinson*, 77.

6. Launius, *Seasons in the Sun*, 20.

7. Fromer, *Rickey and Robinson*, 69.

8. Anderson, "Branch Rickey and the St. Louis Cardinal Farm System," 113. Monetary comparisons are made using Measuring Wealth, at http://www.measuring wealth.com/uscompare (accessed May 18, 2014).

9. Allen, *You Could Look It Up*, 154. See also Halberstam, *Summer of '49*, 25 (in 1949, average salary for a top-flight rookie was $7,000).

10. The definitive biography is Lowenfish, *Branch Rickey*. Others include Fromer, *Rickey and Robinson*.

11. Based on a Kiner television biography broadcast by Root Sports Television Network, Pittsburgh, Pennsylvania, April 23, 2014.

12. Halberstam, *Summer of '49*, 168.

13. O'Toole, *Branch Rickey in Pittsburgh*, 155.

14. Lowenfish, *Branch Rickey*, 519.

15. Lowenfish, *Branch Rickey*, 318 (Rickey's contract, however, still provided for a cash bonus on player sales).

16. See, e.g., Lowenfish, *Branch Rickey*, 284 ("It is better to trade a player a year too early than a year too late").

17. Fromer, *Rickey and Robinson*, 72.

18. Fromer, *Rickey and Robinson*, 54.

19. Lowenfish, *Branch Rickey*, 131.

20. See, e.g., Shirley Povich, "This Morning," *Washington Post*, December 16, 1942 ("Down through the years, when he was general manager of the Cardinals, the money flowed only one way in the deals Rickey made—into the Cardinals' coffers").

21. Roscoe McGowen, "Dean's 1937 Affiliation Is Still Deep History to Baseball Men," *New York Times*, December 8, 1936 ("large amount of cash, probably the Rickey usual of $150,00 to $200,000"). See also Lowenfish, *Branch Rickey*, 246, 285–87.

22. Stockton, *Gashouse Gang*, 66–67.

23. Lowenfish, *Branch Rickey*, 305.

24. Lowenfish, *Branch Rickey*, 314–15.

25. Lowenfish, *Branch Rickey*, 336.

26. Lowenfish, *Branch Rickey*, 336; John Drebinger, "Camilli and Allen Are Sent to Giants in 5 Player Deal," *New York Times*, August 1, 1943.

27. Lowenfish, *Branch Rickey*, 500.

28. "Phillies Get Dickson for Two Players and $80,000 in Deal with Pirates," *New York Times*, January 14, 1954.

29. Associated Press Staff, "Braves Trade Six to Get O'Connell," *New York Times*, December 27, 1943. Cf. John Drebinger, "Dodgers Get Rube Melton in Deal, Sending Allen and $30,000 to Phils," *New York Times*, December 13, 1942 ("The sum involved was $30,000. . . . That puts Rickey in a new light, for in the many years he served as general manager of the Cardinals he invariably was on the receiving end when such a sum changed hands").

30. Arthur Daley, "The Mahatma Speaks," Editorial, *New York Times*, June 15, 1953.

31. Lowenfish, *Branch Rickey*, 500.

32. Lowenfish, *Branch Rickey*, 298. See also Lowenfish, *Branch Rickey*, 260–63 (background on Wentz overture).

33. Lowenfish, *Branch Rickey*, 314.

34. Lowenfish, *Branch Rickey*, 319.

35. A glaring exception, and one that received reams of unfavorable commentary, was the Chesapeake Corporations board allowing chief executive Audrey McClendon to purchase interests in all exploratory oil and gas fields that the company had acquired and, further, to do so with loans from the bank that was the principal lender to the corporation.

36. See generally Halberstam, *Summer of '49*, 201–2.

37. See, e.g., Fromer, *Rickey and Robinson*, 78–79.

38. Lowenfish, *Branch Rickey*, 396.

39. Lowenfish, *Branch Rickey*, 7.

40. Robinson and Duckett, *I Never Had It Made*, xxiii.

41. Fromer, *Rickey and Robinson*, 84.

42. Fromer, *Rickey and Robinson*, 81.

43. Lowenfish, *Branch Rickey*, 382–83.

44. Lowenfish, *Branch Rickey*, 383.

45. See also "Woman Magnate [Effa Manley] Rips Rickey for Raiding the Negro League," *Chicago Herald American*, undated, no file, Wendell Smith Papers, A. Bartlett Giamatti Research Center, National Baseball Hall of Fame, Cooperstown, New York, hereafter referenced as Wendell Smith Papers.

46. Dickson, *Bill Veeck*, 126.

47. Lowenfish, *Branch Rickey*, 453.

48. Branch Rickey, quoted in Fromer, *Rickey and Robinson*, 81–82.

49. Branch Rickey, quoted by Fromer, *Rickey and Robinson*, 96.

50. Lowenfish, *Branch Rickey*, 326.

51. Fromer, *Rickey and Robinson*, 97; Lowenfish, *Branch Rickey*, 350.

52. Lowenfish, *Branch Rickey*, 23. Lowenfish recounts the episode in detail, 22–25. See also Fromer, *Rickey and Robinson*, 106.

53. Lowenfish, *Branch Rickey*, 24.

54. See Lowenfish, *Branch Rickey*, 289–90.

55. Robinson and Duckett, *I Never Had It Made*, 7. Downs died, quite tragically, a few years after Robinson began playing for the Dodgers. Downs became ill while visiting Jackie and Rachel Robinson in Brooklyn. He waited to seek medical care until he had returned to Texas, where the care received was both substandard and too late. Jackie Robinson blamed Reverend Downs's untimely death on racism, widespread in New York as well as in Texas. Robinson and Duckett, *I Never Had It Made*, 69.

56. See Fromer, *Rickey and Robinson*, 98–99. The park's owners did not do away with segregated seating until May 1944.

57. Monte Irvin, quoted in Fromer, *Rickey and Robinson*, 115.

58. Fromer, *Rickey and Robinson*, 115.

59. Fromer, *Rickey and Robinson*, 55.

60. Lowenfish, *Branch Rickey*, 62.

61. Fromer, *Rickey and Robinson*, 49.

62. Lowenfish, *Branch Rickey*, 564.

63. Lowenfish, *Branch Rickey*, 78.

64. Lowenfish, *Branch Rickey*, 565.

65. Fromer, *Rickey and Robinson*, 72.

3. Bill Veeck Compared

1. Veeck and Linn, *Veeck as in Wreck*, 204.

2. Veeck and Linn, *Veeck as in Wreck*, 14.

3. Veeck and Linn, *Veeck as in Wreck*, 24.

4. Veeck and Linn, *Veeck as in Wreck*, 81. See also Veeck, *Hustler's Handbook*, 29.

5. Dickson, *Bill Veeck*, 3. "I have been busted and I have been affluent and I have been busted again." Veeck and Linn, *Veeck as in Wreck*, 196.

6. Simon, *Home and Away*, 32.

7. Veeck and Linn, *Veeck as in Wreck*, 342.

8. Dickson, *Bill Veeck*, 84.

9. Veeck, *Hustler's Handbook*, 160.

10. Veeck and Linn, *Veeck as in Wreck*, 105.

11. Veeck and Linn, *Veeck as in Wreck*, 3.

12. Dickson, *Bill Veeck*, 173.

13. Dickson, *Bill Veeck*, 256 (recollections by Larry Doby Jr. of annual family visits to the Veeck farm).

14. Lou Boudreau, in Boudreau and Schneider, *Lou Boudreau*, 95.

15. Lou Boudreau, in Boudreau and Schneider, *Lou Boudreau*, 95.

16. Feller and Gilbert, *Now Pitching, Bob Feller*, 146.

17. Feller and Gilbert, *Now Pitching, Bob Feller*, 127. See also Veeck and Linn, *Veeck as in Wreck*, 102.

18. Dickson, *Bill Veeck*.

19. Feller and Gilbert *Now Pitching, Bob Feller*, 127.

20. Sickels, *Bob Feller*, 171.

21. Veeck, *Hustler's Handbook*, 110–11.

22. Veeck, *Hustler's Handbook*, 111.

23. Veeck and Linn, *Thirty Tons a Day*.

24. Dickson, *Bill Veeck*, 253.

25. *Washington Post*, February 3, 1963.

26. Veeck, *Hustler's Handbook*, 250.

27. See, e.g., Veeck, *Hustler's Handbook*, 30, 79, 99 et seq.

28. Veeck, *Hustler's Handbook*, 62.

29. Veeck, *Hustler's Handbook*, 99.

30. Vccck, *Hustler's Handbook*, 102.

31. Veeck, *Hustler's Handbook*, 105.

32. Veeck, *Hustler's Handbook*, 99, 40.

33. Veeck and Linn, *Veeck as in Wreck*, 78.

34. Veeck and Linn, *Veeck as in Wreck*, 170.

35. Veeck, *Hustler's Handbook*, 176.

36. Dickson, *Bill Veeck*, 173.

37. Veeck and Linn, *Veeck as in Wreck*, 171.

38. Veeck and Linn, *Veeck as in Wreck*, 182.

39. Dickson, *Bill Veeck*, 44.

40. Dickson, *Bill Veeck*, 173.

41. Veeck and Linn, *Veeck as in Wreck*, 174.

42. Veeck and Linn, *Veeck as in Wreck*, 174

43. Veeck and Linn, *Veeck as in Wreck*, 177.

44. Wendell Smith, "Sports Beat," *Pittsburgh Courier*, September 10, 1949, Wendell Smith Papers.

45. Dickson, *Bill Veeck*, 303.

46. See Dickson, *Bill Veeck*, 312.

47. Veeck and Linn, *Veeck as in Wreck*, 175.

48. Effa Manley (1897–1981), who owned the Newark Eagles with her husband, was a white woman who pretended to be African American. She is one of the more colorful figures in Negro League history. See generally Luke, *Most Famous Woman in Baseball*. Effa Manley is the only woman to be inducted into the National

Baseball Hall of Fame, having been selected by the Negro Leagues Committee in 2006.

49. Luke, *Most Famous Woman in Baseball*, 176. See also *Veeck as in Wreck*, 176.

50. Luke, *Most Famous Woman in Baseball*, 178.

51. Luke, *Most Famous Woman in Baseball*, 177.

52. Reported in Dickson, *Bill Veeck*, 339.

53. Veeck and Linn, *Veeck as in Wreck*, 179.

54. Veeck and Linn, *Veeck as in Wreck*, 179.

55. Dickson, *Bill Veeck*, 312, 339.

56. Simon, *Home and Away*, 26–27.

57. Veeck and Linn, *Veeck as in Wreck*, 180.

4. Doby Breaks the Color Line

1. Hirsch, *Willie Mays*, 234. See, e.g., Fay Vincent, "Back Talk: Larry Doby Played with Dignity and without Bitterness," *New York Times*, June 22, 2003. The former commissioner of baseball (1989–92), who employed Doby from time to time, recalled: "Larry lost patience [when a] heckler called him every name in the book. Larry lost it and started over the barrier toward the fan. His good friend, Bill McKechnie, the [Cleveland] third base coach, grabbed him by the seat of the pants, and said: 'Don't go up there, kid. That will ruin you, not him.'"

2. Jacobson, *Carrying Jackie's Torch*, 32–33. See also Claire Smith, "Larry Doby, Who Broke a Color Barrier, Dies, 79," *New York Times*, June 20, 2003: "When I arrived in Cleveland, Jackie Robinson called and the first thing we discussed was the hotel and food situation. Those were the two most important things. After you play a hard game of ball, and you want to sit down and eat . . . and have your family [or teammates] with you, and you can't, it really bothers you."

3. Luke, *Most Famous Woman in Baseball*, 89.

4. Moore, *Larry Doby*, 10.

5. Moore, *Larry Doby*, 11.

6. Moore, *Larry Doby*, 14; Luke, *Most Famous Woman in Baseball*, 89.

7. Jacobson, *Carrying Jackie's Torch*, 15. Monte Irvin, another racial trailblazer and also in the Hall of Fame, was one of the other four players featured in the book.

8. Jacobson, *Carrying Jackie's Torch*, 31.

9. See Moore, *Larry Doby*, 26.

10. Pluto, *Our Tribe*, 144.

11. Luke, *Most Famous Woman in Baseball*, 122.

12. Luke, *Most Famous Woman in Baseball*, 134–35.

13. Fromer, *Rickey and Robinson*, 94.

14. Luke, *Most Famous Woman in Baseball*, 172 (appendix).

15. Luke, *Most Famous Woman in Baseball*, 136.

16. Shep Jackson, "From the Sidelines," *Cleveland Call & Post*, June 13, 1974.

17. Wendell Smith, "Sports Beat," *Pittsburgh Courier*, July 12, 1947. Wendell Smith Papers.

18. Pluto, *Our Tribe*, 145.

19. Luke, *Most Famous Woman in Baseball*, 136.

20. Wendell Smith, "Sports Beat," *Pittsburgh Courier*, July 12, 1947.

21. See, e.g., the Dollar Times calculator, at http://www.Dollartimes.com (accessed October 10, 2014).

22. At least according to Wendell Smith, Rickey also tried to sign Monte Irvin without payment for his contract with the Eagles, "but Mrs. Manley raised her monotonous howl." Smith, "Sports Beat," *Pittsburgh Courier*, June 28, 1949.

23. Luke, *Most Famous Woman in Baseball*, 138.

24. Pluto, *Our Tribe*, 146–47.

25. Pluto, *Our Tribe*, 148.

26. Pluto, *Our Tribe*, 148.

27. "Larry Doby, Ace Negro Infielder, Signs Contract with Cleveland," *New York Times*, July 4, 1947.

28. Pluto, *Our Tribe*, 149.

29. Pluto, *Our Tribe*, 153.

30. Pluto, *Our Tribe*, 150.

31. Pluto, *Our Tribe*, 150, quoting Whitey Lewis of the *Cleveland Press*.

32. Wendell Smith, "Sports Beat," *Pittsburgh Courier*, July 12, 1947.

33. Wendell Smith, "Sports Beat," *Pittsburgh Courier*, August 30, 1947.

34. Borsvold, *Cleveland Indians*, 38.

35. Pluto, *Our Tribe*, 154.

36. Pluto, *Our Tribe*, 153.

37. Tom Heinrich, "Old Reliable" from Massillon, Ohio, had published a book on playing the outfield, but neither the author nor the interlibrary loan librarian at the University of Pittsburgh has been able to locate a copy.

38. Speaker ranks fifth for career hits all time: 3,584 hits over 22 years. First is Pete Rose, 4,256 hits in 24 years; second is Ty Cobb, 4,189 hits over 24 years; third is Henry Aaron, 3,771 over 23 years; and fourth is Stan Musial, 3,630 hits over 22 years. "Career Leaders & Records for Hits," at http://Baseball-Reference.com (accessed October 20, 2014).

39. Crowe, *Just as Good*, 26 (pagination by the author, unnumbered children's picture book).

40. Mel Allen, quoted in Crowe, *Just as Good*, 11 (pagination by the author).

41. See, e.g., A. S. Doc Young, "Larry Doby Outstanding Star as Indians Win World Series," *Cleveland Call and Post*, October 16, 1984.

42. The episode is recounted by George Vecsey in *Yogi Berra*, 108–9.

43. Jacobson, *Carrying Jackie's Torch*, 8.

44. Jacobson, *Carrying Jackie's Torch*, 7–8.

45. Halberstam, *Summer of '49*, 195. Gowdy remembered Ted Williams as the first in baseball to predict the coming importance of black athletes in American sports. Halberstam, *Summer of '49*, 196.

46. See Barra, *Yogi Berra*, 370.

47. Barra, *Yogi Berra*, 112.

48. Pluto, *Our Tribe*, 153. "He takes [Doby] and Helyn to the best restaurants. He says his door is always open and it's true. He becomes a true friend."

49. Borsvold, *Cleveland Indians*, 71. It could have been, at least partially. Mays came up in 1951 but Banks not until 1953 and Aaron not until 1954.

50. Dickson, *Bill Veeck*, 176.

51. Bryson, *One Summer*, 219.

52. Borsvold, *Cleveland Indians*, 58.

53. Borsvold, *Cleveland Indians*, 61.

54. Borsvold, *Cleveland Indians*, 61.

55. Allen, *You Could Look It Up*, 154.

56. Barra, *Yogi Berra*, 142.

5. Doby's Middle Years

1. Jacobson, *Carrying Jackie's Torch*, 27. "Doby never would identify the bad guys on the Indians and in baseball, the ones who heckled him, shunned him, called him names, and made racist allusions and jokes" (Jacobson, *Carrying Jackie's Torch*, 32).

2. Moore, *Larry Doby*, 184–85, quoting Hall of Fame player and executive Bill White. White had grown up in Cleveland, where Doby was his childhood hero. Then and in ensuing years White found Doby to be "a beautiful, tough and intelligent human being" (185).

3. Moore, *Larry Doby*, 34.

4. Allen, *You Could Look It Up*, 182.

5. Singletary, *Al Lopez*, 109.

6. See, e.g., Glenn Altschuler, "Baseball Great Battled Racism by Embracing Jewish Heritage," *Pittsburgh Post-Gazette*, July 27, 2014, B-5, reviewing Rosengren, *Hank Greenberg*: "A phenomenal baseball player (and, at times, a prescient general manager . . .) Hank Greenberg exhibited great courage, intelligence, and integrity. . . . [He gave] baseball fans, young and old, many reasons to conclude that ability on the baseball field . . . is far more important than skin color, religion or national origin."

7. Rosengren, *Hank Greenberg*, 359. See also Altschuler, "Baseball Great Battled Racism," ("He may well have been the best Jewish player in the history of the major leagues. . . . He exhibited great courage, intelligence and integrity").

8. Rosengren, *Hank Greenberg*, 298–99.

9. Rosengren, *Hank Greenberg*, 357.

10. Dollar Times calculator, at http://www.dollartimes.com (accessed October 23, 2014).

11. Rosengren, *Hank Greenberg*, 316–17.

12. Borsvold, *Cleveland Indians*, 61; Rosengren, *Hank Greenberg*, 317.

13. Greenberg and Berkow, *Story of My Life*, 209.

14. Greenberg and Berkow, *Story of My Life*, 209.

15. Rosengren, *Hank Greenberg*, 327.

16. Rosengren, *Hank Greenberg*, 325–26.

17. Rosengren, *Hank Greenberg*, 326, 334.

18. Rosengren, *Hank Greenberg*, 333.

19. Borsvold, *Cleveland Indians*, 61.

20. Borsvold, *Cleveland Indians*, 62.

21. Greenberg and Berkow, *Story of My Life*, 211.

22. Greenberg and Berkow, *Story of My Life*, 231–32.

23. Greenberg and Berkow, *Story of My Life*, 209; Rosengren, *Hank Greenberg*, 328.

24. See, e.g., Rosengren, *Hank Greenberg*, 327, quoting Stephen Norwood and Harold Brackman.

25. Greenberg and Berkow, *Story of My Life*, 210.

26. Greenberg and Berkow, *Story of My Life*, 210.

27. Rosengren, *Hank Greenberg*, 327.

28. Borsvold, *Cleveland Indians*, 62.

29. Borsvold, *Cleveland Indians*, 61.

30. Jacobson, *Carrying Jackie's Torch*, 29.

31. Pluto, *Our Tribe*, 143.

32. Jacobson, *Carrying Jackie's Torch*, 29, quoting Larry Doby.

33. Jacobson, *Carrying Jackie's Torch*, 33.

34. Luke, *Most Famous Woman in Baseball*, 152.

35. See Pluto, *Our Tribe*, 165–66.

36. See, e.g., Singletary, *Al Lopez*, 148 ("the best rotation in history").

37. Borsvold, *Cleveland Indians*, 60.

38. Halberstam, *Summer of '49*, 79. The other three were Whitey Ford, Hoyt Wilhelm, and Eddie Lopat, all of whom pitched for the Yankees.

39. Allen, *You Could Look It Up*, 179.

40. Barra, *Yogi Berra*, 192.

41. Pluto, *Our Tribe*, 169.

42. Singletary, *Al Lopez*, 171.

43. Singletary, *Al Lopez*, 171.

44. Singletary, *Al Lopez*, 171. The top five ERAS in World Series history are Sandy Koufax, .95, 57 Innings Pitched (IP); Christy Mathewson, .97, 101.2 IP (New York Giants); Waite Hoyt, 1.83, 83.2 IP (New York Yankees); Bob Gibson, 1.89, 81 IP (St. Louis Cardinals); and Curt Schilling, 2.23, 133.1 IP (Philadelphia Phillies, Arizona Diamondbacks, and Boston Red Sox). A surprising sixth is Ken Holtzman, 2.30, 70.1 IP (Oakland Athletics). Graphic, NBC Television, 2014 World Series.

45. Pluto, *Our Tribe*, 171, quoting the late Al Rosen.

46. Pluto, *Our Tribe*, 172.

47. Singletary, *Al Lopez*, 98.

48. Singletary, *Al Lopez*, 104.

49. Singletary, *Al Lopez*, 109.

50. Singletary, *Al Lopez*, 110.

51. *Cleveland Call & Post*, November 5, 1955.

52. Singletary, *Al Lopez*, 113.

53. Moore, *Larry Doby*, 111, quoting Larry Doby.

54. Singletary, *Al Lopez*, 220.

55. Doc Young, "Inside Sports: Why Minoso and Doby Got Traded," *Jet*, December 19, 1957, quoted in Moore, *Larry Doby*, 111.

56. Moore, *Larry Doby*, 116.

57. Pluto, *Our Tribe*, 183.

58. See generally Pluto, *Our Tribe*, 180–82.

6. It Takes a Village

1. Cleveland actually had two, Luke Easter and Doby. Moore, *Larry Doby*, 92.

2. See, e.g., Moore, *Larry Doby*, 101 (table).

3. Colton, *Southern League*, 293, quoting Tom Yawkey.

4. Ribowsky, *Don't Look Back*, 42.

5. Ribowsky, *Don't Look Back*, 42–43.

6. Ribowsky, *Don't Look Back*, 43.

7. 163 U.S. 537, 548 (1896).

8. See generally L. P. Beth, "The White Primary and the Judicial Function in the United States," *Political Quarterly* 29, no. 4 (1958): 366.

9. 163 U.S. 537 (1896).

10. 163 U.S., 544.

11. See generally Hoffer, *"Plessy v. Ferguson" and Inequality in Jim Crow America*.

12. Smith v. Allright, 321 U.S. 649 (1942).

13. See, e.g., Purdum, *Idea Whose Time Has Come*; Risen, *Bill of the Century*. The year 2014 marked the fiftieth anniversary of the Civil Rights Act of 1964.

14. 347 U.S. 483 (1954).

15. Washington's autobiography, *Up From Slavery* (1901), is still widely read today.

16. Dickson, *Bill Veeck*, 31.

17. *New York Times*, February 6, 1933.

18. Lowenfish, *Branch Rickey*, 399–400.

19. *New York Daily News*, February 8, 1933.

20. Catherine Smith, "Tribute to: 'Fay' Young," *Chicago Defender*, November 14, 1953.

21. Dickson, *Bill Veeck*, 36–37.

22. See, e.g., Ribowsky, *Don't Look Back*, 117 (1934), 136 (1935), and 207 (1942). See also Dickson, *Bill Veeck*, 45.

23. Dickson, *Bill Veeck*, 50.

24. Westwood Pegler, *Pittsburgh Press*, August 4, 1938.

25. Tye, *Satchel*, 172.

26. Tye, *Satchel*, 86.

27. Pietrusza, *Judge and Jury*, 412–14; Dickson, *Bill Veeck*, 75. Besides prohibiting the use of Major League uniforms, in 1942 Landis discouraged Minor and Major League clubs from allowing use of their facilities for such events.

28. Dickson, *Bill Veeck*, 73.

29. Dickson, *Bill Veeck*, 73.

30. Bill Veeck interviews with Shirley Povich, *Washington Post*, May 10, 1953; February 6, 1960.

31. Dickson, *Bill Veeck*, 80.

32. Bill Veeck tells the story in his own words in Veeck and Linn, *Veeck as in Wreck*, 147.

33. See Wikipedia article at http://www.wikipedia.org/wiki/world_war_II-casualties -military (accessed February 22, 2014).

34. Fromer, *Rickey and Robinson*, 151.

35. See generally Pietrusza, *Judge and Jury*.

36. See, e.g., Bankes, *Pittsburgh Crawfords*, 124.

37. Eskenazi, *Lip*, 152.

38. Bankes, *Pittsburgh Crawfords*, 124.

39. Lowenfish, *Branch Rickey*, 358.

40. See, e.g., Eskenazi, *Lip*, 170–71: "[Leo] told a reporter that there was a 'gentleman's agreement' among the owners not to hire black ballplayers. This was too much for Judge Landis. He immediately called in Durocher and then issued a statement."

41. Quoted in Pietrusza, *Judge and Jury*, 418.

42. Butts Brown, "In the Grove," *New Jersey Herald News*, July 25, 1942, quoted in Moore, *Larry Doby*, 21. See also Stall, "Actor Robeson Makes Plea for Negro Players," *New York Journal American*, December 9, 1943.

43. Moore, *Larry Doby*, 21.

44. Rowan and Robinson, *Wait until Next Year*, 107.

45. Fromer, *Rickey and Robinson*, 104.

46. Much of this material comes from the account in Dickson, *Bill Veeck*, 89–93.

47. Dickson, *Bill Veeck*, 90.

48. See Dickson, *Bill Veeck*, 90.

49. Dickson, *Bill Veeck*, 92.

50. Tygiel, *Baseball's Greatest Experiment*, 69.

51. Polner, *Branch Rickey*, 171.

52. Lowenfish, *Branch Rickey*, 373, 379.

53. Fromer, *Rickey and Robinson*, 104.

54. Lowenfish, *Branch Rickey*, 396.

7. Shadow of Rickey and Robinson

1. Moore, *Larry Doby*, 167.

2. Joe Morgan as reported in Thomas Singer, "Larry Doby," Baseball.com, June 23, 2003. (Doby died on June 18, 2003.)

3. Ribowsky, *Don't Look Back*, 238.

4. See, e.g., Rosengren, *Hank Greenberg*, 328.

5. Ribowsky, *Don't Look Back*, 313.

6. See, e.g., "Negro Players on Opposing Sides," *Sporting News*, June 23, 1948, 16 (photograph of Doby and Robinson together).

7. Rampersad, *Jackie Robinson*, 217, 233, and 242. Arnold Rampersad is best known as the biographer of Langston Hughes, the African American literary great. See Rampersad, *The Life of Langston Hughes*, vol. 1, *1902–1941: I, Too, Sing America* (New York: Oxford University Press, 1986); and Rampersad, *The Life of Langston Hughes*, vol. 2, *1941–1976: I Dream a World* (New York: Oxford University Press, 1988). He has also authored biographies of other great African Americans, e.g., *The Art and Imagination of W. E. B. Du Bois* (New York: Schocken-Knopf-Doubleday, 1990); *Ralph Ellison: A Biography* (New York: Vintage, 2008), as well as works about other famous African American sports figures, e.g., Arthur Ashe and Arnold Rampersad, *Days of Grace: A Memoir* (New York: Ballantine Books, 1994).

8. Jackie Robinson, quoted by Rampersad, *Jackie Robinson*, 183; see also 203 (similar).

9. Bob Feller to biographer Sickels, *Bob Feller*, 171.

10. Ribowsky, *Don't Look Back*, 265.

11. Ribowsky, *Don't Look Back*, 265.

12. Hirsch, *Willie Mays*, 228.

13. Hirsch, *Willie Mays*, 228.

14. Robinson and Duckett, *I Never Had It Made*.

15. Quoted in Hirsch, *Willie Mays*, 229.

16. Hirsch, *Willie Mays*, 469.

17. Robinson and Duckett, *I Never Had It Made*.

18. Hirsch, *Willie Mays*, 469.

19. See, e.g., Leigh Montville, "Revolutionary Rookie," *Wall Street Journal*, September 20. 2014, C-8. "Robinson, the stoic black second baseman who confounded the bigots and triumphed"; no mention of either Bill Veeck or Larry Doby.

20. *They Were All Stars*, Negro Leagues Baseball Museum, Kansas City, Missouri, narrated by James Earl Jones (visited January 30, 2015).

21. Available online at Paper of Record, at http://www.paperofrecord.hypernet .ca/search.asp (accessed February 2015).

22. Games played available at Baseball Reference, at http://www.baseballreference .com under the respective players' names (accessed February 5, 2015).

23. "Jackie's Wife and Son in Brooklyn Home," *Sporting News*, July 19, 1947, 9.

24. Joan Crosby, "Mrs. Robinson . . . Roams Dodgers Stands, Listening to Fans Size Up Hubby," *Sporting News*, July 19, 1947, 18.

25. Bill Roeder, "22,372 Daily Saw Robinson Play in the West," *Sporting News*, June 4, 1947, 8.

26. See "Jackie Sings as He Plays; Del Ennis Hears a Lullaby," *Sporting News*, May 28, 1947 (Robinson played at first base in his initial Dodger season).

27. See, e.g., "Jackie Just Another Player to Us—with No Favors, Says Chapman: He Must Learn to Take It, Says Phillies Manager," *Sporting News*, May 7, 1947, 6.

28. "'Intentional' Says Stanky; 'Accident' Says Enos of His Spiking of Jackie," *Sporting News*, August 27, 1947, 4.

29. "Robinson Hit by Pitched Ball for the Third Time," *Sporting News*, May 21, 1947, 14; Watson Spoelstra, "Jackie Tops N.L. Players in Being Hit by Pitchers," *Sporting News*, July 9, 1947, 18.

30. "Varied Policies at Hotels Greet Robinson on Trip," *Sporting News*, May 21, 1947, 8.

31. "Jackie Gets Car, Video Set at Game Attended by 26,123," *Sporting News*, October 1, 1947, 11. See also A. Van Pelt, "50,000 fans Cheer Dodgers at Rally: Jackpot for a Pair of Jacks," *Sporting News*, October 8, 1947, 10.

32. "Agent Setting Up Sports and Stage Dates for Jackie," *Sporting News*, October 1, 1947, 34.

33. See Paul Gould, "Jackie Playing to Sellouts: May Net 5 Grand a Week," *Sporting News*, October 29, 1947, 17; "Jackie Robinson Stars [on barnstorming tour]," *Sporting News*, November 3, 1948.

34. See John B. "Old, Los Angeles Showers Robinson with Praise," *Sporting News*, December 24, 1947, 4.

35. "Jackie Robinson Defrosts Newport News Coolness," *Sporting News*, February 25, 1948, 21. See also "Newport News Stages Giant Reception for Jackie but Learns He Is on the Coast," *Sporting News*, January 14, 1948, 15.

36. "Rickey-Robinson Harmonizing Headlines Chicago Writers' Show," *Sporting News*, January 28, 1948, 9; Ed Burns, "Jackie Attends Banquet, Dodger Boss' Request," *Sporting News*, February 1948.

37. "Jackie Heavier as a Sophomore," *Sporting News*, March 24, 1948, 19.

38. Harold Burr, "Jackie Keeps on Jump in Off-Season but Sidesteps Fried Chicken Circuit," *Sporting News*, December 15, 1948, 17.

39. "Jackie to Broadcast Daily Sports Show in New York," *Sporting News*, October 6, 1948, 23. See also "Jackie Pumps Boss Rickey on Radio Program," *Sporting News*, December 1, 1948, 27.

40. Bromberg, "Doby Credits Study in Earning Steady Jog, a Dream Centerfielder," *Sporting News*, October 27, 1948, 5.

41. Oscar Ruhl, "Robinson to Race Doby," *Sporting News*, May 19, 1948, 30.

42. Povich, "Doby's Drives Resemble Babe's Big Blows—Mighty Wallops by Any Standard," *Sporting News*, June 8, 1949, 4.

43. Robinson himself played no part in it. Quite the contrary: when the Dodgers and the Indians played in an exhibition, news reports contain photographs of the two men together, laughing and talking. See, e.g., note 6 for this chapter.

8. The Second Shadow?

1. Leavy, *Last Boy*, 123.
2. Leavy, *Last Boy*, 123.
3. Hirsch, *Willie Mays*, 97.

4. See, e.g., "the Republicans have made a choice. . . . They will hold their [2016] convention in Cleveland," David M. Shribman, "The Choice of Cleveland," *Pittsburgh Post-Gazette*, July 20, 2014.

5. Veeck, *Hustler's Handbook*, 165.

6. Veeck, *Hustler's Handbook*, 165.

7. Veeck, *Hustler's Handbook*, 165.

8. Allen, *You Could Look It Up*, 154.

9. See Infoplease, http:///www.infoplease.com/ipsa/AO113222 (accessed July 30, 2014).

10. "Hall of Fame Welcomes Class of 2014," *Pittsburgh Post-Gazette*, July 28, 2014, D-3.

11. "New York Yankees," http://www.Wikipedia.com (accessed August 31, 2015).

12. One of Mark Hanna's best-known observations is, "There are two important things in politics: one is money, and I forget what the second one is."

13. See Grabowski and Grabowski, *Cleveland Then and Now*, 130. In his book *One Summer*, 303–4, Bill Bryson also recounts the Van Sweringtons' weird story.

14. In a 1938 stunt Cleveland Indians catchers Hank Helf and Frank Pytlak set what they termed the "all-time altitude mark" by catching baseballs dropped from the top of the 708-foot building. See Bruce Anderson, "When Baseballs Fell from on High, Henry Helf Rose to the Occasion," *Sports Illustrated*, March 11, 1985.

15. Grabowksi and Grabowski, *Cleveland Then and Now*, 10.

16. "Van Sweringen Brothers," http:/en.wikipedia.org/wiki/Van_Sweringen_brothers (accessed March 9, 2014).

17. The Van Sweringens' biography is told in Harwood, *Invisible Giants*.

18. "History of the Cleveland Browns," http://en.wikipedia.org/wiki/History_of_the_Cleveland_Browns (accessed August 25, 2014). See also Wendell Smith, "Smitty's Sports Spurts," *Pittsburgh Courier*, September 23, 1946, naming Cleveland professional football coach Paul Brown to his sports honor roll "for having signed two Negro players to play with his team in the All-American Hall Conference." Wendell Smith Papers.

19. See, e.g., Moore, *Larry Doby*, 76–77.

20. Grabowski and Grabowski, *Cleveland Then and Now*, 92.

21. Busta-Peck, *Hidden History of Cleveland*, 92–93.

22. Feagler, *Feagler's Cleveland*, 238.

23. Feagler, *Feagler's Cleveland*, 252.

24. Grabowski and Grabowski, *Cleveland Then and Now*, 47.

25. Nancy Keates, "Hotter in Cleveland," *Wall Street Journal*, August 29, 2014.

26. Busta-Peck, *Hidden History of Cleveland*, 90.

27. See generally Schneider, *Cleveland Indians Encyclopedia*, 319–25.

28. See, e.g., chapter 12 (Mantle) and chapter 14 (Mays).

29. See Doc Young, "Why Minoso and Larry Doby Got Traded: Larry Doby Says Lopez Affected Play with White Sox," *Jet*, December 19, 1957.

30. Rob Edelman, "*What's My Line?* and Baseball," *Baseball Research Journal* 43, no. 2 (Fall 2014): 36.

31. June 24, 1956. Edelman, "*What's My Line?* and Baseball," 38.

32. See generally Edelman, "*What's My Line?* and Baseball," 36–41.

9. Playing in the American League

Epigraph: Although Yawkey later was redeemed: at the urging of Rachel Robinson, the Yawkey Trust donated $3 million to the Jackie Robinson Foundation, which assists young individuals with college scholarship aid. See Budig, *Grasping the Ring II*, 2.

1. Hirsch, *Willie Mays*, 234. The Philadelphia Phillies were last in the American League.

2. Fromer, *Rickey and Robinson*, 102. Green made his Major League debut on July 21, 1959, followed by a second African American, pitcher Earl Wilson (July 28, 1959). See http://www.baseballreference.com/players/g/greenpuo1.shtml (accessed August 31, 2014).

3. Jacobson, *Carrying Jackie's Torch*, 7–8.

4. Jacobson, *Carrying Jackie's Torch*, 8.

5. Halberstam, *Summer of '49*, 206–7.

6. Hirsch, *Willie Mays*, 137.

7. Allen, *You Could Look It Up*, 171.

8. Halberstam, *Summer of '49*, 206.

9. Halberstam, *Summer of '49*, 206.

10. Reported in Fromer, *Rickey and Robinson*, 154.

11. See Fromer, *Rickey and Robinson*, 154. See also the award index at http://www.baseballreference.com/awards/roy_rol.shtml (accessed November 18, 2014).

12. See the award index at Baseballreference.com. Separate awards for each league began only in 1949.

13. Jacobson, *Carrying Jackie's Torch*, 8.

14. Rampersad, *Jackie Robinson*, 208.

15. Veeck and Linn, *Veeck as in Wreck*, 183; Moore, *Larry Doby*, 121.

16. Fromer, *Rickey and Robinson*, 181.

17. Lowenfish, *Branch Rickey*, 488.

18. Veeck, *Hustler's Handbook*, 179.

19. Hirsch, *Willie Mays*, 337.

20. See also Lowenfish, *Branch Rickey*, 429.

21. Fromer, *Rickey and Robinson*, 142.

22. Reported in Fromer, *Rickey and Robinson*, 121.

23. Barra, *Mickey and Willie*, 445.

24. Sickels, *Bob Feller*, 189, 191, and 239.

25. *New York Times*, August 5, 1955.

26. Moore, *Larry Doby*, 110.

27. Hirsch, *Willie Mays*, 5. The five tools are hitting for average, hitting for power, fielding, throwing, and base running.

28. *Time*, July 26, 1953.

29. Hirsch, *Willie Mays*, 179.

30. Hirsch, *Willie Mays*, 179.

31. Of the first fifteen African Americans to play in the Major League All-Star Game, fourteen were players from National League teams. Only one (Larry Doby) was from the American League (Doby was on the All-Star Star roster in 1949, 1950, 1951, 1952, 1953, 1954, and 1955). As Bill Veeck observes, "The National League is superior to the American League. . . . No one even bothers to argue this anymore except a few chronic searchers after lost causes—because the National League stocked up on Negro players while the American League was sitting back and admiring how nicely the Yankees were getting along without them." Veeck, *Hustlers Handbook*, 179.

32. See, e.g., Hirsch, *Willie Mays*, 431.

10. The Long Shadow of Paige

1. Tye, *Satchel*, 298; Ribowsky, *Don't Look Back*, 12.

2. Tye, *Satchel*, 64.

3. Tye, *Satchel*, 97.

4. Barra, *Mickey and Willie*, 168.

5. Paige had a second Major League stint 1951 through 1953, winning eighteen and losing twenty-three for the St. Louis Browns. He also made a token, gimmicky appearance for Kansas City in 1965, at the age of fifty-eight.

6. Tye, *Satchel*, 104.

7. Chester Washington, *Pittsburgh Courier*.

8. Tye, *Satchel*, 164.

9. Tye, *Satchel*, 151.

10. Tye, *Satchel*, 243.

11. Barra, *Mickey and Willie*, 85 (six feet four or six feet five, weighing "about 170 pounds").

12. Regarding the "Iron Lung," see Colton, *Southern League*, 110.

13. Even if he traveled long distance with the team, Paige parted company as soon as the team had arrived in the away city. "We used to get into a team bus waiting to take us to the hotel. Satch always had somebody there in a big shining Cadillac." Ribowsky, *Don't Look Back*, 265 (comment of Cleveland Indians player-manager Lou Boudreau).

14. Tye, *Satchel*, 154.

15. Ribowsky, *Don't Look Back*, 249.

16. See also Ribowsky, *Don't Look Back*, 13 (one hundred no hitters).

17. Ribowsky, *Don't Look Back*, 37, 249.

18. Tye, *Satchel*, 253.

19. Tye, *Satchel*, 262.

20. Dickson, *Bill Veeck*, 184, recounting Satchel Paige describing his "nothin' ball."

21. Tye, *Satchel*, 262.

22. Tye, *Satchel*, 147.

23. Veeck and Linn, *Veeck as in Wreck*, 45.

24. Tye, *Satchel*, 256.

25. Ribowsky, *Don't Look Back*, 24 (comment of Bill Veeck).

26. Tye, *Satchel*, 74.

27. Ribowsky, *Don't Look Back*, 298.

28. Tye, *Satchel*, 132.

29. Tye, *Satchel*, 49.

30. Ribowsky, *Don't Look Back*, 73.

31. Ribowsky, *Don't Look Back*, 99.

32. See Dunkel, *Color Blind*.

33. Ribowsky, *Don't Look Back*, 94–95, 87.

34. Tye, *Satchel*, 143.

35. Tye, *Satchel*, 145.

36. Tye, *Satchel*, 62.

37. Tye, *Satchel*, 90.

38. Tye, *Satchel*, 155.

39. Ribowsky, *Don't Look Back,* 198.

40. Tye, *Satchel*, 62.

41. Tye, *Satchel*, 66.

42. Tye, *Satchel*, 91.

43. Tye, *Satchel*, 216.

44. Doby to Charles Dexter, in Dexter, *Baseball Has Done It*, 61.

45. Doby as remembered by Indians catcher Jim Hegan, Moore, *Larry Doby*, 68.

46. Veeck moved the Indians' spring training from Florida to Tucson, Arizona, particularly so that Doby would have an easier time as he broke through the American League color barrier. Ribowsky, *Don't Look Back*, 265. It backfired: the Indians' hotel discriminated against Doby blatantly and for many years.

47. Moore, *Larry Doby*, 77.

48. Moore, *Larry Doby*, 77.

49. Ribowsky, *Don't Look Back*, 265 (Paige scared Doby off by keeping a loaded gun).

50. Moore, *Larry Doby*, 18.

51. Tye, *Satchel*, 216.

52. Tye, *Satchel*, 267 (comments of Indians teammate Steve Gromck).

53. Moore, *Larry Doby*, 168.

54. Moore, *Larry Doby*, 169.

55. Moore, *Larry Doby*, 169.

56. Moore, *Larry Doby*, 169.

57. Moore, *Larry Doby*, 172.

58. Moore, *Larry Doby*, 196–97.

59. Tye, *Satchel*, 209.

60. Tye, *Satchel*, 211.

61. Tye, *Satchel*, 177.

62. Tye, *Satchel*, 92.

63. Tye, *Satchel*, 97.

64. Tye, *Satchel*, 81.

65. Tye, *Satchel*, 89.

66. Tye, *Satchel*, 244.

67. Tye, *Satchel*, 253.

11. Should Paige Have Been First?

1. Lowenfish, *Branch Rickey*, 382.

2. Tye, *Satchel*, 207.

3. Tye, *Satchel*, 181.

4. Ribowsky, *Don't Look Back*, 232, 230.

5. Lowenfish, *Branch Rickey*, 102–6.

6. Fromer, *Rickey and Robinson*, 80.

7. Lowenfish, *Branch Rickey*, 94.

8. Bouton, *Ball Four*, 54.

9. See Bissinger, *Classic Mantle*, 16.

10. Barra, *Mickey and Willie*, 111.

11. Barra, *Mickey and Willie*, 141.

12. Ribowsky, *Don't Look Back*, 206.

13. Ribowsky, *Don't Look Back*, 206.

14. Ribowsky, *Don't Look Back*, 207.

15. See Measuring Worth, at http://www.measuringworth.com/uscompare (accessed March 16, 2015) ($1.7 million in economic status and $4.2 million in economic power).

16. Ribowsky, *Don't Look Back*, 208.

17. See, e.g., Ribowsky, *Don't Look Back*, 223, 253 (Paige-Feller barnstorming tour).

18. Ribowsky, *Don't Look Back*, 208.

19. Quoted in Ribowsky, *Don't Look Back*, 98.

20. See, e.g., Wendell Smith, "Paige Thumbs Nose at His Public Here—the 'Great Satchel' Loafs in the Dressing Room While 10,000 Wait for Him to Make Appearance—the Same Old Paige," *Pittsburgh Courier*, June 26, 1943.

21. Tye, *Satchel*, 301–2.

22. Ribowsky, *Don't Look Back*, 12.

23. Ribowsky, *Don't Look Back*, 14.

24. See Tye, *Satchel*, 301.

25. Ribowsky, *Don't Look Back*, 51.

26. Ribowsky, *Don't Look Back*, 39.

27. Ribowsky, *Don't Look Back*, 234.

28. Veeck and Linn, *Veeck as in Wreck*, 182.

29. Ribowsky, *Don't Look Back*, 269.

30. Ribowsky, *Don't Look Back*, 274.

31. See Ribowsky, *Don't Look Back*, 160.

32. Ribowsky, *Don't Look Back*, 268.

33. As told to Mark Ribowsky, in Ribowsky, *Don't Look Back*, 269.

34. Dickson, *Bill Veeck*, 228–33; Ribowsky, *Don't Look Back*, 316.

35. *Collier's*, June 13, 1953; Ribowsky, *Don't Look Back*, 301.

36. *Time*, July 19, 1948.

37. Ribowsky, *Don't Look Back*, 303.

38. Ribowsky, *Don't Look Back*, 123.

39. Ribowsky, *Don't Look Back*, 137.

40. Ribowsky, *Don't Look Back*, 280.

41. Ribowsky, *Don't Look Back*, 238.

12. The Mantle Shadow?

1. Barra, *Mickey and Willie*, 5, 91, 204.

2. Leavy, *Last Boy*, 72.

3. Leavy, *Last Boy*, 37.

4. Bissinger, *Classic Mantle*, 61, 94.

5. *New York Times*, March 1969.

6. Barra, *Mickey and Willie*, 7.

7. Leavy, *Last Boy*, 256.

8. Leavy, *Last Boy*, 94.

9. See generally Mantle et al., *Hero All His Life*.

10. Bissinger, *Classic Mantle*, 59.

11. Bissinger, *Classic Mantle*, 25.

12. Leavy, *Last Boy*, 64–67; Barra, *Mickey and Willie*, 93–94.

13. Leavy, *Last Boy*, 65.

14. Lowenfish, *Branch Rickey*, 577.

15. Lowenfish, *Branch Rickey*, 70.

16. Lowenfish, *Branch Rickey*, 13.

17. Barra, *Mickey and Willie*, 131.

18. Bissinger, *Classic Mantle*, 49.

19. Leavy, *Last Boy*, 11.

20. Barra, *Mickey and Willie*, 133–34.

21. Barra, *Mickey and Willie*, 9.

22. Leavy, *Last Boy*, xv.

23. Bissinger, *Classic Mantle*, 67.

24. Allen, *You Could Look It Up*, 145.

25. Leavy, *Last Boy*, 21–22.

26. Halberstam, *Summer of '49*, 5.

27. Barra, *Mickey and Willie*, 134.

28. Leavy, *Last Boy*, 240.

29. Barra, *Mickey and Willie*, 151.

30. Barra, *Mickey and Willie*, 253. Cf. the New York Giants in 1951 and rookie Willie Mays, discussed in chapter 14.

31. Bissinger, *Classic Mantle*, 28.

32. Bissinger, *Classic Mantle*, 39; *New York Times*, April 1951.

33. Barra, *Mickey and Willie*, 129.

34. Leavy, *Last Boy*, 21.

35. Barra, *Mickey and Willie*, 119.

36. Barra, *Mickey and Willie*, 135.

37. Barra, *Mickey and Willie*, 93.

38. Barra, *Mickey and Willie*, 164.

39. Merlyn Mantle to Jane Leavy, in Leavy, *Last Boy*, 80.

40. Leavy, *Last Boy*, 80.

41. Barra, *Mickey and Willie*, 133.

42. Barra, *Mickey and Willie*, 142.

43. Hirsch, *Willie Mays*, 144.

44. Bissinger, *Classic Mantle*, 23–24.

45. Barra, *Mickey and Willie*, 197.

46. Leavy, *Last Boy*, 19.

47. Leavy, *Last Boy*, 15.

48. Leavy, *Last Boy*, 58.

49. Barra, *Mickey and Willie*, 195.

50. Leavy, *Last Boy*, 115.

51. Barra, *Mickey and Willie*, 139.

52. Barra, *Mickey and Willie*, 37.

53. Bissinger, *Classic Mantle*, 10.

54. See, e.g., Allen, *You Could Look It Up*, 183–84.

55. *New York Journal American*, May 16, 1957.

56. Leavy, *Last Boy*, 172.

57. Leavy, *Last Boy*, 169.

58. See, e.g., Bouton, *Ball Four*, 29–31.

59. Bouton, *Ball Four*, xx.

60. Bissinger, *Classic Mantle*, 107.

61. See generally Leavy, *Last Boy*, 341.

62. Leavy, *Last Boy*, 294.

63. Leavy, *Last Boy*, 326.

13. The Mantle Legend

1. Leavy, *Last Boy*, 59; Barra, *Mickey and Willie*, 194.

2. Bissinger, *Classic Mantle*, 49.

3. Bissinger, *Classic Mantle*, 49.

4. Tyler Kepner, "500 a Reminder of How Good Pujols Is," *Pittsburgh Post-Gazette*, April 27, 2014, c-3.

5. Leavy, *Last Boy*, 88.

6. Joe Trimble, *New York Daily News*, April 11, 1953; Leavy, *Last Boy*, 88.

7. Barra, *Mickey and Willie*, 9.

8. Leavy, *Last Boy*, 99. sabr researchers fixed the distance as between 500 and 520 feet. Barra, *Mickey and Willie*, 192.

9. Leavy, *Last Boy*, 153.

10. *New York Times*, April 4, 1953; Leavy, *Last Boy*, 254.

11. Leavy, *Last Boy*, 155.

12. Leavy, *Last Boy*, 83, 149.

13. Leavy, *Last Boy*, 150.

14. Leavy, *Last Boy*, 251.

15. Moore, *Larry Doby*, 75.

16. Leavy, *Last Boy*, 62.

17. Leavy, *Last Boy*, 152.

18. Leavy, *Last Boy*, 116.

19. Leavy, *Last Boy*, 106.

20. See, e.g., "Meniscal Tears," in *Mayo Clinic Family Health Book*, 2nd ed. (1996), 876–78. Today, of course, the surgery is performed as an arthroscopic rather than open knee procedure and is therefore less intrusive.

21. Leavy, *Last Boy*, 107.

22. Leavy, *Last Boy*, 107.

23. Leavy, *Last Boy*, 109.

24. Barra, *Mickey and Willie*, 7.

25. Barra, *Mickey and Willie*, 174.

26. Barra, *Mickey and Willie*, 285.

27. Bissinger, *Classic Mantle*, 13.

28. Bissinger, *Classic Mantle*, 61.

29. Leavy, *Last Boy*, 288–89.

30. Barra, *Mickey and Willie*, 309.

31. Barra, *Mickey and Willie*, 248.

32. Barra, *Mickey and Willie*, 214.

33. Barra, *Mickey and Willie*, 285.

34. Leavy, *Last Boy*, 221.

35. Leavy, *Last Boy*, 224.

36. Leavy, *Last Boy*, 222.

37. Bissinger, *Classic Mantle*, 37.

38. Leavy, *Last Boy*, 223.

39. Leavy, *Last Boy*, 234.

40. Leavy, *Last Boy*, 227.

41. Barra, *Mickey and Willie*, 294.

42. Bissinger, *Classic Mantle*, 37.

43. Leavy, *Last Boy*, 197.

44. Yankee teammate Stan Williams to Jane Leavy, in Leavy, *Last Boy*, 241.

45. All quotations from Leavy, *Last Boy*, 239.

46. Leavy, *Last Boy*, 187.

47. Leavy, *Last Boy*, 238.

48. See, e.g., Leavy, *Last Boy*, 247.

49. Hirsch, *Willie Mays*, 139.

50. Leavy, *Last Boy*, xiv.

51. Leavy, *Last Boy*, 316.

14. Mays and "The Catch"

1. Hirsch, *Willie Mays*, 47.

2. Recounted in Eskenazi, *Lip*, 266; Hirsch, *Willie Mays*, 179.

3. Reported in Budig, *Swinging for the Fences*, 96.

4. Hano, *Day in the Bleachers*.

5. Barra, *Mickey and Willie*, 9.

6. See, e.g., Barra, *Mickey and Willie*, 263 (in 1958 Giants fans voted Orlando Cepeda team MVP even though Mays outhit Cepeda, .327 with 29 HR versus .312 with 25 HR).

7. See Hirsch, *Willie Mays*, 315.

8. Hirsch, *Willie Mays*, 258.

9. See, e.g., Barra, *Mickey and Willie*, 17.

10. Hirsch, *Willie Mays*, 469.

11. Hirsch, *Willie Mays*, 6.

12. See Hirsch, *Willie Mays*, 302: "Mays's team in 1955 might have been the finest club in baseball history. It had four future Hall of Famers—just in the outfield! Henry Aaron, Larry Doby, Monte Irvin and Mays divided the playing time; future Hall of Famers Roy Campanella and Ernie Banks were at catcher and shortstop. Former rookies of the year Junior Gilliam and Joe Black played [second] and pitched; the best pitcher was Don Newcombe."

13. See, e.g., Dickson, *Bill Veeck*, 173; Hirsch, *Willie Mays*, 146; Veeck and Linn, *Veeck as in Wreck*, 175; Veeck, *Hustler's Handbook*, 79.

14. Fromer, *Rickey and Robinson*, 125.

15. Hirsch, *Willie Mays*, 146.

16. Hirsch, *Willie Mays*, 146.

17. Hirsch, *Willie Mays*, 390.

18. Hirsch, *Willie Mays*, 65.

19. *Pittsburgh Courier* (1951).

20. Barra, *Mickey and Willie*, 126.

21. Barra, *Mickey and Willie*, 122.

22. Recounted in Eskenazi, *Lip*, 249.

23. Hirsch, *Willie Mays*, 13.

24. Hirsch, *Willie Mays*, 31.

25. Recounted in Hirsch, *Willie Mays*, 46.

26. Hirsch, *Willie Mays*, 16.

27. Barra, *Mickey and Willie*, 151.

28. Hirsch, *Willie Mays*, 119.

29. Eskenazi, *Lip*, 249.

30. Eskenazi, *Lip*, 249.

31. Eskenazi, *Lip*, 19.

32. Barra, *Mickey and Willie*, 122.

33. Quoted in Hirsch, *Willie Mays*, 105.

34. Hirsch, *Willie Mays*, 105.

35. Eskenazi, *Lip*, 224.

36. Barra, *Mickey and Willie*, 9.

37. Hirsch, *Willie Mays*, 102.

38. Hirsch, *Willie Mays*, 110.

39. Hirsch, *Willie Mays*, 12.

40. Hirsch, *Willie Mays*, 121.

41. Quoted in Hirsch, *Willie Mays*, 112.

42. Quoted in Hirsch, *Willie Mays*, 113.

43. Quoted in Hirsch, *Willie Mays*, 91.

44. Hirsch, *Willie Mays*, 111.

45. Barra, *Mickey and Willie*, 155.

46. Barra, *Mickey and Willie*, 169.

47. Recounted in Eskenazi, *Lip*, 250.

48. Barra, *Mickey and Willie*, 423.

49. Hirsch, *Willie Mays*, 111.

50. Hirsch, *Willie Mays*, 120.

51. Hirsch, *Willie Mays*, 120.

52. Hirsch, *Willie Mays*, 121.

53. Barra, *Mickey and Willie*, 113.

54. Barra, *Mickey and Willie*, 167.

55. Barra, *Mickey and Willie*, 132.

56. Barra, *Mickey and Willie*, 155.

57. Barra, *Mickey and Willie*, 214.

58. Hano, *Day in the Bleachers*, 116.

59. Hano, *Day in the Bleachers*, 116.

60. Hano, *Day in the Bleachers*, 121.

61. Hano, *Day in the Bleachers*, 119.

62. Hano, *Day in the Bleachers*, 124; Hirsch, *Willie Mays*, 193.

63. Hano, *Day in the Bleachers*, 123.

64. Hirsch, *Willie Mays*, 204.

65. Hirsch, *Willie Mays*, 205.

66. Barra, *Mickey and Willie*, 415.

67. Barra, *Mickey and Willie*, 212.

68. Hano, *Day in the Bleachers*, 122.

69. Sickels, *Bob Feller*, 239.

70. Moore, *Larry Doby*, 102. See also Sickels, *Bob Feller*, 239 (Bob Feller pointed out a catch by Doby that Feller thought was a "superior play" when compared to Mays's famous catch).

71. Eskenazi, *Lip*, 276–77.

72. Hirsch, *Willie Mays*, 204.

73. Barra, *Mickey and Willie*, 260.

74. Barra, *Mickey and Willie*, 264.

75. Hirsch, *Willie Mays*, 274.

76. Prescott Sullivan in the *San Francisco Examiner*, Summer 1958, recounted in Hirsch, *Willie Mays*, 293.

77. Bud Spencer, in the *San Francisco News* (1958).

78. *Sports Illustrated*, September 26, 1960, quoted in Hirsch, *Willie Mays*, 327.

79. Willie Mays, quoted in Hirsch, *Willie Mays*, 293.

80. Einstein, *Willie's Time*, 12.

81. Barra, *Mickey and Willie*, 204.

82. Barra, *Mickey and Willie*, 230.

83. Bouton, *Ball Four*, 22.

84. See Hirsch, *Willie Mays*, 5.

85. Hano, *Day in the Bleachers*, 116.

15. Robinson, Doby, and the Media

1. Daniel Henninger, "Where Have You Gone, Derek Jeter?," *Wall Street Journal*, September 25, 2014, A-19.

2. Franklin Lewis, *Cleveland Press*, October 26, 1955.

3. See, e.g., Boudreau and Schneider, *Lou Boudreau*, 97; Freedman, *Early Wynn*, 62; Sickels, *Bob Feller*, 172 (Boudreau), 234–30 (Bob Feller).

4. Bouton, *Ball Four*, 40.

5. Lowenfish, *Branch Rickey*, 368; Fromer, *Rickey and Robinson*, 125 (Robinson at first base).

6. Consider, for example, Andy Carey's fielding statistics: in 1954, 120 games, 15 errors, .967; in 1955, 135 games, 22 errors .954; in 1956, 131 games, 21 errors, .948; and in 1957, 81 games, 5 errors, .977.

7. Bill White, *Uppity: My Untold Story about the Games People Play* (New York: Grand Central, 2011), 123.

8. Moore, *Larry Doby*, 177.

9. Easter had played briefly in 1949, registering forty-five at-bats in twenty-one games played.

10. Moore, *Larry Doby*, 92.

11. Moore, *Larry Doby*, 92.

12. Interview with the late Al Rosen, in Moore, *Larry Doby*, 92.

13. Moore, *Larry Doby*, 92.

14. Fromer, *Rickey and Robinson*, 160.

15. Lowenfish, *Branch Rickey*, 466.

16. Fromer, *Rickey and Robinson*, 177.

17. Moore, *Larry Doby*, 172.

18. Fromer, *Rickey and Robinson*, 177.

19. Fromer, *Rickey and Robinson*, 161.

20. These and other facts are gleaned from the Wendell Smith Papers (visited September 18, 19, and 20, 2014).

21. See, e.g., letters dated December 19, 1945; January 14, 1946; July 27, 1946; November 27, 1946; February 4, 1947; June 3, 1948; and July 5, 1949, on file at the National Baseball Hall of Fame Library.

22. Letter from Wendell Smith to Branch Rickey, dated December 19, 1945, Wendell Smith Papers.

23. See, e.g., Tim Weir, "Smith: A Baseball Pioneer Worthy of Honor," *USA Today*, February 7, 1994 ("the most important roommate Jackie Robinson ever had").

24. Wendell Smith, Sports Beat, *Pittsburgh Courier*, August 1, 1950.

25. Wendell Smith, Sports Beat, *Pittsburgh Courier*, February 3, 1951. The players and their salaries were Jackie Robinson, $35,000; Larry Doby, $28,000; Roy Campanella, $20,000; Don Newcombe, $18,000; Luke Easter, $15,000; Sam Jethroe, $15,000; and Monte Irvin, $12,000.

26. Wendell Smith, Sports Beat, May 24, 1947.

27. Jerome Holtzman, "Wendell Smith—A Pioneer for Black Athletes," *Chicago Tribune*, June 22, 1974.

28. Dickson, *Bill Veeck*, 339.

29. Henninger, "Where Have You Gone?"

30. Greenberg and Berkow, *Story of My Life*, 205.

31. Bernard Kahn, sports editor, *Daytona Beach Evening News*, quoted in Rosengren, *Hank Greenberg*, 336.

32. Dickson, *Bill Veeck*, 162.

33. Dickson, *Bill Veeck*, 159.

34. Dickson, *Bill Veeck*, 157.

35. Moore, *Larry Doby*, 167.

36. Bill White, quoted in Moore, *Larry Doby*, 185.

37. Interview with Ken Singleton, August 9, 1980, in Moore, *Larry Doby*, 133.

38. Boudreau and Schneider, *Lou Boudreau*, 97.

16. Doby's Later Years

1. Freedman, *Early Wynn*, 71.

2. Bill Veeck to the Chicago press, as reported in Moore, *Larry Doby*, 119.

3. Moore, *Larry Doby*, 120.

4. See, e.g., "Sox Buy Hotel to End Race Ban," *Chicago American*, November 9, 1961 (the Sarasota Terrace Hotel next to the facility where the Sox had moved their training).

5. Moore, *Larry Doby*, 123.

6. Neff et al., *New Sports Encyclopedia*, 477–78.

7. Even opponents sought Doby's instruction. Dusty Baker, then an outfielder with the Atlanta Braves, would visit with Doby after Atlanta-Montreal games, seeking advice about hitting. See, e.g., Moore, *Larry Doby*, 133.

8. Moore, *Larry Doby*, 132.

9. Jacobson, *Carrying Jackie's Torch*, 35.

10. Budig, *Swinging for the Fences*, 91.

11. Budig, *Swinging for the Fences*, 90.

12. Budig, *Swinging for the Fences*, 92.

13. *Cleveland Plain Dealer*, October 3, 1974.

14. Budig, *Swinging for the Fences*, 92.

15. Jacobson, *Carrying Jackie's Torch*, 37.

16. Robinson and Anderson, *Frank*, 11.

17. Robinson and Anderson, *Frank*, 11.

18. Robinson and Anderson, *Frank*, 11.

19. Moore, *Larry Doby*, 140.

20. Moore, *Larry Doby*, 140.

21. Moore, *Larry Doby*, 140.

22. Moore, *Larry Doby*, 142.

23. Jacobson, *Carrying Jackie's Torch*, 47.

24. See, e.g., Jean Hollands, *Same Game, Different Rules: How to Get Ahead without Being a Bully Broad, Ice Queen, or "Ms. Understood"* (New York: McGraw Hill, 2002), 163–64.

25. Carol A. Gallagher and Susan K. Golant, *Going to the Top: The New Road Map for Success from America's Leading Women Executives* (New York: Penguin Books, 2000), 109.

26. Moore, *Larry Doby*, 147.

27. See generally Helyar, *Lords of the Realm*.

28. Moore, *Larry Doby*, 151.

29. Moore, *Larry Doby*, 151. It is interesting that many of the players who not only refused any notion of a boycott but also welcomed the first black players (Robinson and Doby) were from California, where more-enlightened attitudes prevailed. They included Ted Williams (hometown, San Diego), Bob Lemon (Long Beach), Duke Snider (Compton, near Los Angeles), Dom DiMaggio (San Francisco), and several others.

30. *Chicago Tribune*, July 1, 1978.

31. *Chicago Tribune*, August 17, 1978.

32. *Chicago Tribune*, August 20, 1978.

33. Moore, *Larry Doby*, 159; *Chicago Tribune*, October 20, 1978.

34. See Budig, *Grasping the Ring*, 11.

35. Budig, *Grasping the Ring*, 13.

36. Budig, *Grasping the Ring*, 11.

37. Budig, *Grasping the Ring*, 11.

38. Moore, *Larry Doby*, quotation on the book's cover.

39. Budig, *Grasping the Ring*, 13.

40. Budig, *Grasping the Ring*, 13.

41. Budig, *Grasping the Ring*, 13.

42. *New York Times*, April 4, 1998.

43. Transcript on file with the author.

44. Budig, *Grasping the Ring*, 17.

17. Doby, Robinson, and Racism

1. Singletary, *Al Lopez*, 214.

2. Robert W. Creamer, *Stengel: His Life and Times* (New York: Simon & Schuster, 1984), 282.

3. Fromer, *Rickey and Robinson*, 30.

4. Lowenfish, *Branch Rickey*, 356.

5. Smith, *Red Smith on Baseball*, 15.

6. For a detailed account, in Robinson's own words, see Robinson and Duckett, *I Never Had It Made*, 18–23.

7. Lowenfish, *Branch Rickey*, 368.

8. Lowenfish, *Branch Rickey*, 375–76.

9. Fromer, *Rickey and Robinson*, 15.

10. Fromer, *Rickey and Robinson*, 177.

11. Moore, *Larry Doby*, 26, 60.

12. Dickson, *Bill Veeck*, 128.

13. Lowenfish, *Branch Rickey*, 404.

14. Rowan and Robinson, *Wait until Next Year*, 170.

15. Lowenfish, *Branch Rickey*, 403.

16. *New Jersey Afro-American*, December 28, 1946.

17. Moore, *Larry Doby*, 47.

18. Doc Young, *Cleveland Call & Post*, October 18, 1947.

19. Moore, *Larry Doby*, 84.

20. Lowenfish, *Branch Rickey*, 419.

21. Fromer, *Rickey and Robinson*, 127.

22. Lowenfish, *Branch Rickey*, 351.

23. Fromer, *Rickey and Robinson*, 137.

24. Fromer, *Rickey and Robinson*, 144.

25. Fromer, *Rickey and Robinson*, 146.

26. Lowenfish, *Branch Rickey*, 430.

27. Moore, *Larry Doby*, 72.

28. Moore, *Larry Doby*, 48.

29. Boudreau and Schneider, *Lou Boudreau*, 96.

30. Moore, *Larry Doby*, 82.

31. Moore, *Larry Doby*, 4.

32. Freedman, *Early Wynn*, 62.

33. Freedman, *Early Wynn*, 33.

34. Moore, *Larry Doby*, 88.

35. Moore, *Larry Doby*, 88.

36. Lowenfish, *Branch Rickey*, 431.

37. Moore, *Larry Doby*, 92.

38. Hirsch, *Willie Mays*, 146.

39. Fromer, *Rickey and Robinson*, 123; Robinson and Duckett, *I Never Had It Made*, 52.

40. Lowenfish, *Branch Rickey*, 422–25.

41. See Durocher and Linn, *Nice Guys Finish Last*. See also Durocher, *Dodgers and Me*.

42. Lowenfish, *Branch Rickey*, 502.

43. See, e.g., Lowenfish, *Branch Rickey*, 150.

44. Boudreau and Schneider, *Lou Boudreau*, 95.

45. Boudreau and Schneider, *Lou Boudreau*, 96.

46. Boudreau and Schneider, *Lou Boudreau*, 96

47. Boudreau and Schneider, *Lou Boudreau*, 96

48. Boudreau and Schneider, *Lou Boudreau*, 108.

49. Boudreau and Schneider, *Lou Boudreau*, 144.

50. Boudreau and Schneider, *Lou Boudreau*, 149.

51. Boudreau and Schneider, *Lou Boudreau*, 127.

52. Moore, *Larry Doby*, 50.

53. Goldman, *Forging Genius*, 118.

54. Allen, *You Could Look It Up*, 277.

55. Allen, *You Could Look It Up*, 172.

56. Allen, *You Could Look It Up*, 171.

57. Allen, *You Could Look It Up*, 173.

58. Allen, *You Could Look It Up*, 173.

59. Singletary, *Al Lopez*, 218.

60. Allen, *You Could Look It Up*, 109 &, 169.

61. Singletary, *Al Lopez*, 214.

62. David Halberstam, *October 1964* (New York: Villard Books, 1994), 110.

63. Singletary, *Al Lopez*, 214: "Solly Hemus, the abusive, driven manager of the St. Louis Cardinals from 1959 to 1961, was labeled a racist by two of his players, Bob Gibson and Curt Flood."

64. Doc Young, "Why Minoso and Doby Got Traded: Larry Doby Says Lopez Affected Play with White Sox," *Jet*, December 19, 1957.

65. See, e.g., Singletary *Al Lopez*, 222.

66. Singletary, *Al Lopez*, 223.

67. Paul Dickson, introduction to Moore, *Larry Doby*, x.

68. Dickson, *Bill Veeck*, 131.

69. Dickson, *Bill Veeck*, 339.

70. Moore, *Larry Doby*, x.

71. Moore, *Larry Doby*, x–xi.

72. Singletary, *Al Lopez*, 216.

73. Singletary, *Al Lopez*, 218.

74. Singletary, *Al Lopez*, 218.

75. Moore, *Larry Doby*, 104.

76. Singletary, *Al Lopez*, 226.

77. *Cleveland Plain Dealer*, October 26, 1955.

78. Singletary, *Al Lopez*, 176.

79. Freedman, *Early Wynn*, 73 (quoting pitcher Early Wynn).

80. Freedman, *Early Wynn*, 73.

81. Moore, *Larry Doby*, 118.

82. Peary, *We Played the Game*, 379.

83. Singletary, *Al Lopez*, 220.

84. Goldman, *Forging Genius*, 195.

85. Moore, *Larry Doby*, x.

86. Moore, *Larry Doby*, xi.

18. A Seldom-Remembered Pioneer

1. Coverdale, *Whitey Ford*, 32; see also 34, 56, and 61 (memorable Doby home runs off Ford).

2. Barra, *Mickey and Willie*, 184.

3. Barra, *Mickey and Willie*, 184.

4. Feller and Gilbert, *Now Pitching, Bob Feller*, 16 (along with Joe DiMaggio, Ted Williams, Hank Greenberg, and Jimmy Foxx).

5. Leavy, *Last Boy*, 134.

6. Hirsch, *Willie Mays*, 111.

7. Although Hirsch rates Mays 1955 barnstorming team as possibly "the finest club in baseball history. It had four future Hall of Famers—just in the outfield! Henry Aaron, Larry Doby, Monte Irvin and Mays divided the playing time," Hirsch, *Willie Mays*, 302.

8. Halberstam, *Summer of '49*, 165–66.

9. Winchester, *Men Who United the States*, 412.

10. Winchester, *Men Who United the States*, 13.

11. Winchester, *Men Who United the States*, 165.

12. Halberstam, *Boys of Summer*, 165.

13. The first game of the 1949 World Series (Yankees versus Dodgers) has been thought to be the first game to reach a television audience of 10 million. Arguably, the biggest attraction of that first game was the starting pitcher for the Brooklyn Dodgers, Don Newcombe, who was also black, had been named Rookie of the Year for 1949, stood six feet five, and was crafty and mean, at least when on the pitching mound. Halberstam, *Summer of '49*, 286. From the earliest days as teammates on the Newark Eagles to playing together in Japan and Doby's selection for the

National Hall of Fame, Newcombe and Doby were the closest of friends. See, e.g., Moore, *Larry Doby*, 122, 169–71, and 173–74.

14. Winchester, *Men Who United the States*, 415.

15. Quoted in Leavy, *Last Boy*, 136.

16. Lowenfish, *Branch Rickey*, 467.

17. Moore, *Larry Doby*, 121.

18. See, e.g., Budig, *Grasping the Ring*, 14–15.

19. Quoted in Jacobson, *Carrying Jackie's Torch*, 37.

20. Fay Vincent, "Larry Doby Played with Dignity and without Bitterness," *New York Times*, June 22, 2003.

21. Halberstam, *Summer of '49*, 302.

Postscript

1. Lewis, *Moneyball*.

2. See generally James, *Bill James Handbook 2015*; James, *Solid Fools Gold*.

3. See, e.g., Lewis, *Moneyball*, 86.

4. "Only two [baseball statistics] . . . are inextricably linked to baseball success; on-base percentage and slugging percentage. Everything else [is] far less important." Lewis, *Moneyball*, 127, quoting Paul DePodesta.

5. Lewis, *Moneyball*, 38.

6. Lewis, *Moneyball*, 3.

7. Quoted in Lewis, *Moneyball*, 58.

8. Lewis, *Moneyball*, 90.

9. "The pitcher's plate shall be 10 inches above the level of home plate." Major League Baseball Official Rules, Rule 1.04, available at http://www.mlb.com/mlb/downloads/2014/official_baseball-rules (accessed February 18, 2015).

10. Bryson, *One Summer*, 219.

Bibliography

Allen, Maury. *You Could Look It Up: The Life of Casey Stengel.* New York: Times Books, 1979.

Anderson, Donald R. *Branch Rickey and the St. Louis Cardinal Farm System: The Growth of an Idea.* Madison: University of Wisconsin–Madison, 1985.

Bankes, Joseph. *The Pittsburgh Crawfords.* Jefferson NC: McFarland, 2001.

Barra, Allen. *Mickey and Willie: Mantle and Mays, the Parallel Lives of Baseball's Golden Age.* New York: Crown, 2013.

———. *Yogi Berra—Eternal Yankee.* New York: Norton, 2009.

Berkow, Ira. *Hank Greenberg: Hall of Fame Slugger.* Philadelphia: Jewish Publication Society, 1991.

Bissinger, Buzz. *The Classic Mantle.* New York: Stewart, Tabori & Chang, 2010.

Borsvold, David. *Cleveland Indians: The Cleveland Press Years, 1920–1982.* Charleston SC: Arcadia, 2003.

Boudreau, Lou, with Russell Schneider. *Lou Boudreau: Covering All the Bases.* Champaign IL: Sagamore, 1993.

Bouton, Jim. *Ball Four: My Life and Hard Times Throwing the Knuckle Ball in the Big Leagues.* Cleveland OH: World, 1970.

Boyer, Mary S. *The Good, the Bad, and the Ugly: The Cleveland Indians.* Chicago: Triumph Books, 2008.

Bryson, Bill. *One Summer: America, 1927.* New York: Doubleday, 2014.

Budig, Gene A. *Grasping the Ring: Nine Unique Winners in Life and Sports.* Lincoln: University of Nebraska Press, 2008.

———. *Grasping the Ring II: Nine People Who Matter.* Lincoln NE: Bison Books, 2010.

———. *Swinging for the Fences: Nine Who Did It with Grit and Class.* Lincoln: University of Nebraska Press, 2012.

Burk, Robert F. *Marvin Miller, Baseball Revolutionary.* Champaign: University of Illinois Press, 2015.

Busta-Peck, Christopher. *Hidden History of Cleveland.* Charleston SC: History Press, 2011.

Campanella, Roy. *It's Good to Be Alive.* Lincoln: University of Nebraska Press, 1959.

Colton, Larry. *Southern League: A True Story of Baseball, Civil Rights, and the Deep South's Most Compelling Pennant Race.* New York: Grand Central, 2013.

Coverdale, Miles, Jr. *Whitey Ford: A Biography.* Jefferson NC: McFarland, 2006.

Crowe, Chris. *Just as Good: How Larry Doby Changed America's Game.* Illustrated by Mike Benny. Sommerville MA: Candlewick, 2012.

Dexter, Charles, ed. *Baseball Has Done It.* New York: Lippincott, 1964.

Dickson, Paul. *Bill Veeck: Baseball's Greatest Maverick.* New York: Bloomsbury, 2012.

Dunkel, Tom. *Color Blind: The Forgotten Team That Broke Baseball's Color Line.* 2013. Reprint, New York: Grove Press, 2014.

Durocher, Leo. *The Dodgers and Me: The Inside Story.* Chicago: Ziff-Davis, 1948.

Durocher, Leo, with Ed Linn. *Nice Guys Finish Last.* New York: Simon & Schuster, 1975.

Einstein, Charles. *Willie's Time: A Memoir.* New York: Penguin, 1992.

Eskenazi, Gerald. *The Lip: A Biography of Leo Durocher.* New York: William Morrow, 1993.

Falkner, David. *Great Time Coming: Jackie Robinson from Baseball to Birmingham.* New York: Simon & Schuster, 1993.

———. *The Last Yankee: The Turbulent Life of Billy Martin.* New York: Simon & Schuster, 1992.

Feagler, Dick. *Feagler's Cleveland: The Best from Three Decades of Commentary by Cleveland's Top Columnist.* Cleveland OH: Gray, 1968.

Feller, Robert, with Bill Gilbert. *Now Pitching, Bob Feller: A Baseball Memoir.* Birch Lane Press, 1990.

Fountain, Charles. *Under the March Sky: The Story of Spring Training.* New York: Oxford University Press, 2009.

Freedman, Lew. *Early Wynn, the Go-Go White Sox, and the 1959 World Series.* Jefferson NC: McFarland, 2007.

Fromer, Harry. *Rickey and Robinson: The Men Who Broke Baseball's Color Barrier.* New York: Taylor Trade, 1982.

Goldman, Steven. *Forging Genius: The Making of Casey Stengel.* Washington DC: Potomac Books, 2005.

Golenbock, Peter. *Wild, High and Tight: The Life and Death of Billy Martin.* New York: St. Martin's Press, 1994.

Grabowski, John J., and Diane E. Grabowski. *Cleveland Then and Now.* San Diego: Thunder Bay Press, 2002.

Greenberg, Hank, with Ira Berkow. *The Story of My Life.* Chicago: Ivan R. Dee, 1989.

Halberstam, David. *Summer of '49.* New York: HarperCollins Perennial Classics, 1989.

Hano, Arnold. *A Day in the Bleachers.* New York: Thomas Growell, 1955.

Harwood, Herbert H., Jr. *Invisible Giants: The Empires of Cleveland's Van Sweringen Brothers.* Bloomington: Indiana University Press, 2003.

Helyar, John. *The Lords of the Realm: The Real History of Baseball.* New York: Random House, 1994.

Hirsch, James. *Willie Mays: The Life, the Legend.* New York: Scribner, 2010.

Hoffer, William J. H. *"Plessy v. Ferguson" and Inequality in Jim Crow America*. Lawrence: University of Kansas Press, 2000.

Jacobson, Steve. *Carrying Jackie's Torch: The Players Who Integrated Baseball—and America*. Chicago: Lawrence Hill Books, 2007.

James, Bill. *The Bill James Handbook 2015*. Chicago: ACTA Sports, 2014.

———. *Fools Rush In: More Detours on the Way to Conventional Wisdom*. Chicago: ACTA Sports, 2014.

———. *Solid Fools' Gold: Detours on the Road to Conventional Wisdom*. Chicago: ACTA Sports 2011.

Kahn, Roger. *The Boys of Summer*. Reissue ed. New York: Harper Perennial Modern Classics, 2006.

———. *Rickey and Robinson: The True, Untold Story of the Integration of Baseball*. Emmanus PA: Rodale Books, 2014.

Kahn, Roger, with Red Barber, *The Jackie Robinson Reader: Perspectives on an American Hero*. New York: Plume, 1998.

Kiner, Ralph, with Danny Peary. *Baseball Forever: Reflections on Sixty Years in the Game*. Chicago: Triumph Books, 2004.

Kirwin, William. *Out of the Shadows: African American Baseball from the Cuban Giants to Jackie Robinson*. Lincoln NE: Bison Books, 2005.

Lamb, Chris. *Blackout: The Untold Story of Jackie Robinson's First Spring Training*. Lincoln: University of Nebraska Press, 2004.

Launius, Roger. *Seasons in the Sun: The Story of Big League Baseball in Missouri*. Columbia: University of Missouri Press, 2002.

Leavy, Jane. *The Last Boy: Mickey Mantle and the End of America's Childhood*. New York: Harper, 2010.

Lewis, Michael. *Moneyball: The Act of Winning an Unfair Game*. New York: W. W. Norton, 2004.

Lowenfish, Lee. *Branch Rickey: Baseball's Ferocious Gentleman*. Lincoln: University of Nebraska Press, 2007.

———. *The Imperfect Diamond: The Story of Baseball's Labor Wars*. Lincoln: University of Nebraska Press, 2010.

Luke, Bob. *The Most Famous Woman in Baseball: Effa Manley and the Negro Leagues*. Washington DC: Potomac Books, 2011.

Mantle, Merlyn, Mickey E. Mantle, David Mantle, and Dan Mantle. *A Hero All His Life: Merlyn, Mickey Jr., David, and Dan Mantle; A Memoir by the Mantle Family*. New York: HarperCollins, 1996.

Moore, Joseph Thomas. *Larry Doby: The Struggle of the American League's First Black Player*. Mineola NY: Dover, 2011. Originally published as *Pride against Prejudice: The Biography of Larry Doby* (New York: Greenwood Press, 1988).

O'Toole, Andrew. *Branch Rickey in Pittsburgh*. Jefferson NC: McFarland, 2000.

Peary, Danny. *We Played the Game: 65 Players Remember Baseball's Greatest Era, 1947–1964*. New York: Hyperion, 1994.

Pennington, Edward. *Billy Martin*. New York: Houghton Mifflin, 2015.

Pietrusza, David. *Judge and Jury: The Life and Times of Judge Kenesaw Mountain Landis*. New York: Taylor Trade, 2001.

Piscik, Andy. *The Best Show in Football: The 1964–1955 Cleveland Browns*. Lanham MD: Taylor Trade, 2007.

Pluto, Terry. *The Curse of Rocky Colavito: A Loving Look at a Thirty-Year Slump*. New York: Simon & Schuster, 1994.

———. *Our Tribe: A Baseball Memoir*. New York: Simon & Schuster, 1999.

Pluto, Terry, with Tom Hamilton. *Glory Days in Tribe Town: Jacobs Field 1994–1997*. Cleveland OH: Gray, 2014.

Polner, Murray, *Branch Rickey: A Biography*. New York: Oxford University Press, 1982.

Purdum, Todd S. *An Idea Whose Time Had Come*. New York: Henry Holt, 2014.

Rampersad, Arnold. *Jackie Robinson: A Biography*. New York: Alfred Knopf, 1997.

Ribowsky, Mark. *Don't Look Back: Satchel Paige in the Shadows of Baseball*. New York: Simon & Schuster, 1994.

Risen, Clay. *The Bill of the Century*. New York: Bloomsbury, 2014.

Roberts, Sam. "Faster than Jackie Robinson: Branch Rickey's Sermons on the Mound." *New York Times*, April 13, 1997.

Robinson, Frank, with Dave Anderson. *Frank: The First Year*. New York: Holt, Rinehart, & Winston, 1976.

Robinson, Jackie. *Baseball Has Done It*. With an introduction by Spike Lee. New York: J. B. Lippincott, 1963.

Robinson, Jackie, with Alfred Duckett. *I Never Had It Made: An Autobiography of Jackie Robinson*. New York: Fawcett, 1974.

Rosengren, John. *Hank Greenberg: The Hero of Heroes*. New York: New American Library, Penguin Group, 2013.

Rowan, Carl, with Jackie Robinson. *Wait until Next Year*. New York: Random House, 1960.

Schneider, Russell. *The Boys of the Summer of '48*. Champaign-Urbana IL: Sports Publishing, 1998.

———. *The Cleveland Indians Encyclopedia*. Philadelphia: Temple University Press, 1996.

Sickels, John. *Bob Feller: Ace of the Greatest Generation*. Washington DC: Brassey, 2004.

Simon, Scott. *Home and Away: Memoirs of a Fan*. New York: Hyperion, 2000.

———. *Jackie Robinson and the Integration of Baseball*. Hoboken NJ: Wiley & Sons, 2007.

Singletary, Wes. *Al Lopez: The Life of Baseball's El Señor*. Jefferson NC: McFarland, 1999.

Smith, Red. *Red Smith on Baseball: The Game's Greatest Writer in the Game's Greatest Years*. Chicago: Dee, 2000.

Stockton, J. Roy. *The Gashouse Gang and a Couple of Other Guys*. New York: A. S. Barnes, 1945.

Tye, Larry. *Satchel: The Life and Times of an American Legend*. New York: Random House Trade, 2010.

Tygiel, Jules. *Baseball's Greatest Experiment: Jackie Robinson and His Legacy*. 25th anniversary ed. New York: Oxford University Press, 2008.

Veeck, Bill. *The Hustler's Handbook*. New York: Putnam & Sons, 1965.

Veeck, Bill, with Ed Linn. *Thirty Tons a Day: The Rough-Riding Education of a Neophyte Racetrack Operator*. New York: Viking, 1975.

———. *Veeck as in Wreck*. New York: Putnam & Sons, 1962.

Warmund, Joram, and Joseph Dorinson, eds. *Jackie Robinson: Race, Sports and the American Dream*. New York: Sharpe, Armonk, 1998.

Washington, Booker T. *Up from Slavery*. 1901. Reprint, New York: Dover, 1955.

Winchester, Simon. *The Men Who United the States*. New York: HarperCollins Perennial Classics, 2013.

Index

The italicized locators *fig. 1*, *fig. 2*, and so forth, refer to photographs in the gallery.

images of, *fig. 2, fig. 3*; and lodging discrimination, 224–25; military service of,
24, 136; motives for integration, 16–21;
at Ohio Wesleyan, 19, 22–23; and player
trading, 11–16; preparing Robinson for
integration, 6, 53, 178, 217–18, 219, 226;
recruiting techniques, 40, 259n22; rela-
tionship with Veeck, 33–35; role in farm
clubs, 12–13, 24; role in integration, 73–
74, 84, 88; salary of, 10, 11–12, 14–15,
254n20, 255n29; on scouting practices,
149; and Wendell Smith, 198; on *What's
My Line?*, 112
Rickey and Robinson (Fromer), 73, 90, 113
Rickey and Robinson (Kahn), 93
Rigney, Bill, 187
Risberg, Swede, 85
Rizzuto, Phil, 112
Roberts, Sam, 9
Robeson, Paul, 87–89
Robinson, Eddie, 223
Robinson, Frank, 39, 172, 207–10
Robinson, Jackie, Jr., 96, 240
Robinson, Jackie Roosevelt: as All-Star
player, 241; background of, 45; barnstorming tours, 91, 97–98; baseball
awards, 114; baseball statistics, 91, 100,
193; books about, ix, 5, 93; compared
to Doby, 90–93, 99–100, 240–41; criticism of Willie Mays, 174; education of,
136; films about, ix, 5, 55, 73–74, 93, 220,
221; image of, *fig. 4*; impact of TV coverage on, 240; and Leo Durocher, 179;
media coverage of, 93–98, 111, 119, 197,
198, 239; military service of, 136; overshadowing Doby, 93, 119; personality
of, 41, 217–18, 240–41; preparation for
integration, 6, 216–18, 219–20, 225–26;
professionalism of, 144; racism faced
by, 55, 97, 116–17, 219–20, 221–22, 224–
25, 235–36; recruited by Rickey, 40, 51;
relationship with Doby, 44–45, 66–67,
91, 258n2, 265n43; responses to racism,
41, 92, 196–97; and Reverend Downs,
20, 256n55; role in baseball's integration, ix–x, 17–18, 32–33, 73–74; salary of, 277n25; on Satchel Paige, 132;

Satchel Paige's criticism of, 135–36; dur-
ing spring training, 130; teammates'
responses to, 193, 220–22, 278n29; and
Wendell Smith, 178, 198; on Yankees's
racism, 114
Robinson, Mack, 90
Robinson, Rachel (Jackie's wife), 96
Rockefeller, John D., 104, 106
Rodriguez, Alex, 234
Roosevelt, Theodore, 84
Rose, Pete, 85, 259n38
Rosen, Al: 1954 World Series, 182–83; base-
ball statistics, 63, 67, 193; Hank Green-
berg's treatment of, 63–64, 66; images
of, *fig. 13*; with the Indians, 57–58, 63–
64, 110; on Luke Easter, 195; treatment of
Doby, 53, 192, 224; on Veeck, 32
Rotisserie Baseball, 243–44
Royals, 6, 219–20, 225
Ruth, Babe, 81, 133, 161, 167
Ryan, Ellis, 39, 62, 227

sabermetrics, 243–47
SABR (Society of American Baseball
Research), 243
Sain, Johnny, 55, 192
salaries. *See* player salaries
San Diego Padres, 204–5
Santa Rita Hotel, 65, 130, 175, 224, 225,
235–36
Satchel (Tye), 127, 135
Schilling, Curt, 261n44
Schmidt, Mike, 235
scouting, 149, 244–45
Seattle Mariners, 254n7
Segui, Phil, 207, 209
Seitz, Peter, 210
Selig, Bud, 214
Senators, 162
Shaker Heights community (Cleveland),
105
Sheehan, Bill, 187
Shepard, Bert, 17
Shotton, Burt, 226
Sickels, John, 32, 184
Simon, Scott, 28, 42
Singletary, Wes, 215, 229, 233